ALL OUR FAMILIES

DISABILITY LINEAGE AND THE FUTURE OF KINSHIP

OUR

FAMILIES

JENNIFER NATALYA FINK

BEACON PRESS
BOSTON

BEACON PRESS
Boston, Massachusetts
www.beacon.org

Beacon Press books
are published under the auspices of
the Unitarian Universalist Association of Congregations.

25 24 23 22   8 7 6 5 4 3 2 1

This book is printed on acid-free paper that meets the uncoated paper
ANSI/NISO specifications for permanence as revised in 1992.

Text design and composition by Kim Arney

Library of Congress Cataloging-in-Publication Data

Name: Fink, Jennifer Natalya, author.
Title: All our families : disability lineage and the future of kinship /
Jennifer Natalya Fink.
Description: Boston : Beacon Press, [2022] | Includes bibliographical
references and index. |
Summary: "All Our Families: Finding OurDisability Lineages argues that
disability is stigmatized because it is delineated-excised from our understanding
of family, cut out from the story a family tells about itself, and proposes how
finding and integrating disability in our family would transform our lived
experiences of both family and disability"—Provided by publisher.
Identifiers: LCCN 2021047963 | ISBN 9780807003954 (hardback) |
ISBN 9780807003978 (ebook)
Subjects: LCSH: People with disabilities—Family relationships. | Families.
Classification: LCC HV1568 .F55 2022 | DDC 362.4/043—dc23/eng/20211004
LC record available at https://lccn.loc.gov/2021047963

For Nadia Sohn Fink

and

For all our families:
chosen and inherited, past and future

CONTENTS

LOOKING FOR LINEAGE

I'm seven. I'm walking through room after room in my grandparents' cavernous Long Island house, looking for my cousin. "Cousin, cousin," I call, wishing I knew his name. "Cousin . . . XY," I call. I know he's a boy, and I'm a geneticist's daughter. Chromosomes count.

Cousin XY visits me in dreams. He has his father's eyes.

My Cousin XY was born in 1972 with Down syndrome—and immediately abandoned to a state institution. He was listed only as Baby XY. I always knew my aunt and uncle had "given away" their son at birth. His very existence was explained to me as a tragedy. A crisis. An aberration that perhaps science could one day prevent. In the hospital on the day he was born, his mother refused to look at his face: "Take him away."

His—my—grandfather, a family doctor, the family medical expert, was firm: "Give him up. You can start over. You have a right to real children; he will be happier there."

Where was *there*? I often wondered where my cousin was, who he was. Silence and two neurotypical children quickly replaced him in the family narrative. On the rare occasions when his existence came up, "everyone gave them away" was repeated as a gospel truth. And indeed, in the 1970s, institutionalization, abandonment, and excision from the family narrative was still too often the fate of those labeled incurable at birth.

But I discovered that wasn't the whole truth. As with most families, the story of my family's disability lineage had far more strands than I realized. In 2017, when I was visiting a far-flung branch of my family in Manchester, UK, I discovered that there was another cousin in my family with Down syndrome, also on my father's side, buried in plain sight: Rhona. Born in Scotland in 1946, two decades before Cousin XY, Rhona lived in apparent happiness, first with her nuclear family in Glasgow and then in a group home called Cosgrove, which her mother helped found, for disabled Jewish people. True to her name—Rhona means "joy" in Hebrew—she lived a joyous, Jewish life.

Two of my family members had been written out of the family story. De-lineated from our lineage. I mourned what I never had: both a lived relationship with my cousins and a family myth that could include them. I wondered how the knowledge of a rich, deep history of disability in my family would have changed my experience of my own daughter's diagnosis at age two as a disabled, nonspeaking autistic person. If I had grown up playing with Cousin XY, would we have experienced her disability as part of the warp and woof of our lineage, instead of as a personal disaster, rending us from the fabric of family?

These were the questions that led me to think about disability lineage and what the implications of repressing, hiding, finding, and celebrating it might be for disabled people and their families everywhere. By cutting me off from knowledge of my disabled cousins, I had no source of disability knowledge and history in my family. Their lives were treated as extraordinary, disposable, and traumatic—so traumatic that the very fact of them was hidden, erased from the story our family told about itself.

This is typical of how disability is narrated in the family myths passed down from one generation to another. Disability is erased, repressed, covered over. Families de-lineate—destroy the connections between generations of disabled people, their families, and their caretakers. Our disabled kin are not merely misrepresented. They are written out of the story.

By examining the ways families excise disability from their stories, I began to see how disability is fundamentally shaped by this omission. The way we assign meanings to bodies and minds, establish norms, and otherize and stigmatize according to perceptions of ability is inseparable from how we name and claim our kin. Family is defined and produced by eradicating disability lineage, often making the inevitable appearance of disability within a given family a crisis: a trauma to be erased, effaced. Unwritten. I refer to this process as de-lineation: the separation of disabled people from their lineage. The word "delineate" literally means to mark off with lines, and thus separate. It includes the word "lineate," derived from "lineage"—family ancestry. The de-lineation I'm examining here is sometimes literal, as with the institutionalization of my cousin XY; it is sometimes rhetorical, as with the suppression of my cousin Rhona and her disability from the family narrative. "Delineate" also means to describe or portray—a form of inclusion. So within the word itself lies the potential to re-lineate: to sew a family member back into the fold. To describe, portray, and, thus, connect.

The concept of disability lineage, which is at the core of *All Our Families*, offers a way of reimagining the possibilities for our relationship to disability and family. If we found and reclaimed our disabled ancestors, our understanding of family, self, and bodymind would be profoundly altered. We'd have an archive of the vast variations of bodyminds in our past to draw on, which would help us value the diversity of our current kin. As I traced my own disability lineage and examined why it hadn't been incorporated into the story my family told about itself, I became more convinced that the erasure of disability lineage is one of the primary ways that disabled people are rendered "other" to their own families. Our current misunderstanding and pathologizing of disability rests on this exclusion of our disabled kin. In exploring what it means to recuperate disability lineage, I use my own journey to open up the possibilities for inclusion and redefinition for all families and bodyminds.

I invoke Eli Clare's term "body-mind" here to denote how mind and body are inseparable, and how any nonphobic understanding of disability is predicated on an acknowledgment of that indissoluble relation.[1] However, I prefer a nonhyphenated neologism, *bodymind*, to truly honor the inextricable nature of embodiment and consciousness.

Disability is entwined not only with the relationship between body and mind but also with other formations of identity. While I have considered how disability is shaped by multiple vectors of power and difference such as race, gender, and sexuality, I am limited, like all critics, by my own positionality. White, middle-class, Jewish, queer, not disabled (yet). Of course these broad categories don't tell the whole story. My heritage is Eastern European, Brazilian, and Scottish; I am married to a Korean American, gender nonconforming person; my daughter is biracial, Korean and Jewish; and our extended family stretches around the globe.

This is what I know about my family. Some of our origins remain unknown, untraceable. Race, class, religion, sexuality, and gender complicate these categories. As a queer person, I claim a sort of familial-national affiliation and family of choice with queers all over the world—and the experiences of oppression and liberation in which this identity is rooted. I also have privileges that shape my identity in ways that are hard to see and painful to own. I benefit from all the hidden violence against BIPOC (Black, Indigenous, and People of Color) people that constitutes white privilege—and from the ableism woven into how we produce raced bodies. While like most people over fifty, many of my bodily functions are impaired, I am still deemed "normative enough" not to be sorted as disabled. At least not yet. I am critical of such sorting systems, and this book explicates some of the ways these categories and sortings perpetuate ableism and rupture lineage. But nonetheless, it's important to mark that I do not share the experience of being regarded as disabled by my culture.

I am the parent of a disabled child—a positionality that is often overprivileged in discourses about disability and families. Mothers in particular, for reasons related to our misogynistic care-work system, often center stories about disability on the burdens of care. Moreover, nondisabled parents of disabled children have a complex relationship to disability activism—and to their disabled children. While it was just such parents who initiated many of the early disability activist initiatives, their perspective has often been the only one included in public discussions of disability, standing in the place of the voices of disabled people themselves. Though in some instances the interests and agendas of (nondisabled) parents of disabled people have been congruent with those of disabled people, that is not always the case. As Allison C. Carey, Pamela Block, and Richard K. Scotch have argued in their landmark study of parents of children with disabilities, while disabled-led organizations stress pride, autonomy, and disability identity, parent-led organizations "stress cure and maximal normalization, striving to erase rather than embrace disability."[2] Parents often wield power and influence not only in their own families but in the public sphere, their accounts of disability superseding those of their disabled children.

All Our Families resists these tropes, instead centering the narrative on disabled people themselves wherever possible. But it is nonetheless emergent from the particularities of a white disability parenting experience by a nondisabled person. I have tried to consider these limitations, and I include and center the views of disabled BIPOC from diverse, multiply marginalized positionalities. As part of that commitment, I have, whenever possible, cited activists and artists who themselves identify as disabled, rather than nondisabled theorists. Imperfectly, I have attempted to be true to the mandate "Nothing about us without us" of the disability rights movement.

Though I intend for this project to encompass the broadest possible understanding of disability, and not to privilege some forms of disability over others, much of my analysis centers on intellectual and developmental disabilities, particularly those which are innate rather than acquired, such as Down syndrome and autism. This is a reflection of my own lineage, but I have also chosen this focus because of the ways our society's ableism is often most acute and genocidal in relation to such disabilities. As disability philosophers such as Eva Feder Kittay have noted, intellectual disabilities—which are not curable, are inherited, and may require lifelong relations of dependency—provide the most profound challenges to normative ideas regarding whose life is worth living. It is precisely *because* of this that intellectual disabilities offer the greatest opportunities for radically rethinking ableism.[3]

To expand the modes of expression as well as kinds of people represented, I have used accessible, popular forms of discourse such as blogs, personal essays, and journalistic essays rather than rely only on the abstract, expert analysis of scholars. This is a commitment to plain language—to writing that is accessible to the widest possible range of bodyminds—and to centering the people who are most affected by disability lineage and its erasure: disabled people themselves.

In addition to conventional scholarship, I include the work and thinking of disability justice activists, as I found that they had more to say about what to actually *do* about ableism than the scholars who dissected it. This emerging thinking—occurring in the wake of the twin emergencies of the global coronavirus pandemic and the crisis of police violence and state marginalization of BIPOC highlighted by the Movement for Black Lives—strikes me as far more exciting, lively, diverse, and concrete than anything coming from the academy. Of course there are many scholars in the field of disability studies who themselves identify as disabled, and I have drawn from their work as well, but I want to place my book's lineage in the tradition of activism as well as scholarship. As numerous BIPOC scholar-activists like Angel Miles, Akemi Nishida, and Anjali J. Forber-Pratt have pointed out, too much of disability studies scholarship is dominated by white, middle-class professors like myself and fails to examine how disability is produced intersectionally.[4]

I aim to foreground the ways race works to construct disability in families, and the ways that disabled BIPOC and their families are shaped specifically by disability lineage and its repression, particularly in relation to the overpolicing of public space. Many communities are pushing against multiple forms of oppression, providing rich sources of innovative, creative reimaginings of family and disability. The numerous powerful reinventions and extensions of kinship systems in Black communities provide one model for how disability lineage may be woven into all our families. My own experiences of queer family making, which in my case involves both adoptive and biological parentage as well as biracial and interfaith blending, led me to look beyond nuclear and biological models of kinship. I hope *All Our Families* initiates multiple, contested conversations about what it means to include diverse bodyminds in all kinds of families.

METHODS AND MENDINGS

I've drawn on a wide range of methods here, ranging from disability studies, crip theory, critical race theory, and disability justice activism, to queer theory. This eclectic blend of ideas and sources has helped shape my argument. In addition to consulting public records and archives, I interviewed extended family members in Scotland. There, I also visited Cosgrove Care, the institution Rhona's mother founded, where I interviewed its current director, Heather Grey, who gave me context and history about disability and care in Scotland.

One of the most transformative interviews for this project was not with a relative but with a professional care worker: Kathy, the person who spent the most time, most intimately, with Rhona during her adult life at Cosgrove.[5] Talking to Rhona's caregiver was as generative for understanding my disability lineage as was talking to her surviving sister and niece! This transformed my thinking, leading me to think more critically and deeply about care and all the raced, gendered fears that organize its system. Care work is the hidden twin of disability, and to re-lineate disability into our family stories is to see care work in all its racist, misogynistic rhetoric.

I've threaded my story—my family—throughout this book. This is an important component of my feminist, crip-queer disability politics, and also a means of performatively enacting the work of repair that I claim disability lineage can do. Including ourselves, our positionalities, our multiple roles and lives in our scholarship has been a fundamental precept of feminist scholarship for more than four decades. Situating and embodying the author—usually at the beginning and end of a scholarly text—is now as conventional a form of address as the abstracted, impersonal universal academic voice used to be. Disability studies scholars such as Alison Kafer have argued for extending that to situating our own experiences of embodiment and disability *inside* our texts, as part and parcel, instead of segregating body from text.[6] Disability lineage needs to be woven into the rhetorical cloth, not segmented and segregated, relegated to the realm of the anecdotal and personal. I consider my use of my own family's repressed and recovered disability lineages throughout this book a part of the argument I'm making here. The transformative power of naming and claiming our disability lineage—and the disastrous consequences of its denial—are explored in all their complexity.

This book is composed of two parts. The first half of the book explores the concept of disability lineage. I outline why it can be an innovative and useful framework for tracing how disability came to be experienced as an individual trauma to a singular family, rather than a common, collective, and normal experience of all families. Our disability *mishpacha*—extended kinship system—already exists; I argue it needs to be re-lineated, reclaimed. By excluding disabled people from the myths and stories families tell about their ancestors and origins, disability remains a trauma that keeps on happening, since its antecedents are repressed from the narrative. I then examine the mechanisms of its repression, rooted in racist and anti-Semitic sorting systems we've inherited from the German Nazis and US Reconstruction-era white supremacists. By examining the racist and sexist systems of distributing and (de)valuing care, both informal and professional, I expose how they shape the repression and fear of disability lineage. I discovered that the caregiver, and lineages of caregiving, are also expunged from family narratives, in ways deeply connected to underlying racist and misogynistic systems of power.

The implications of this double erasure are examined, as well as its profound connections to how genetics and the reproduction of disability is figured in both scientific and popular discourse. I argue that the popular account of genetic inheritance is scientifically inaccurate. It also perpetuates the systemic shame and blame of disabled people and their families, leading to the repression and fear of disability lineage. The pathologizing and excision of disabled people from the public sphere is a direct inheritance of these ableist, racist systems. I explore how disabled people themselves have re-lineated disability in public to challenge this privatization and marginalization of disability, paying particular attention to the realms of fashion and performance, online and off, as they are ripe sites for disability culture and family re-lineation.

In the second half of the book, I move to reimagining care—and disability—as shared and how this might reshape our understanding of lineage, kinship, and disability. I look to mutual aid and disability justice models and argue for connecting them to the familial so that disability can be shared and integrated, passed down in the story a family makes about itself as well as in the larger community. As disability justice lawyer, activist, and scholar Talila A. "TL" Lewis notes, ableism is always already intersectional; "these constructed ideas of normality" that ableism perpetuates "are deeply rooted in anti-Blackness, eugenics, misogyny, colonialism, imperialism, and capitalism."[7] Ableism is also embedded in our gendered, neocolonial, racist care structures. I examine some of the ways that care work and care workers could be reorganized and revalued to combat this endemic inequality, building on the work of disability scholars and justice activists. But I also argue that without the naming and claiming of disability lineage, the systemic racism and sexism that confounds and constructs disability will never be undone. The eradication of disabled people from their family stories is itself racist and misogynistic; this systemic inequality is inseparable from the de-lineation of disabled people that produces them as an exception to the white, heteronormative family rule.

I end by connecting the familial disability lineage I am proposing we value and share to a more collective ancestral one, linking the inherited family lineage to the kind of crip kinship for which disability justice activists have argued. Kinship, I suggest, has already been transformed by queer and BIPOC families in ways that could prove transformative for understanding and integrating our disability lineage into our present family systems. Families of origin, I propose, need not be opposed to the chosen family if we extend our understanding of family to encompass a more layered, extended kinship system. By reclaiming our personal disability lineage, we open up the possibility of connecting it to a larger communal ancestry, with powerful political and social implications for all our family and kinship systems. Drawing on the work of mutual aid movements, I argue for a reconnection of the family disability narrative to the collective disability justice one, and suggest ways such a reconnection would make for a more inclusive, more flexible structure of care and community. I draw on concepts from universal design to imagine how we might begin to connect our collective and familial disability lineages. The rich possibilities for such an open, flexible disability *mishpacha* are explored and celebrated.

This book names and diagnoses a problem and then proposes some possible solutions. *Solutions*: that term terrifies me; both in its horrific echoes of Hitler's final solution to the "problem" of being Jewish and in the arrogant assumption that I have a solution to ableism and its enactment across generations, or that a single solution will fit all families. Disabled people are all too familiar with rhetoric that poses them as a problem in need of a solution. Instead, I close by proposing some means of repairing the damaging rhetoric that leads to de-lineation, and multiple strands of possibilities for exploring how to re-lineate. In the appendix, I provide some concrete suggestions for readers about how to find, claim, integrate, and pass down their own disability lineages.

I hope *All Our Families* provides the spark for a larger conversation about how to connect disability, community, family, and ancestry, rather than providing definitive answers or "solutions." By putting family lineage and disability ancestry in dialogue, I hope to create a more sustainable future for all our families. Though not all disability lineages can be fully reclaimed, the very act of assuming that our families always included disabled people can be transformative.

Every family story is a disability story, if you choose to so tell it. This book is for all families with disabled kin. Which is all families! Though it too often has been repressed and denied, all families have disability lineages. I wrote this for my brilliant daughter, who ableism threatened to de-lineate. For Cousin XY and Cousin Rhona, who, as I thread them back into our family, join me in sowing the seeds for a more inclusive future. A mixed metaphor: the best kind for the complex work of re-lineation.

When I shared the topic of this book with my daughter and asked her how she felt about my writing it, Nadia typed with a teenaged eyeroll, "It's your book—it's not mine. It's good for you to write yours, Mom. I'll write my own story!" She already has, in her blog posts, videos, and poems. My hope is that by finding and honoring our disability lineages, all disabled people will be empowered to name and claim their own stories and connect them to the larger kinship lineage in which they are entangled.

This book is a provocation. An incitement to challenge how we imagine family, kinship, and all the bodyminds they can contain. The multitudes we were, and those yet to come. I write for those who will come after me, in hopes that my daughter may be a part of the disability lineage that threads us together across generations. I write for Cousin XY and Cousin Rhona, imagining them back into the story, mending the broken thread, kithing back together my kin. And I write for all the disabled ancestors, in all our families, who we might sew back into the patchwork quilt of our family's story: an unfinished tapestry in which to wrap our children's children's children.

CHAPTER 1

DISABILITY AS TRAUMA, FAMILY LINEAGE AS REPAIR

My grandfather's white-pillared house was brimming with kin. The kitchen was overflowing at all hours with great aunts, second cousins, and grandmothers—whatever relatives were living under his roof at that moment. Everyone congregated around the kitchen as my grandmother cooked. The fancy dining room with the chandeliers and champagne carpet never got used.

Though my gruff grandfather argued with everyone, his household included far-flung family members in his ever-expanding *mishpacha*—Yiddish for family, extended family, and that aunt who's really just your mother's best friend. Along with his wife and four children, my grandfather's house included relatives ranging from my grandmother's widowed sister and her two young children, to my grandmother's elderly mother, who helped cook, clean, and mind the children. Yet his own grandson with Down syndrome wasn't welcome there. Cousin XY—his grandson, my first cousin—never sat around that crowded kitchen table. In fact, he wasn't allowed to be part of our family at all.

My grandfather, Benjamin Fink, understood kinship to extend far beyond the nuclear family. This wasn't due to any particular generosity of spirit on his part. Despite being a highly educated doctor, he had a tough-guy, unvarnished demeanor. After serving as a doctor overseas in World War II, he was content to turn his Long Island home into his castle, from which he doled out medical advice by day in his practice, attached to the house, and after hours to the extended family, friends, and patients gathered around his table for my grandmother's cooking. The whole house smelled of chicken fat and medicine, a heady mixture of rubbing alcohol and those human aromas it is meant to eradicate.

Like many postwar American Jews, my grandfather's sense of family included almost anyone whose lineage connected to his. While many Jewish American families in this period took in "refugees"[1]—distant family members who were Holocaust survivors—my family had more pedestrian kin to tend to: US-born relatives, unable to support themselves for one reason or another. Of course there were tensions—all the usual drama and chaos of an extended family living under one roof. But I grew up feeling like it was only natural that Aunt Dora, my grandmother's widowed sister who taught me how to knit, lived with my grandparents. I made no distinction between Aunt Dora and my more immediate family members: they were all family to me. *Mishpacha.*

Many of those Grandpa Ben included under his gabled roof were women with few resources, who didn't provide any income to the household. Grandmothers, widows. Small, unruly children. In fact, it was precisely those who were the most vulnerable, the least able to provide for themselves, who ended up in my grandfather's house. Their care needs were part of what qualified them for inclusion. It is all the more striking to me that my grandfather insisted that my aunt and uncle abandon their own child at birth simply because he had an extra chromosome.

Even this expansive, flexible notion of family had a limit: disability. While this nonnuclear *mishpacha* was capacious enough to include a variety of dependent adult women and their kids, it couldn't include a grandchild with an extra chromosome. My grandfather insisted that my Cousin XY be "given away" at birth, permanently de-lineated from his loosely defined family simply because he had a disability, making him a member of the largest minority group on earth. Cared for first by a retired nurse, then by an institution, his exact whereabouts soon disappeared as he vanished from the family story. He was gone, severed from our *mishpacha*.

Though the radical de-lineation and institutionalization my cousin XY experienced in the 1970s (the tail end of the era of mass institutionalization of disabled people in the US) is no longer as common as it once was, the cultural and psychological de-lineation of disabled people from the notion of family persists. At every stage of the life cycle, from birth to death, families continue to define themselves against disability, viewing disability as a crisis: an extraordinary, tragic event rather than an ordinary part of family life. Nowhere is this more evident than in how disabled children are figured and feared in our culture—even before they are born.

THE SPECTER OF DISABILITY: FEAR OF A CRIP KID

Twenty percent of all people have a disability. That makes disabled people the largest minority group in the world. Less than 4 percent of disabilities are congenital.[2] Disability at birth is one of the most unlikely ways of acquiring disability, and a rare outcome of any pregnancy. Yet this congenitally disabled child looms large over how we conceive of family— even before we conceive! Couples considering whether to have a child routinely debate whether they would be able to tolerate a disabled child. I heard many such conversations when I was considering having a child. I *had* many such conversations.

It's hard to imagine prospective parents blithely announcing that they would have a child only if they could be guaranteed to be heterosexual and cisgendered, yet it's common for otherwise liberal people to say that they want a child only if they are not disabled—and then launch into a discussion of what level of disability they might "permit." The internet exposes these anxieties in their rawest form. Almost every anonymous online forum about parenting, such as Quora, contains endless threads proclaiming, "I don't want a child with a disability. Back me up, ladies!"[3] Whether one could accept a child with a disability is often posed as the litmus test of whether one should be a parent at all. "If I don't want a child with a disability, should I even have children?" goes another popular and predictable thread.

Such exchanges reflect the dominant view of disability as traumatic and rare, rather than a normal part of human existence that adds to the diverse fabric of our communities. Michael Oliver suggests this "personal tragedy theory of disability" is so widespread, so unquestioned, that it shapes every facet of how we think of human value.[4] It's naturalized not only in how we value humans but also in how we think about our own families. Disability is what we define our families *against*.

"Disability" is never really defined in these conversations. It's a place-holder for our fears. Our limits. Our denial. Because disabled people are excluded from our notion of family, when we start imagining ourselves as parents, we literally cannot conceive (all puns intended) of our own future child as disabled. In fact, as disability activists have noted, not only are disabled people the largest minority group in the world, but anyone who lives long enough will also be disabled at some point in their life. Nonetheless, the family continues to define itself against disability, otherizing its disabled members and experiencing them as a trauma to the very fabric of family.

I should know. When my daughter was diagnosed at age two and a half with autism, I felt like the world had stopped. And yet it turned. The afternoon of her diagnosis, while watching her play happily in the yard, my partner and I exchanged a teary glance. It was a gorgeous autumn day, complete with a bright yellow sun shining over my shining, happy daughter. Suddenly, my child and I were stripped of our identities. Who were we? "Autistic." It felt like a wound. A blunt object had hit us. Torn us. Traumatized us.

A trauma is defined as "a deeply distressing or disturbing condition." The example the dictionary offers is telling: "a personal trauma like the death of a child." Except nobody had died; nothing had changed.[5] "Personal": not collective or political. This was an individual event. Or so our culture led us to believe. The second definition suggests the medicalized experience of disability: "physical injury." Except nobody was sick. There was no injury.

Distressing, injurious: an injury. Personal, individual, private. Something one doesn't want to make public. All of these definitions suggest that trauma is an interruption to the normal, healthy course of life. A rupture—physical or emotional. Yet nothing, except the story we were telling about our daughter and her identity, and our expectations about who she was and might become, had changed. We were experiencing the *diagnosis* as a trauma, not her disability. This rupture, this diagnosis, introduced a radical difference into the spine and spleen of our family. She was something other than us: autistic, disabled. Our family felt flayed.

I struggled to make sense of what the hell had just happened as I looked over the exorbitant developmental pediatrician's bill and read the diagnosis, a bunch of numbers with decimal points followed by a single damning word: autism. This all seemed unprecedented, without context. I felt marked, labeled, cut off: our family sorted into the "not normal" category. I knew that, of course, other families had people with disabilities in them; I even knew of disabled people shamefully hidden away in my extended family. I knew *of* Cousin XY, and his eradication from my family. *But I didn't know him.* My grandfather's de-lineation of my cousin from our sprawling *mishpacha* had left me bereft of my disability lineage. I had no lived sense of how disability could be incorporated and woven into the fabric of my own family.

Nor did I have a narrative that could help me wrap my mind and arms around a disabled child. No family story of how disability could be woven into a loving family life. Quite the opposite: the story my family told itself of disability was one of trauma, rupture, and de-lineation, defined by the absent presence of Cousin XY in my grandfather's house.

My experience is typical of parents and other family members who experience a diagnosis of a child that sorts them into the "disabled" category. It is also a common experience for family members who receive a disability diagnosis of an elder. Medical researchers have found that older adults often resist receiving diagnoses that might enable them to access medications and benefits, for "despite their clear benefits, diagnostic labels also serve as cues that activate stigma and stereotypes."[6] It is so common, this feeling of trauma, rupture, stigma, and an outsideness to the narrative of family itself, that there are numerous popular and scholarly accounts attempting to make sense of this. Most of them want to make sense of the identity category of disability, rather than that of the family and how it definitionally excludes disability. Even meta-analyses of disability identity, such as the American Psychological Association's "Thinking About Disability Identity," presume that disability is traumatic, a rupture with the family.[7] While many explore cultural and genetic inheritance and expectations, none explore disability lineage—our inherited sense of disabled people as a central part of the story of our family and its ancestry.

Our very definition of the family excludes disability lineage. Our sense of what a family is—who constitutes it, what kinds of bodyminds it can hold, and, crucially, the history of whose it has held—is defined by this exclusion. Despite the fact that one-fifth of all the planet's people are formally recognized as disabled, meaning that more or less everyone else is related to a person with a disability, we continue to construct our sense of family and its lineage in such a way that we are stunned, shocked, and traumatized by the incredibly common, collective, and familial experience of disability.

OF APPLES, ABLEISM, AND OTHERING

The literature for families with disabled children—usually directed toward an implicitly nondisabled parent—perpetuates these notions of disability as a traumatizing event, a rending of the familial cloth. Andrew Solomon's popular study of parenting and difference, *Far from the Tree*, exemplifies this tendency to view a child's disability as an isolated trauma outside the "normal" narrative of family and its lineage. His argument exposes the ableism governing even supposedly progressive beliefs about inclusivity in families.

Solomon describes identities that children receive from their parents as vertical and those they don't as horizontal. Vertical identities, Solomon argues a bit too neatly, are not only those biological traits passed down genetically from parent to child, like hair color or a propensity for math, but also shared cultural norms such as language and faith. I am Jewish because my parents are Jewish. Yet we value only *some* traits as formational; Solomon points to blondness and myopia as traits passed down from parent to child that do not form a basis for a shared identity.

Solomon opposes vertical identity to the more vexing concept of horizontal identity. Whereas everyone has vertical identities, only some people have horizontal identities, "an inherent or acquired trait that is foreign to his or her [sic] parents and must therefore acquire identity from a peer group."[8] These horizontal identities are notable for their eccentric and exceptional nature—not everyone has them—and that they may be *either* acquired or inherent.

Disabilities that are significant enough to count as disabilities are deemed horizontal in Solomon's account because they, unlike, say, myopia, are unfixable. Incurable. That which is deemed incurable is also rendered as other to the family and its lineage. Such disabilities render the child an outsider in their own family. The parent must then work to love, accept, and integrate this foreign bodymind into the nation-state of the "normal" family.

Disability scholars and activists instead emphasize the way that societies *make* a particular impairment disabling, whether it's vertically or horizontally inherited. For example, I am legally blind in one eye but can see reasonably well with glasses; our society doesn't consider that disabling. A wheelchair user who can move just fine if there's a ramp provided, on the other hand, is viewed as disabled. The barriers are social and cultural; it is those barriers, not the impairment itself, that render a particular person with a specific impairment disabled. Originating with British activist Michael Oliver, this model shifts the focus to the barriers to inclusion. "Disabling barriers and attitudes" are the problem, not the impairment. A disability's origin in or outside the family, the disabled person's difference from the family, should not then define whether the disability is identity forming. The social barriers to inclusion, not the impairment or its lineage, are what defines the disability as such—hence it is termed the "social model." It is often posed against the "medical model" of disability, which views the impairment itself as the problem—as a personal tragedy, an individual trauma. Even many doctors and nurses now embrace the social model; a 2014 nursing journal, for example, notes how this model "challenges the view of disability as an individual problem . . . and instead focus[es] on the barriers and attitudes that are disabling."[9]

trunk. In Rosemarie Garland-Thomson's terms, the normate is the semi-fictional nondisabled person, "the constructed identity of those who, by way of the bodily configurations and cultural capital they assume, can step into a position of authority and wield the power it grants them."[14] These bodyminds require a category deemed "disabled" to give them meaning and to authorize their power to sort, label, and de-lineate.

The family that believes itself to be normative *needs* a disabled child—if only an imaginary one, that much-discussed figure saturating the discourse of pregnancy—to define it as such. As TL Lewis notes, the fear of disability defines *all* people, not just those who are categorized as disabled.[15] The family sorts and separates the disabled child. They are incorporated only as a singular, unprecedented, disruptively and traumatically pathological other. The bad apple against which the rest define themselves. That parents themselves might be disabled—either currently or inevitably, if they should live so long, in the future—is effaced by this paradigm. In fact, approximately one in ten parents have a disability.[16] But this is not part of our rhetoric of disability and family. The tree demands the far-flung apple to confirm its superiority and normativity.

When Solomon's tome began making the rounds of parents in my circle in 2012, three years after my daughter's diagnosis, I couldn't quite articulate why I found it so problematic. To be honest, I found it revolting. My disgust was twofold: I didn't want my child to be one of those "far from the tree" weirdos. And as a bisexual, queer feminist in a biracial family, deep in the lived politics of my marrow, I felt how much his binary formulation of difference perpetuated an ableist myth of normativity. A normative family is disrupted by the arrival of a child with an uninherited otherness, and must learn to accept and incorporate this creature into its fold. The ways this child's difference might connect to differences in bodyminds in previous generations is unexamined. The ways the supposedly normative bodyminds of the parents and siblings are themselves idiosyncratic, particular, and unprecedented are effaced.

The stark delineation between the "normal" family and the disabled child forecloses finding and connecting to the family's disabled ancestry, to the parents' eventual disability, and to imagined future generations with disabled family members and caregivers. Disability lineage is unimagined and unimaginable, ensuring that the trauma experience of disability will be repeated, repeatedly reproducing itself, paradoxically, as unprecedented.

This model is not only ableist; it also perpetuates ideas about value and embodiedness that are profoundly racialized and racist. Blond hair, one of Solomon's examples of a difference that doesn't matter or create identity, is actually quite definitional in a colorist and racist society. In Nazi Germany, blond hair was sometimes the difference between life or death for Jews: a powerful, genocidal sorting mechanism indeed.[17] TL Lewis argues that disabilities never exist in a vacuum; ableism is "a system that places value on people's bodies and minds based on societally constructed ideas of normalcy, intelligence, excellence, and productivity. These constructed ideas are deeply rooted in anti-Blackness, eugenics, colonialism, and capitalism."[18] The cultural norms defining family against its disabled members are not only ableist but also profoundly racist.

The salient, defining quality of horizontal identities is that they are not inherited from the family, by either biological or cultural transmission. Such a definition depends on a deep knowledge of one's cultural and biological family history—one that the people of the United States, a nation of descendants of migrants, immigrants, dispossessed indigenous folks, and the formerly enslaved, cannot entirely know. Without knowing our disability lineages, all of our children's disabilities will seem unprecedented, uninherited, singular. Traumatic. But it is the very system of sorting and dividing the supposed normate from the pathologized disabled other that creates the condition of that traumatizing dislocation from lineage.

It might seem, then, that rather than name and claim our differences—and our children's—we should simply erase them in a warm, fuzzy blanket of acceptance. But as Tom Shakespeare and other disabled disability studies scholars insist, differences are real, embodied, material, and emotional. The construct of disability is a valuable one for naming and claiming specific embodied, en-minded experiences. As critics of the social model argue, claiming that barriers to inclusion are the only things that define disability marginalizes the embodied, complex experiences of disability.

But some differences, Solomon and others suggest, are *really* different. Can't we at least arrive at a spectrum of difference? Why not measure the difference, the distance from the tree? As a bisexual woman who is often measured and rendered "less queer" than a gay person, and a parent of a child "on the spectrum," as the popular euphemism goes, I am well aware of the impulse to spectrumize—and the profound violence this does. The problem is that any spectrum of identity creates linear and absolute values. Spectrums have two defining ends. The Kinsey Scale makes a bisexual person—a perfect five like me—less queer than a hard-gay ten, say, in its one-to-ten scale of sexual orientation.[22] In both my ecstatic pleasure in queer culture and sex, and my oppression by discriminatory laws and phobic people, I am queer as folk. Queer as a perfect Kinsey ten. When I'm engaged in queer sex or being beaten by cop, my five-ness is irrelevant. Queer scholars suggest that the only people such spectrum regimes help are those who exist outside of them—the heteronormates who need to invent such numeric, linear systems precisely as a strategy to dehumanize queers and define themselves against us. So spectrumizing and scaling disability serve only to further marginalize.

Another common move under the guise of disability acceptance is parental mourning. In the literature on disability parenting, there's a lot of airtime given to mourning that "normal" child the (normal?) parent presumably expected, and a lot of energy given to binarizing differences, sorting which ones define the child as an "other" to the family. Indeed, psychotherapist Pamela Bartram has studied how to transform parental melancholy, a sort of permanent gloom rooted in guilt and shame about having a disabled child. "For parents," she argues, "the hidden idea is that incurable disability has occurred through some fault of theirs, . . . they have failed, continue to fail and can only imagine a future dominated by a sense of perpetual failure because the child can never be repaired."[23] Bartram normalizes the "distress and sadness you would expect in such circumstance" in having a child diagnosed with a disability, making the disability itself distressing, not the systemic oppression of ableism. Instead of challenging the expectation of a "normal" (never defined) child, she offers suggestions for how parents can let go of the idea that the disabled child is a symptom of their own moral failure, grieve the loss of the "ideal" child who never was, and come to a begrudging acceptance of their disabled child. She never questions why curability is the marker of difference, or why the common experience of disability is configured as outside the norm of family. Rather, a rueful acceptance of the damaged goods—the disabled child—by the parents is encouraged.

The disability itself remains a trauma to be overcome. It should be grieved, processed correctly with the help of an expensive therapist, rather than left to fester as a shameful, stigmatized site of melancholy. The child's "incurability" and difference remain the cause of the trauma, not the social barriers that make the impairment challenging. That a child's diagnosis and disability are traumatic remains unquestioned. Just as disabled people are often expected to fit their experiences into a narrative of overcoming their disability, the parents, too, must likewise overcome their despair.

Reading Bertram made me feel a strange sense of cognitive dissonance. On the one hand, my daughter was a site of joy for me: a specific individual like and unlike me, whose disability was inextricably linked with her unique and delightful being. On the other, her disability was a site of despair that couldn't be overcome through familial love because the very definition of family that I had inherited depended on her de-lineation. When I brought this dilemma to my own therapist, I found a similar model to Bertram's was the only available one on offer. I was to "process" my feelings in the private space of a therapist's office in order to move out of trauma and arrive at an individual, dour state of acceptance of the damaged goods. My daughter's joyful, irreducible, complex being and society's disabling, alienating effects on us were not part of our forty-five-minute hour. Nor was any value placed on us joining a disability community or seeing ourselves as part of a larger, collective identity.

As I kept searching for an account that would help me make sense of all this, I found a third version of the disability-as-parental-trauma narrative: a stoical approach that attempts to elide the power of ableism in defining disability. Around the time my daughter received her diagnosis, one popular example floating around the internet was an essay by Emily Perl Kingsley, the parent of a now-adult child with Down syndrome, titled "Welcome to Holland."[24] Though first published in 1987, this essay has had remarkable staying power: it was proffered by multiple well-meaning friends and doctors upon hearing of my daughter's diagnosis. Instead of bad and good apples, bad melancholy and good grieving, "Holland" attempts to normalize having a child with a disability through the metaphor of a flight planned for one lovely holiday destination—say, Italy—and landing in another: Holland. In witty, upbeat prose, Perl Kingsley argues that these are equally lovely but different places, and that there need be no trauma in parenting a child with a disability, but simply surprise at arriving at this other, unexpected place: the Magical Land of Disability. "The important thing," she opines, "is that they haven't taken you to a horrible, disgusting, filthy place, full of pestilence, famine and disease. It's just a different place."[25] One can imagine Solomon and Bartram applauding the inclusivity and acceptance of the disabled child and the family's journey. It was indeed a relief, when I first read this piece, to hear something other than despair and mourning.

"Holland" has an obvious appeal: it allows the parent to imagine disability as a neutral form of difference. Such a concept anticipates more recent work to conceptualize autism as a form of neurodiversity rather than pathology. Like Cyrée Jarelle Johnson, who argues for "autism neutrality"—for disability as fact rather than a source of affective shame or pride—"Holland" moves beyond pathologizing the disabled person.[26] But this paradigm elides how parenting a child with a disability may have real, material, intrinsic challenges. More profoundly, it ignores how disability—and the disabled child—is reviled by the family and the society in which it is embedded: devalued, debased, and dehumanized.

The ways a family might stretch, change, and grow, the real, material challenges of care in an ableist society, the shame and stigma of disability that cuts families off from their own extended families and communities: all are glossed over in this account. The sorting mechanism that defines which disabilities are extraordinary, incurable, and other to the family lurks just beneath the upbeat prose: if a child's disability proves challenging, requires extensive supports and resources, and demands emotional as well as material labor, is that child then "horrible, disgusting, filthy"? The language of disgust is first named and then denied. Though Perl Kings-ley's article aims to present a destigmatizing view, in line with her lifelong work advocating for inclusive and humane representations of disabled people such as her son on *Sesame Street* and elsewhere, her article unin-tentionally perpetuates a false vision of disability and parenting.[27]

Moreover, surprise is still central to this model of stoic acceptance, trauma, and shock repackaged in a more benign form of false equivalency. If disability is a common, normal, ordinary facet of human existence, why should it be surprising? Faced with the difference the diagnosis of disabil-ity introduces into the family narrative, the family is encouraged to sim-ply deny its radically irreducible nature and repackage the disabled child as another kind of equally delightful brand of normate. Eliding differ-ence—and the ableist social conditions that make its incorporation and acceptance nearly impossible—is no better than pathologizing it. After reading this account, instead of arriving in Holland or Italy, I felt like I was stranded at the airport alone with my family. Similar accounts in memoirs by parents of children with disabilities left me cold; the journey from trauma to acceptance never addressed why or how disability was traumatizing in the first place, or its de-lineating effects.[28]

In some respects, Perl Kingsley's, Bertram's, and Solomon's responses to disability mirror those of queer theorist Anna Cvetkovich in that they focus on the *response* to trauma as a means of depathologizing it. In her thoughtful examination of queer cultures that have formed in response to various traumas, Cvetkovich argues, "Thinking about trauma from the same depathologizing perspective that has animated queer understand-ings of sexuality opens up possibilities for understanding traumatic feel-ings not as a medical problem in search of a cure, but as felt experiences that can be mobilized in a range of directions, including the construction of cultures and publics."[29] While Cvetkovich's resistance to pathologiz-ing and curing resonates with that of many disability justice activists, the definition of the "event" of disability as traumatic remains uninter-rogated. Similarly, in popular disability parenting accounts, the parents and normative family become the producers of the cultural response to an event whose traumatic nature remains a given.

Both Perl Kingsley and Solomon are attempting such a depathologizing of disability. Their models try to imagine the production of a parenting and family culture that could incorporate disability. But the initial fact of disability as traumatic remains unquestioned, so these models unintentionally repathologize and de-lineate disabled people. Under the guise of acceptance, these narratives perpetuate the idea that a disabled child is a trauma to be overcome: a radical, unprecedented other against which the family can define itself and then congratulate itself for deigning to accept—though that acceptance leaves the child as inexorably other. Disability is rendered extraordinary and exceptional to the normal fabric of family. The child is *rendered*.

THREADING THE FAMILY NEEDLE: FROM ERASURE TO REPAIR

At the end of a life spent producing trenchant critiques of systems of power such as homophobia, seeking them out in hidden places in literary texts with paranoid precision and zeal, the literary theorist Eve Kosofsky Sedgwick began writing about disability and repair. This brilliant critic, famous for her sharp, incisive critical rhetoric, disabled by both breast cancer and its treatment, her mind fuzzing with chemo, wrote of the possibility—and necessity—of criticism as a form of repair. A reparative criticism would be in her words "additive and accretive": where paranoid criticism tears down, finds fault in, and interrogates (that favored word of literary critics!), reparative criticism builds, adds, adores. It opens up to a collective praxis, Sedgwick suggests. "What we can best learn from such [reparative] practices are, perhaps," she concludes, striking an uncharacteristically tentative tone, "the many ways selves and communities succeed in extracting sustenance from the objects of a culture—even a culture whose avowed desire has often been not to sustain them."[30] Like Sedgwick, I seek repair. So even as I expose and analyze the systematic forms of oppression that have disconnected us from our disability lineage with all the critical, scholarly, perhaps slightly paranoid argumentation in which I was trained, I want also to forge a more tentative and loving rhetoric of repair.

It was that spirit of repair that brought me to my own disability lineage in the first place. It is not only the objects of a culture that can be sources of repair and sustenance, but also the individuals: the lives from which we've been de-lineated. Their stories. To find this lineage, to even understand its necessity, I have had to surface it. Even when there are no names. We push against the void, explore the institutions and records that rendered this person as a number. In naming Cousin XY, I am reclaiming him for me. For my daughter.

It's not simple; the void is still there. A tree with absent branches.

In seeking our disability lineages, we forge transgenerational, intimate relations. Like trees, we seek to communicate across generations via complex networks of roots. Sometimes we have to graft, sometimes we dig, sometimes we sew. This is the work of repair. In Jewish tradition, every person is tasked with "*tikkun olam*," repair of the world.

A reparative disability lineage might not only expose the violently ableist systems of oppression that literally separated disabled people from their families while rhetorically separating them from the very notion of family, but would also build, limb by limb, cousin by cousin, a more just, joyful, and inclusive sense of extended kinship. Such a reparative lineage would welcome and incorporate disabled people into the family fold. A *mishpacha* for all. If I had known my own disability lineage, that autumn diagnosis day would perhaps have glistened more brightly, knowing that my daughter was connected to Cousin Rhona, Cousin XY, and untold others. I would have listened to what the disabled members of my lineage had to say about their own experiences of family, kinship, community, disability, and identity.

Instead of narrating disability as trauma and disabled people as traumatized, the complexity, resilience, and joy of disabled lives must be part of the story. We do not need more models of disability "acceptance," in which individuals are asked to tolerate their disabled brethren in private—to incorporate them into ableist family frameworks. Rather, we need to reject the notion that disability is traumatic, individual, exceptional, and rare and instead examine why disability has been delineated as such. In rejecting the trauma model, I hope we can forge a disability lineage that repairs this rupturing and allows us to learn from our disabled ancestors. To understand why I—and countless millions of other families—experienced my daughter's diagnosis and disability as traumatic, we need to denaturalize the notion of disability as trauma and explore how it *was made* traumatic. And by whom. The origins of the racist, misogynist, and ableist systems that this delineation serves must be exposed. That takes us to the Nazis. And racist Reconstruction-era America.

But even as we explore the oppressive sorting systems that de-lineated disabled people from their family story, let's keep in mind the ways disabled people pushed back, connected, included, and forged their own kinship systems, as well as the incipient possibilities for lineating that these catastrophic, violent separations suggest. How the roots were always seeking each other, the tree canopies touching. The way the discarded fruit seeds the orchard.

CHAPTER 2

NAZIS, SORTING, AND SEGREGATION

DELINEATING THE FREAKISH

Our contemporary practice of segregating disabled family members from our lineage—and from society writ large—can be directly traced back to twentieth-century German fascism. Disability studies scholars have examined in depth the origins of constructions of disability in Nazi-era rhetoric and practices. However, the effects of this fascist rhetoric on disability in families has not been examined fully—nor its reverberations on our current understandings of disability lineation. Disability's central role in defining who is and isn't considered family is directly linked to fascism and its aftermath.

Historian Carol Poore has examined how, unlike Jews, communists, and other targets of dehumanization in Nazi culture, disabled people were viewed as an *internal* threat to "Aryan" Germans: "The existence of large numbers of degenerate 'Aryan' Germans endangered the heredi- tary health of the body politic (Volkskorper) from within."[1] The family, Poore notes, was the site of intense scrutiny for this internal—what we would now call genetic—contamination. German families were forced to produce family trees proving that they contained not only no Jewish ancestors but also no disabled ones. Our current rhetoric of "good genes," and the de-lineating, ableist consequences of its supposed opposite for disabled people, is rooted in this fascist vision of the family.

Moreover, historians David Mitchell and Sharon Snyder have uncovered how the Nazis developed both the notion of the concentration camp and the mechanics of it in killing centers at hospitals for disabled people. Disabled people were first separated from the general hospital population and then, in the T4 program, exterminated in gas chambers. The Nazis worked out both their ideology and their methods, later scaled up in Auschwitz and other concentration camps, on disabled people. Though the details are gruesome and shocking, the rhetoric is familiar:

> Between 1939 and 1945, Nazi doctors, under the guise of medical advancement, killed 300,000 disabled children and adults. . . . Disabled "patients" were identified by clinicians, psychiatrists and social workers, and required to register with Nazi officials. Diagnostic records characterized them as "useless eaters," "lives unworthy of living" and "burdens upon themselves and the nation's resources."[2]

While the language may be shocking today, the underlying notion of evaluating a human's right to exist based on how independent they are persists. As Robert McGruer points out, we no longer use terms like "useless eater" to describe those who cannot contribute to capitalism's labor force; instead, we've created a category called "severely disabled" to denote expendability.[3] The persistence of sheltered workplaces where disabled workers are paid subminimum wages and segregated from "nondisabled" workers exemplifies this.[4] The act of ableist sorting—giving the state or the doctor or the family the power to divide humans into two categories and murder, mistreat, and marginalize those in one of them—is itself rooted in fascism.

The very categories of disability we create to describe bodymind variation reflect our desire to mark some people as human and redeemable and others as disposable: discarded from society, separated from their families, cut off from their lineage. Historian Edith Sheffer has argued that the twentieth-century creation of the categories of autism and Asperger's syndrome by Nazi sympathizer Hans Asperger were made purely as a means of sorting disabled children into those to be "reformed" and experimented upon (Asperger's), and those to be marked for killing (autistic).[5] Today, we know that neurologically, there is no fundamental difference between people with so-called Asperger's syndrome and autism; therefore the *DSM-IV*, the diagnostic manual for psychiatrists, no longer recognizes Asperger's as a diagnostic category.[6] There is simply no scientific basis for the distinction between Asperger's syndrome and garden-variety autism. Dr. Asperger's construction of these two categories was part of the larger Nazi project of dividing and murdering.

This numbering, marking, and labeling of disabled people was the first step in the larger Nazi project of genocide. As Mitchell and Snyder describe:

> They [disabled people] were loaded into vans with black-painted windows—nicknamed "death buses" by local children—and transported to the killing centers, countryside hospitals and institutions just outside of picturesque cities such as Dresden and Potsdam. In Berlin, "death committees" of physicians determined whether disabled people should be released, or, if their documents were marked with an ominous red cross, taken to their deaths.[7]

Once in the death centers, the Nazis experimented with the best, cheapest, and fastest methods of mass murder. They quickly moved from starvation to cramming disabled bodies into small rooms and adding gas. Mitchell and Snyder grapple with why it was so easy for the Nazis to do this to disabled people, and why there continues to be less outrage on behalf of these victims and prosecution of the perpetrators than on behalf of other targets of Nazi genocide. Their work exposes how fundamental ableism is to other forms of oppression—and its genocidal consequences.

It is disturbing to trace a direct line between the genocidal actions of German Nazis and the seemingly benign, mundane acts of my suburban Jewish American family in 1970s America. But it is undeniable that our contemporary American concepts of disability and family were forged by fascists. Unless we face this disturbing history and its foundational power in shaping diagnostic categories, institutionalization, and our concepts of family and disability, we are doomed to repeat it. Cousin XY's erasure in my family's lineage is directly linked to the black-windowed vans of T4: to Asperger and the rest. Mitchell and Snyder's evidence is as unequivocal as it is horrific. That is our legacy. Mine, and my daughter's.

The desire to construct some bodies as disabled and disposable and others as not, to sort and segregate, is not merely some leftover from the most extreme aspects of German fascism. It is rooted in American culture as well. These two forms of hatred are disturbingly connected. As scholars such as James Q. Whitman have argued, Hitler actually drew on US models of racial segregation—models that deployed racialized, ableist notions of the normate (presumed white) to justify the systemic segregation and dehumanization of African Americans—to construct his anti-Semitic rhetoric.[8]

Numerous BIPOC disability studies scholars have similarly examined how American racism and ableism co-constructed one another, before and after the Nazi era, with disproportionate consequences for BIPOC communities. As Isabella Kres-Nash argues, "The existence of the economic system of slavery relied on the social idea that African Americans lacked sufficient intelligence to participate or compete on an equal basis in society with white Americans. This idea was confirmed with the creation of several diseases specific to Black people," among them drapetomania—the "disease" of running away from one's owner.[9]

Moreover, long after Reconstruction, Black disability continues to be disparaged and pathologized, while the disabling conditions of systemic racism that make Black disability both disproportionately prevalent and "more disabling" in effect than similar impairments in other populations is erased and effaced. Black, queer, crip scholar-poet Cyrée Jarelle Johnson traces how, from the antebellum outbreak of smallpox disproportionately affecting Black people due to living conditions produced by systemic racism to our recent COVID-19 pandemic, "Black illness is treated as inevitable and attributed to some inherent racial inferiority," rather than to the racist conditions that produce it in disproportionate amounts and effects.[10]

This all-American sorting of bodies as ill or disabled according to their race was borrowed by the German Nazis, retooled to fit anti-Semitic ideas about Jewish intrinsic illness, weakness, and disability, piloted on the bodies of disabled Germans of all religions, and implemented on a mass scale on Jews. The fascist rhetoric of the Nazis, rather than being originary, borrowed much of the racist-ableist rhetoric of post–Civil War US culture and then sent it back to the US in ways that continue in current rhetoric about disease and disability.

After World War II and the vanquishing of the Nazis by the Allies, it is ironic—and tragic—that the fascist sorting systems and discourse of family fine-tuned by the Nazis were then deployed on disabled people in the US through institutionalization and de-lineation. In the hyper-industrialized culture of post–World War II America, disability was viewed as a symptom of unhygienic otherness that needed to be segregated, institutionalized, and de-lineated from the white family. As the state returned white women workers to the home, medical discourse and institutional care replaced home care. Doctors replaced mothers as the makers and markers of who was "healthy" and white enough to be included in that family.[11] Mass institutionalization of white disabled people in segregated institutions, often employing underpaid BIPOC care workers, and the continued disabling and pathologizing of Black people through racist ideas of health, produced Blackness itself as a disability. In effect, disability became a kind of racialized, dehumanized specter of the two-parent, single-breadwinner, white middle-class family.

At the same time, in part *because* of these new forms of de-lineation and segregation, the disability rights movement gained traction. After the war, the ranks of disabled veterans swelled, and the Barden-LaFollette Act of 1943 expanded vocational, educational, and rehabilitative services for some veterans and other disabled people—those sorted as not *too* disabled.[12] However, this incipient civil rights movement for some (white, war veteran) disabled people was coupled with increasing segregation and dehumanization of other (Black, "severely" or congenitally) disabled people.

Mass institutionalization of disabled people from the post–Civil War era until the late 1970s was the less-than-final solution to those sorted as having "severely disabled" bodyminds. Kim Nielson convincingly argues that as the US struggled to define itself as a nation after the Civil War, and as a modern one at that, the debate over whose bodies and minds should count increasingly was played out by defining, controlling, and institutionalizing those bodyminds deemed disabled.[13] Segregated insane asylums helped construct Black desires for freedom and agency as a form of disability, echoing the antebellum invention of drapetomania.[14] Asylums, almshouses, and prisons were built on a mass scale to define and contain those the state wished to marginalize. As Ivan Brown and John P. Radford argue, "The institutional era needs to be understood not only as the operation of a series of large and separated building complexes [for disabled people] but also as a state of mind"—one that led to separating permanently the vast majority of people with intellectual or other "severe" disabilities from their families and communities.[15]

Segregated educational institutions such as Gallaudet, set up for people with particular disabilities, proliferated as well, amid debates over who was included in the universe of supposedly universal public education. Whereas home care and integration in the community had previously been the norm in the US, the industrialization and modernization that came in the wake of Reconstruction, as well as debates about who qualified as a citizen, led to mass segregation and institutionalization of those labeled as disabled. My grandfather thought he was being modern—enlightened, humane—by insisting on institutionalization!

The parallel, segregated spaces of institutions defined, marginalized, and segregated disabled people, separating them from their families and communities. This often led to horrific abuse. It almost always resulted in de-lineation. However, in some cases, like educational institutions such as Gallaudet, these segregated spaces also afforded disabled people unprecedented opportunities for community building, self-determination, and the forging of a collective identity as disabled. Disabled people were not merely passive victims of this attempt to define citizenship against disability. Many disabled people became activists and leaders for the larger cause of disability rights. Paul Strachan, for example, founded the American Federation of the Physically Handicapped in 1940 and created a sea change in policies, laws, and practices regarding the employment of disabled workers. Gallaudet (and its predecessor, the National Deaf-Mute College) produced numerous activists and innovators such as Agatha Tiegel, whose work as a disability advocate, educator, and feminist helped transform the opportunities available to deaf women.[16] But the success of these exceptional few happened in concert with the mass institutionalization of the majority of disabled people who were not deemed fit to work—and hence not human. People with intellectual and developmental disabilities suffered enormously from this system, as they were considered ineducable, unsocializable, warehousable. Their families were instructed to disown them.

While many families simply abandoned their children to institutions, some families maintained complex ties to their children, both de- and re-lineating them. My own family's embrace of institutionalization demonstrates the complexity of how these bonds were severed, forged, repaired, and severed again as the institution replaced and ruptured the family.

LEGACIES OF INSTITUTIONALIZATION: COUSIN RHONA

In the summer of 2017, I was in Manchester, England, visiting friends, and thought I'd call on a family member I remembered from childhood: my grandfather's cousin Myron. I had last visited Myron and his family in Manchester when I was eight, when my dad was on sabbatical doing research in the UK. I remembered a drafty Victorian house, a teen's room covered in Beatles paraphernalia, and the names of Myron's children. I contacted them; they suggested I meet with their aunt Vera, Myron's sister, as Myron was too senile to meet new-old family members.

So I met Auntie Vera in Heathlands Village, a Jewish residential care home for older people with the charm of a country estate. She was warm, as sharp as a ninety-two-year-old tack can be, and eager to share the minute details of our family history. Vera had clearly put some care into the stylish sweater-and-pants ensemble with a brooch and the exact same semi-cat's-eye sunglasses my own grandmother used to wear. "Darling! You look just like your grandmother. Those curls!" She hugged me tightly, leaving a pink lipstick kiss on my cheek. Out came the faded photo albums she'd been curating for the past half century.

Her daughter Ann was there, clearly the organized eldest child who managed her mother's care and remembered everyone's birthday with a brisk let's-get-on-with-it English efficiency. While Auntie Vera appeared happy to have any relative, however distant, as a visitor, Ann understandably wanted to know a little more about me and my intentions. Who was this far-flung Fink, and what did she really want? So I told her about Finks near and far, and, along with details about our various marriages, divorces, and professional accomplishments, mentioned my daughter's disability.

It's the face that counts. If pity and fear shadow their eyes, I know instantly: This person is uncomfortable with disabled people. This person does not have a healthy, lived relationship to disability. This person will see me as a hero for loving my own daughter. And I know what's next: a sort of amateur intake, wherein they ask a series of questions to ascertain if my child qualifies as human. How disabled she is. How far from the tree she's fallen. If their face does not change, and there is perhaps even a nod of acknowledgment, then I know we're okay. That while they might describe their experiences using different language than I would, they have a lived, not entirely phobic relationship to disability. Usually, the shadow appears and I know exactly where we're heading.

But there was no shadow in Anna's blue eyes. And yes, there was the nod. "Lots of that in our family, isn't it?" she noted matter-of-factly.

"Disability? Yes," I acknowledged.

"Do you know about Rhona?" No trace of anxiety or fear: just a clear, firm tone.

"Rhona?" I'd never heard such a name.

"She had Down syndrome," Anna said in a careful tone. She looked into my eyes, searching for the shadow.

"She was my sister," Auntie Vera proclaimed with a certain pride. "Always so clean," she added, trying to ward off the shadow.

I was confused. "There was another child? A sister—to Myron, and to you, Auntie Vera?"

"Oh, yes. Rhona: our wee sister. Mum founded Cosgrove for her, and we still contribute. Your grandfather never said a word about her, eh?" She half smiled, half grimaced. My mouth knows that expression too well.

Out came a whole other set of photo albums. A spirited little girl in glasses, with a giant grin. In every picture she is with her siblings, parents, and extended family, apparently loved and embraced by them. Then the same child, still surrounded by family, who's now a round-faced teen with characteristic Down syndrome features. They used to call such features "mongoloid," believing they looked Mongolian. I remember hearing my grandfather refer to Cousin XY that way, one of the only times that I ever heard him mentioned. I thought of my daughter, who is half Asian, who is often assumed by white people to have Down syndrome.

"They never told you about Rhona? Even when you were here in the '70s, visiting with Myron?" Ann frowned; Auntie Vera's face froze in that half smile, half grimace.

"Never."

Ann looked down at her hands. "Now didn't your grandfather have a son who had a child with Down syndrome?"

Cousin XY. They knew about XY! Somehow this was shocking to me. I quickly explained how he was given away at birth. Abandoned to the state. Presumably institutionalized. Possibly dead.

"A shame," they both tsked. Tsk, tsk. It felt good to tsk away the trauma with these strangers, my family.

A thought seized me: "Did my grandfather know about Rhona?"

Auntie Vera grinned her charming grin. "Let me show you something, my dear." Out came more photo albums, and one particular photo.

It's a family affair. Wedding? Bar mitzvah? Something of the sort. The event long forgotten, but its image is captured for all eternity in this black-and-white photo. There's Myron, looking every bit the suave, successful psychiatrist in an ever-so-English three-piece bespoke suit. Standing beside him is my grandfather, much as I remember him: a bit rumpled, but with the same ginormous, face-eating grin you'll find living on the faces of my father, myself, and my daughter.

And there, seated to the left: Rhona. Hands together, dressed in a fine taffeta plaid number, smiling. Visibly disabled. Visible to all, in public. Integrated into the world of mid-twentieth-century, middle-class Jewish ritual life. Included. Looking rather pleased with it all.

"Oh, yes, Ben knew Rhona. He and Myron were great friends, you know. Not just cousins. Both men of science and all. Ben wanted Myron to come to the US, was going to sponsor their immigration, but because of Rhona, they stayed." Because of Rhona. "Better care for Downs people in Scotland, you know."

So my grandfather's unrelenting pressure on my aunt and uncle to abandon their son, my cousin XY, had a context. A history. A lineage. A taffeta dress.

"What became of Rhona?" The question was out of my mouth before I realized how rude it might seem.

"Well, she's dead now, died in 2001. Born in 1946, when I was already a young lady of twenty! But she lived in Cosgrove. Lived well." Auntie Vera explained with enormous pride how in 1963 her mother enlisted the local reverend, I. K. Cosgrove—as well as their local (non-Jewish) member of Parliament and wealthier Jewish philanthropists—to start an assisted living center for Jewish people. For Rhona.

It was *because* of Rhona that my grandfather so vehemently insisted on de-lineating Cousin XY. After learning about Rhona, I wanted to know my family's full disability lineage and to connect, if possible, with Cousin XY. I'd known about him since his birth, when I was six. But I had never thought of him as part of my family. Part of my disabled family and its lineage.

By sharing a bit about the process of how I partially refound Cousin XY, I want to demonstrate how reintegrating *what we already know* about our disabled family members can powerfully combat ableism and create a living disability lineage, even in the face of institutionalization, abandonment, and repression. Finding our disability lineage is as much about what was always hiding in plain sight as it is the discovery of new information. Moreover, the absences, gaps, and aporias—what remains unknowable and unrecoverable—are as significant a part of the family story as what we can recover.

In my case, I found a little of both: substance and silence. What could be found, what was lost. To find out more about Cousin XY, I began with the internet. I knew from experience that asking my family about him would be met with a set response: he was given away, better off for it, that's all we know, he's not really your family. So I turned to the internet and its web of lives, searching the birth records for Cousin XY, knowing only his sex, year and place of birth, and his parents' names. Fink, Samuel A. and Carol P.[17] Male. I typed in the date, city, and state of his birth. With a few keystrokes, I was drowning in a sea of Finks. An ocean of newborn male Finks. David, Terrence, Frank. Frank Fink? There's a terrible idea for a name.

As I swam deeper in this endless ocean of data, an art project came to mind: Christian Boltanski's *The Reserve of Dead Swiss* (1990), sometimes translated as *All the Dead Swiss*.[18] In this conceptual artwork, Boltanski presents forty-two portraits of randomly selected Swiss citizens who died in a recent year. He blows up their portraits, and illuminates them with light bulbs, but gives us no context. No information to understand what we're seeing. Why these particular dead Swiss, what is their importance? I interpreted *All the Dead Swiss* as a sort of commentary on Holocaust memorials: on the impossibility—and necessity—of remembering ordinary citizens who remain only as numbers. "All the Live Finks," I thought as I sorted through reams upon reams of newborn Finks.

Then I saw it: Samuel Fink. My uncle's name. Listed as deceased. I was momentarily confused: We Jews do not name our sons for the living. Only the dead.

Now, neither my uncle nor Cousin XY were dead in 1972, and I know for a fact that my aunt and uncle refused to see or name their son. But the state did. The state Christianized him, gave him his father's name, and made "You are dead to me" a living truth. Cousin XY didn't actually die, but the state allowed his identity as a Jewish male individual to die. For his life in my family to end.

This erasure of Cousin XY in my family narrative—and in the state's official records—is by no means unusual, and was the norm in the 1970s, when Cousin XY was born. Institutionalization disconnected both of my cousins from the family story. But when a family cuts a disabled member out of the narrative, the disabled family member does not disappear—instead, they suffer needlessly in institutions or as a resident in the family home who ghosts its peripheries, while the other family members lose the joy—and complexity—of knowing and caring for that particular individual. This is not simply my personal opinion; research suggests that disabled individuals live longer, healthier, and more productive lives when they stay part of their families. Even the best institutions dehumanize and limit their lives.[19]

It's easy to understand why my family feared that Rhona would be converted to Christianity without her consent, and would want to found a Jewish institution for her care. The souls of the disabled were often the price of institutional care in the UK in the twentieth century. At the time of Rhona's institutionalization, there was no separation of church and state in the UK; all public institutions required their residents to practice Christianity. Forced conversions were perfectly legal. Disabled people were vulnerable to institutional abuse of all kinds, including spiritual abuse.[20] As disability historians note, institutions for the disabled have notoriously forced Christianization and conversion on their disabled residents in the global north, in those countries in which separation of church and state was not written into the law.[21] In Scotland, this forced conversion and Christianization continued until the 1980s. And while this has ended as official practice in most state institutions in the global north, spiritual abuse has been exported by missionaries to much of the rest of the world, where Christian missions are often the primary sources of institutional, long-term care for disabled people.

Even in contemporary America, private, religiously affiliated institutions are often the best—and in some cases the only—sources of care for the disabled. Catholic Charities and Jewish Family Services are some of the largest and oldest providers of direct services to people with disabilities at all stages in the life cycle. In smaller towns and cities, these are often the primary providers of such services, and even in metropolitan areas, religious organizations often provide the best quality of such services, due to their vast resources and tax-free status.

In my own upper-middle-class, diverse, secular community, the *only* provider of overnight respite care for disabled families, where parents can drop off their disabled children for a night or two of respite from their caregiving duties, is a fundamentalist Christian, Protestant church–affiliated place called Jill's House.[22] When I explored this option for my family, I was shocked to learn that bedtime prayers praising Jesus are mandatory for all who stay there. Instead of professional caregivers, Christian teens and young adults provide both physical and "spiritual" care. Is this really so different from the forced Christianization of Rhona's era? Even today, there is no secular alternative, much less a Jewish one. Many of my secular peers in the autistic family community regularly drop off their disabled children at Jill's House for a night or two of respite. But the thought of my daughter, the burgeoning Torah scholar, being forced, however kindly, to pray to a god that is not hers for a redemption (from her disability?) that she does not want is so upsetting, so dehumanizing, that we have never used Jill's House's otherwise well-regarded respite care. Which means we have never been able to access any respite care at all.

It is no wonder that my Scottish relatives sought to provide Rhona a Jewish alternative to such forced professions of faith. What is astounding is how successful they were. Rhona was not just not Christian: she lived the life of a Jewish woman. Because of my relatives' advocacy, Rhona was able to practice her religion and determine her own spiritual path. To do so involved moving mountains: founding an entire institution, persuading the local Christian gentry that this was a legitimate and spiritually sound project, obtaining the property for such a venture, and funding it. Otherwise, Rhona's Jewishness would have been denied, erased, destroyed: purchased as the price of care.

Rhona means joy in Hebrew. And as I learned from Auntie Vera and Anna, Jewish life was Rhona's greatest joy: lighting candles, saying the prayers. It was in order to provide her with an adult Jewish life that this family started Cosgrove. Auntie Vera conveyed how proud she was of her family's role in creating this Jewish institution.

This Jewish institution. Any institution, however wonderful, is still, well, an institution. I celebrate these women, their bravery in insisting that Rhona's life had value, that she could be part of their family, part of that dinner my grandfather attended. That she exercised not just the right to life but also the right to a Jewish life. Rhona's mother stands in a long tradition of mothers of disabled children who, as disability theorist and Down syndrome parent Michael Bérubé notes, ignored the "experts" who advised them to abandon their children entirely to institutions.[23] Her mother raised Rhona with dignity and care at home. She then founded a humane institution in which Rhona could live out her adulthood with her spirituality and culture intact. That was no small accomplishment for a middle-class postwar Jewish woman in an extremely ableist, Christian, and patriarchal culture.

Yet we can't celebrate Cosgrove uncritically. Institutions institution-alize. That's what they're there for. They segregate those in their care from the rest of society and perpetuate a definition of the family as that which is free of disability. They are a legacy of the German Nazis and the American segregationists, an irony not lost on me when I consider this compli-cated legacy. I have to also think about this anti-Semitic history, how it still haunts the care of the disabled and the rhetoric of institutional care, even now, even for my daughter.

It is because of institutionalization that I was cut off from my disabil-ity lineage, and my daughter was disconnected from her disabled elders. This is not an innocent omission but rather the erasure of a person, a cul-ture. A lineage. Knowing Rhona, even knowing *of* her, would have altered my understanding of family and enabled me to see my daughter and her disability, lineating it in the story of family.

However liberal and shiny these institutional spaces might have been, they were part of a genocidal system of sorting, segregating, and ostraciz-ing disabled people from their families. They also separated their fam-ilies from any sense of connectedness to disabled people. Cosgrove was founded to segregate. Rhona did not choose to live there. However Jewish and generous Cosgrove may have been, its very existence was profoundly, fundamentally shaped by the logic of the Nazis—as was the eradication of my cousin XY from my family.

Today, many such institutions, including Cosgrove (now Cosgrove Care), have evolved to embrace an independent living framework that centers the needs of their disabled residents, provides them maximum au-tonomy, and serves most of their clients in their own families and households. Disabled adults may need and want to live apart from their families, as do many nondisabled adults. They may need supports and even group settings to do so successfully, and there are many excellent examples of group homes that center the disabled person in every facet of life. Cosgrove Care has evolved into one of such exemplary institutions. Disability activists have worked hard to close the worst of congregate care institutions and transform the rest. In my own community in the Washington, DC, area, Main Street—a nonprofit organization whose motto is "Inclusivity Redefined"—works to created supported living environments for disabled adults in well-maintained apartment buildings that also include nondisabled adults.[24] Activists stress social integration, autonomy, and community; Main Street reflects these values in its slogan "Bring Your Independence." Its community-building activities, café, community center, and mix of disabled and nondisabled residents all support the integration of its diverse bodyminds. These "supported living communities" by all accounts are a world away from the horrific human warehouses of the past.

But supported living communities of people with disabilities can still result in a de-lineation from the family. Without re-lineating disability to our kinship systems, rethinking how we define family and why we exclude and marginalize our disabled family members, even the most progressive and "client-centered" approach is ultimately dehumanizing. The result, in the mid-twentieth century, led to a sorting of my cousins, a final institutional solution separating them from their families and lineage. One was deemed as not worth keeping at home and one was not worth keeping at all. In the twenty-first centuries, the story is more complicated, but despite mass deinstitutionalization, disability is still widely de-lineated.

Deinstitutionalization of people with disabilities, which happened as a result of the disability rights movement of the 1970s, and '80s, may have ended the most extreme and brutal forms of this sorting, but not its rancid rhetoric.[25] It persists in our understanding and definition of family. While mass institutionalization of disabled people is no longer the norm, our continued desire to cure, sort, abort, and segregate our disabled kin far, far away from us (perhaps in a cushy "wellness center") is the legacy of this ableist de-lineation. As the double erasures of Cousin

XY and Cousin Rhona demonstrate, the family continues to define itself by repressing its disability lineage. Our very sense of family—and disability—is a product of these racist, ableist sorting systems born of Nazism. That is why I keep returning to the scene of the crime: T4 and the fascist birth of the institution.

THE RED CROSS: INVERTING NATIONALISM, FREAKIFYING THE NORMATE

An odd detail in Mitchell and Snyder's recounting of the origins of genocide swims to the surface: the red cross. The Nazi German state marked disabled people who were deemed incurable with a red cross, the international symbol of borderless medical care—the irony surely unintentional. All the disabled individuals, like all the Swiss dead of Boltanski's art installation, were first carefully documented and numbered. Then they were marked for extinction with that red cross. In so marking, they were deindividuated, dehumanized, and selected for extermination. We know all this because their numbers were so carefully recorded. This separating and sorting found its way into the very foundation of diagnostic categories of mental health in the twentieth century: as we have seen, Asperger's syndrome was invented to preserve some bodies to be "cured"—operated on, medicated, tested—while other bodies were marked for death.

But the red cross itself offers another, more complex story. By following that one little detail—that red cross—we might open up some new ways of working through these old problems of identity, classification, and cure as they play out in public policy and in the private space of Auntie Vera's photo album. This odd emblem of a red cross that the Nazis appropriated for their horrific purposes from the humanistic Red Cross organization might, surprisingly, offer some possibilities for this rethinking. For imagining another narrative.

The Red Cross predates the Nazi's red cross. It was started in Switzerland in 1863, originally called the International Committee for the Relief of the Wounded, and was part of the first Geneva Convention, where the concept of a neutral medical body on the battlefield tasked with the care of the wounded emerged. Buried in that history is a flag. An inverted flag. "Its emblem," the official website of the International Red Cross proclaims, "[is] a red cross on a white background: the inversion of the Swiss flag."[26] The red cross that the Nazis appropriated to mark the documents of the disabled, to replace their names and individuality with a signifier marking them for their future murder, is an inverted nationalist Christian symbol.

At its founding, the Red Cross both invokes nationalism—which creates the flags under which the state conducts warcraft—and reverses it. The cross, symbolizing Christ's blood and mercy, takes center stage and absorbs all the red from the flag: the territory it represents, the bloodied bodies of the men who wage war under its aegis. The Red Cross, a symbol of the neutral act of caring for the war injured, is still under the sign of a flag—specifically of Switzerland, which remained neutral in both world wars.[27] But the *cross*, not the flag, is red. The flag itself is white: a blank page, the flag of no nation. Free of blood and theology.[28] The Red Cross and its flag wave over all, regardless of country, and under its auspices bodies are cared for indiscriminately. As Benedict Anderson demonstrates, nations are imagined communities, cultural artifacts created to produce a collective identity that exists only *through* this imagining.[29] The community of care that the Red Cross imagines both transcends the individual nation and invokes it through its very use of the flag— the emblem of nation. But this flag unifies rather than demarcates. It waves over all with no sorting by nation, by ability, by whether you are to be cured or cared for. The original motto of the Red Cross—"In War, Charity"—emphasizes care: aid to those in need, regardless of category. Regardless of curability.

This is precisely what I am arguing for: care, not cure. And to push the Red Cross model a bit, not toward charity, with its stench of pity and hierarchy, either. Care: integrating disability into the family and by extension society, rather than separating or sorting. But we can't entirely get away from marking and sorting, from states with their flags and crosses and the internationalism that pushes against it. At its core, care is always engaged in a complicated, sometimes inverted relationship to the state and its institutions.

I want to keep the Red Cross and its flag in mind in envisioning what true inclusion in family lineage would look like. That the Nazis appropriated this emblem of care as a mark of incurability—and hence meriting only destruction in a gas chamber—serves to remind us of how pernicious the sorting of humans is. How even neutral or positive symbols can be misused. Sorting might seem neutral, but the very need to mark otherizes and delineates. Yet nonetheless, I suggest reclaiming this symbol for disabled people and their families.

This may seem just another instance of label proliferation, of yet another group demanding rights and recognition at the cost of integration into society. If the goal is to acknowledge our disability lineage, if all our families include multiple forms of disability across generations, if disability is the rule of human experience, not the exception to it, why do we even need the term "disability"—why mark some as disabled, marking them like the goddamned *Nazis*, if we will all experience disability if we live long enough? Yet if we don't mark, flag, label, name, will disabled people once again be marginalized and even eliminated?

The Red Cross flag helps provide a model for navigating this conundrum. Disability activist and writer Tom Shakespeare explores some possibilities similar to those of the Red Cross flag for reimagining disability. The social model of disability suggests, as Shakespeare argues, that "the difference between disabled people and non-disabled is not that we have bodies or minds which do not work, but that we are an oppressed minority."[30] This seems like a solid, straightforward argument for using the term "disability" to denote not impairment, but rather the minority status in society of those who are so impaired. But Shakespeare then rather spectacularly undoes that logic, arguing, "An embodied ontology would argue instead that there is no qualitative difference between disabled people and non-disabled people, because *we are all impaired*."[31] He goes on to cite the Human Genome Project's discovery that every person's genetic code contains mutation, as well as the "empirical" fact that we will all face some sort of impairment or disability as we age. The Red Cross flag similarly unites us under care.

Why even retain the term "disabled," then, if we are all impaired, mutated, uniquely deviating from the nonexistent yet all-powerful norm? Among disability activists and scholars, there is a lively debate about how to name and claim identity as someone minoritized by and potentially discriminated against because of impairment without perpetuating a system that disables some bodies and denies the impairment of others. Such a privileging, ranking, and sorting of bodies can only, in this view, ultimately perpetuate ableism. They argue for eliminating the whole category of disability, as its rhetoric cannot be separated from the ableism that produced it.

Rosemarie Garland-Thomson and Eli Clare present nuanced theoretical elaborations of this position, Clare arguing for a valuing of all bodyminds and Garland-Thomson deconstructing the normate-disabled binary that invented and pathologized "disabled" in the first place.[32] Crip pride activists offer a more politicized sense of how to resignify and expand notions of disability. They instead suggest that, just as LGBTQ+ people have expanded the category of "gay" to include basically any sexual identity besides straight and have embraced the derogatory umbrella term "queer" as a rallying political cry of pride, disabled people should expand the category and reclaim "crip." "Crip" is a term, as activist-scholar Carrie Sandhal suggests, that "is fluid and ever-changing" and can more readily be expanded to "include not only those with physical impairments but those with sensory or mental impairments as well."[33] Alison Kafer argues that "crip" has a political function, pointing to the constructed and changeable ways that disability is mobilized differently at various historical and cultural moments: "Claiming crip can be a way of acknowledging that we all have bodies and minds with shifting abilities, and that such shifts have political and social meanings and histories."[34] So while we may all have diverse, varying abilities and bodyminds, the social and political context values and sorts them differently, in different historical moments, for different purposes.

Disability justice activists like Mia Mingus have adopted a "both and more" approach, arguing for the inclusion of all bodyminds, with all the specificity of disability and the radical deconstructive force of crip. As she eloquently suggests, this involves "moving away from an equality-based model of sameness and 'we are just like you' to a model of disability that embraces difference, confronts privilege and challenges what is considered 'normal' on every front."[35] It also means engaging with embodiment: the material conditions, challenges, and lived experiences of particular bodyminds. "What do we do with bodies that have limitations, that are different (no matter how much we want to change them)?" asks Mingus pointedly in "Changing the Framework." "How do we acknowledge that all bodies are different, while also not ignoring the very real ways that certain bodies are labeled and treated as 'disabled?'"[36] This involves a radical reframing of how disability gets defined, and by whom, which honors rather than elides difference. As the title of her piece suggests, this means changing the framework, not just the labels produced inside it.

But despite the way these important conversations challenge and reframe how we define and value disability, the fundamental question of sorting remains. Do we continue to perpetuate a binary system—one instantiated by the German Nazis, inflected by American racists—of sorting people into disabled or abled, knowing the disastrous (segregating, institutionalizing, genociding, dehumanizing) consequences for individuals, families, and communities? Or do we relinquish the term "disabled" and the identity it marks and holds, the forms of oppression it names, the community it can build, the pride and self-determination it enables?

The paradoxical emblem of the Red Cross flag offers a both-and way out of this conundrum. As long as we still need to fight ableism, some term is needed to distinguish those who are minoritized on the basis of their physical, mental, and/or cognitive differences from those who are majoritized. However imperfect and fraught they may be, we need terms to mark this difference. Identity is necessary. But on whose terms? Without markers of identity, those minoritized and oppressed cannot organize, fight for, and *value* their identities. Similarly, some term is needed to mark that we still do sort some people as disabled, while others (who may also be impaired—as Shakespeare suggests, we are all in some sense impaired, atypical, *sui generis* mutants) we do not. "Flag" is also a verb: an act of marking. Denoting a special case. Noticing difference. Whether that marking is genocidal and delineating or empowering and affiliating is up to us.

Lest this all seem too abstract, let me bring it back home. To my home. If we didn't have the term "disabled," how could my daughter reclaim Rhona and Cousin XY as part of her specific heritage? Her disability lineage? The *un*marking of Cousin XY has in fact rendered him largely unreclaimable. Unnamed, erased. Dehumanized, in a more totalizing, absolute fashion than the term "disabled" possibly can. So I vote for flagging. Naming. Marking. But the way we organize that marking—and the terminology and marks used to do so—matters. It needn't be the singular, stigmatizing marking of the Nazis and racists. Naming and claiming can be fluid, collective, lineating.

The Red Cross flag offers an emblem for the neutral marking of disability. It also links it to care. Rather than simply rejecting flags, labels, identities, let's embrace and redefine them. Let's keep them fluid, in motion. This is in keeping with a new model of disability emerging from activists such as TL Lewis and Mia Mingus that retains disability as a term, identity, and marker. These disability justice activists argue for disability identity as both fluid and collective. After all, disability is experienced by everyone over their lifetime, either through their care of others or their own experiences. It is fluid, dynamic: shared.

Disability identity therefore need not be static. As Sharon Barnartt argues, "Disability is often described in a way that suggests that it is a permanent and relatively stable state. Even when it is described as being socially constructed, the implication is that impairment leads to a permanent status of being 'disabled.'"[37] She argues that disability is much more fluid and complex than this, as the relationship between impairment and disability is neither predictable nor fixed. Disability can be reconceived as a set of embodied experiences produced in relation to both intrinsic impairment and external forces, while *also* being a powerful form of self-identity. Moreover, by imagining disability as collective rather than a "flaw" of a particular bodymind and as a shared experience involving care, interdependency, family, and community, it can be a source of joy and connection rather than segregation and shame.

A flag, by nature, waves. It is in motion. Who waves it, what does it wave over? That is negotiated. Mutable, and mutational. It is this radically mobile and mutational aspect of the flag that I want to explore. To name and claim for disability. For that, I'll need to borrow from the hippies. And the Brazilians.

OS MUTANTES—WE ARE ALL MUTANTS: MOBILIZING OUR DISABILITY LINEAGE

In the late 1960s in Brazil, Tropicalia was far more than merely a musical genre: it was a social movement—enacted through music. Its psychedelic aesthetic aimed to critique the ruling military dictatorship and invent a new, freer, more equal way of being in the world. Tropicalia bands fused indigenous Brazilian folk music traditions (with multiple points of origin in Portugal and Africa) with contemporary psychedelic US and UK pop forms. Through their trippy sound and psychedelic appearance, they hoped to offer a new model for a more peaceful, more equal society. If this sounds like a frivolous hippie fantasy to you, please note that Brazil's ruling dictatorship took it very seriously, exiling some of its most prominent members, such as Caetano Veloso, and banning Tropicalia from public spaces.[38]

One prominent band to emerge from this movement was Os Mutantes, "The Mutants." I'm invoking Os Mutantes because their embrace of mutants and rejection of normativity, combined with their deep mining of Brazil's hybrid indigenous musical cultures, provides a creative way of thinking about how to refashion identities in ways that grow our roots and lineages without dividing, sorting, and segregating. Mutation and monstrosity are central to ableist discourses of disability. By creatively mobilizing the marking of difference, flying the freak flag of mutation and mutability rather than deploying it as a static, segregating marker, Os Mutantes suggest how the marking of disability can be re-marked, remade, and reimagined. Most of all, disability can be re-lineated by mo-

NAZIS, SORTING, AND SEGREGATION | 43

bilizing some of the ableist markers, institutions, and paradigms that produced it in the first place. To do so requires creativity and imagination, as well as laws and institutions.

Instead of depending only on the state and legal mechanisms, increasingly disability justice activists are demanding that we challenge and change all the other, more subtle aspects of society that perpetuate ableism and lead disabled people to be functionally marginalized, even when legally included. This more complex form of inclusion requires fundamental cultural and structural changes. "Inclusion is not like a light switch that simply gets turned on or off," notes the organization Respectability. "It is more like a dimmer switch that you push forward into the light."[39] This requires rewiring the inherited symbols and systems that produced "ability" and "disability" as structuring terms in the first place. I am suggesting that one way a more complete form of inclusion can be enacted is through a kind of red crossing: an inversion of the symbols that were designed to mark, sort, segregate, and dispose of the disabled. Some models of such a re-marking can be found in the embrace of the mutant by Os Mutantes, and of the freak flag in the 1960s.

"Let your freak flag fly" remains a popular phrase in the US, used to encourage nonconformity. Like Os Mutantes, its origins lie in the '60s hippie movement—and its music. The first known use of the term is by musician David Crosby in the song "Almost Cut My Hair," written for the Crosby, Stills, Nash, and Young album *Déjà Vu*. In the lyrics, Crosby captures a moment of self-doubt—and temporary disability. He doesn't know why he doesn't conform: why he lets his "freak flag fly" and doesn't cut his hair. He then blames his desire for conformity on having had the flu. Significantly for our purposes, it is a temporarily disabling illness that makes him meditate on his hair nonconformity, and subsequently leads him to ponder both his freak flag and the community to whom he and his hair pledge allegiance. A kinship of freaks, an extended family of no nation, is loosely united by this hirsute flag.

Like the Red Cross flag, the freak flag potentially offers a playful means of marking the collective identity of disabled people while keeping it in motion, loosely defined, open to change. Freaks and the discourse to descend: "Only then do I see the swirl marks that glaciers left in the granite, tiny orange newts, . . . my shaky balance gives me this intimacy with the mountain. I would lose so much if that imaginary cure pill actually existed."[43] Our differences—including our impairments—are part of the unique lens through which we each see the world. If we let go of the binary between the curable and incurable, we begin to loosen the chokehold of the human-inhuman binary we inherited from the racists and Nazis as well.

What would science, care, and yes, cure, look like if they *weren't* ruled by the thirst for normativity? Can there be a science aimed at reducing pain and suffering that honors our bodymind differences? What might the radical recent discoveries of genetics look like through such a lens? So many discussions about disability are shadowed and framed by cure. To change and challenge this, we need to reimagine this relationship to health, science, genetics, and disability. I take Clare's radical rethinking, therefore, as a starting point for a radical reclamation of disability lineages. In reclaiming my cousins XY and Rhona for my family, I am rejecting the sorting and shaming, the stigmatizing marking that unnames and dehumanizes. I hope to shift the conversation from the simplistic binaries in which they so often get stuck, and instead embrace a science and ethics of brilliant imperfection. To fly its freak flag, Red Cross logo clearly visible, with perhaps a Muslim crescent, a Trans pink-and-blue pattern, and a Jewish star intersecting it, woven together in its fluid fabric.

CHAPTER 3

GENES AND GENOCIDE

THE JUNK SCIENCE OF ABLEISM

The fear of "*os mutantes*" runs deep. As deep as a prenatal needle as it plunged into my bulging stomach. "No!" I cried.

I was having a standard test, *the* standard genetic test, the one almost everyone, especially women of "advanced maternal age" like myself at thirty-nine, has when they are pregnant to find out if they have a child who is likely to have Down syndrome. It is a common test. A marvel of science. It is one of the few such tests offered to pregnant people. Besides the sex, the only information one receives about one's fetus is whether it is likely to have Down syndrome. The cardinal information every pregnant woman receives is about disability—for the tacit reason that she may abort the fetus if it has the "wrong" number of chromosomes.

I was having the test everyone has. Chorionic villus sampling, or CVS. "As common as the drugstore," my OB-GYN quipped. Yet it felt wrong. I knew that if the fetus had an extra chromosome, I would keep it. I knew it in my bones. In my uterus. But there I was, having a needle plunged directly into said uterus despite being certain that I would keep said fetus no matter what. Every doctor, every relative, even my spouse had urged me to get this test. "Don't you at least want to know?" she asked, not unreasonably. This was hard logic to fight: after all, knowledge is power, even if it comes in the form of a needle. It wasn't the tiny chance of the needle causing complications or even a miscarriage that was freaking me out. It wasn't even the test itself, but rather the cultural ideas about disability that it carried.

I didn't have the tools to articulate any of this yet. My resistance seemed irrational. Hormonal! As the tears streamed down and the nurse offered reassurances that there was very little chance that my fetus would be "wrong," and that of course I would have "options" if there was something "wrong," I got even more upset. I had always thought of myself as a rational, pro-science person. I'm a geneticist's daughter, after all. But I was perplexed by everyone's belief that I needed to know the chromosome count of my baby in utero. And everyone was equally perplexed by my certainty that I didn't want this knowledge, and that I would keep my fetus regardless of what the test revealed.

"Everyone," of course, means my pro-choice liberal friends, family, and medical practitioners. Almost half of everyone else thinks exactly the opposite, and believes it perhaps even more ardently.[1] Because it isn't really knowledge that we're debating here. It's whether we think a given fetus is normal enough to be allowed to survive. For the record, I am 100 percent pro-choice. Nobody is served—children least of all—by women being forced to bear children they don't want. As someone who nearly died during pregnancy and childbirth, I am well aware of their profound physical and emotional risks and costs. But I am as concerned about the genocidal effects of prenatal testing and abortion on disabled lives as I am about access to abortion, reproductive healthcare, and family planning. *How* we make choices both at the beginning and at the end of life has been ruled by a regime of ableism that harms us all.

Choices aren't made in a vacuum. The space around the right to choose to terminate a pregnancy is densely populated by ableist conceptions of what makes a life worth living, and by the segregationist impulses that ableism engenders: to sort lives into those worth living and those not, even before they begin. On both sides, the discussion is not only incredibly polarized but is also based on faulty, ableist reasoning.

Our culture's squeamishness with disabled people parenting—and possibly reproducing their own disabilities—points to the web of ableist ideas undergirding the endless debates about abortion and genetic testing. There's a long, fascist history of controlling the reproductive lives of disabled people that haunts us still. While in Nazi Germany, deaf people were sterilized by the state, in the postwar era, deaf parents throughout the world were simply discouraged from reproducing at all and blamed if their children were deaf.[2]

In our post–ADA era of deinstitutionalization, when it is no longer as common to separate disabled children from their parents by placing them in institutions and schools, reproductive ableism may be subtler. There is still controversy about people with Down syndrome and other developmental or intellectual abilities being "allowed" to have consensual sex, get married, and have children. As recently as 2019, a prominent journalist, Judith B. Newman, wrote blithely about her plans to sterilize her autistic son without his consent. While there was public outrage from both autistic people and their families, the fact that Newman's book was published by a major press demonstrates how systemic this genocidal thinking remains.[3] Though, according to the National Research Center for Parents with Disabilities, there are 4.1 million disabled parents in America, they face incredibly high child removal rates: 70–80 percent for parents with psychiatric disabilities and 40–80 percent for those with intellectual disabilities—despite no evidence that they abuse or neglect their children at higher rates than the general population. News articles on people with disabilities parenting always make it seem like a rarity and frame it as a "should they or shouldn't they?" rather than focusing on the barriers ableism places in the way of their parenting. Journalists rarely normalize disabled people parenting by noting its long history and frequency.

A similar ableism saturates all our conversations about disability, reproduction, and abortion. Too often the abortion debate allows fears of an "unhealthy" fetus to fuel the problematic, sometimes genocidal logic of choice. In my own family, most discussions about abortion began and ended with Cousin XY. In fact, it was one of the only times he was ever mentioned. Nobody ever said explicitly that he should have been aborted;

instead, they mouthed it implicitly a hundred different ways. If only there had been amnio or the less-invasive sequential integrated screening test. If only there had been a cure. If only he hadn't been born. If only, if only.

Something about this whole conversation didn't sit right with me. Even as a kid, I knew that there was something wrong with the idea that only certain kinds of bodies and minds should live. That only a fetus with the "right" number of chromosomes should be viewed as viable. As valuable. At the same time, I knew that a fetus wasn't a person, shouldn't have the same rights as a person, and that for women to have a shot at any semblance of equality, they had to always, unequivocally, have the right to choose to terminate a pregnancy: safely and legally, for any reason. For all the reasons you've heard a million times, whether or not they are persuasive to you, I was and remain pro-choice.

Yet, despite claiming to be all about empowerment and equality, the abortion rights movement seemed never to get to the many ways that abortion has been used as a tool of ableism. Of segregation and genocide before life even begins. *If only Cousin XY hadn't been born* was the hidden message of my pro-choice family. What a tragedy.

It was not the extra chromosome that made it a tragedy, though; it was the segregationist ableism that sorted him into the not-really-human pile at birth. His life was determined not worth living in our family before we even had the chance to meet him. If we'd had a different framework for understanding disability, perhaps we would have allowed ourselves to know him. To love him. If we'd had a lived experience of the joys as well as the challenges of knowing a family member with a disability, we wouldn't have felt that he was better off never born. Even if my aunt had been able to choose to end the pregnancy (the testing indicating the presence of an extra chromosome wasn't available at the time), if she had a fuller understanding of disability as a normal part of life, perhaps by knowing her own disabled lineage, this decision wouldn't have lived in her—in me— shaping our family in such disastrous ways.

Sorted, separated, institutionalized. Aborted. That's the last we hear about the children ableism abandons, unless the old canard "It's for the best for everyone" is trotted out. We occasionally hear from the children, but not from the abandoning parents. Their shame supersedes storytelling. They, too, are sorted, marked unsayable. Their tales untellable.

Parents who abandon, institutionalize, or simply marginalize their disabled children from their families not only harm those children but also do tremendous harm *to themselves*. My family was damaged not by disability but by exclusion, abandonment, and the silences and lies that covered up this original crime. There is a profound bedrock of unhappiness upon which XY's family formed. I can't say more about how anyone but me lived his legacy, but I can say that I imagined that I, too, might be given away if my imperfections were uncovered. I felt his absent presence, XY's: In my grandparent's house. At family gatherings, where he was missing at the Seder table as we recited the questions of the four sons, especially that one who knows not what to ask. Was that him? At night, listening to my family wash the dishes, fight about the laundry, and do all the mundane and profound things that form a family. My cousin was there, a structuring absence. A void. A question mark.

There's not a single moment when my thinking changed about disability, abortion, prenatal testing, and the whole mess of how we choose to make or end a potential life. The seeds were always there: seeing how my family suffered, feeling the present absence of Cousin XY at family gatherings. Experiencing my own abandonment when I came out to my supposedly liberal parents. Working with disabled kids during the summer between college and grad school—and finding it pretty similar to working with any group of kids. Meeting devout Catholics at Georgetown who truly valued all lives at every stage of the life cycle (though we disagreed where it began and ended) certainly helped me complicate my own black-and-white thinking.

But really, it was my daughter. Experiencing the ordinary joys of every parent watching her kid eating an ice cream, giggling over a knock-knock joke, composing a poem (via a letter board). Embracing the individual whose life enriches mine so deeply, so profoundly that I can't imagine life without her. Something in me got rearranged. A hard, rigid view of value softened. It also meant confronting both explicit articulations of ableism, such as "Wouldn't you rather, at the end of the day, have a child without a disability?" and its more polite cousin, "If you could wave a wand and just get rid of the autism, not the kid, wouldn't you do it?" To get to an authentic no meant undoing my own ableism. There's no magic wand for that.

Too often, the antidote to this sense of disabled lives as tragic, traumatic, and valueless is the promotion of the "supercrip": the disabled individual who does something amazing. But the most radical position—the one we must use our testing, engineering, and designing of genes and lives to support—is that ordinary disabled lives are precisely that: ordinary. Full of small moments of joy and despair that make any life.

It's easy to look at exceptional disabled lives and say, what if Cousin XY were Madeline Stuart, a supermodel who happens to have an extra chromosome along with extra sass on the runway? What if Cousin XY inherited his dad's great sense of humor and became a successful comedian like Edward Barbanell, who makes hilarious jokes about his extra chromosome as part of his act? What if, like my dad, Cousin XY turned out to be a short Jewish guy who played varsity basketball? Or like Karen Gaffney crushed it not only in the Special Olympics but also on the motivational speaking circuit?

"Five Amazing People with Down Syndrome Who Do Extraordinary Things," "Seven Inspiring People with Down Syndrome Who Do Amazing Things." The internet is full of this sort of "inspiration porn"—where nondisabled people circulate pictures, memes, and stories of disabled people doing extraordinary things. Every time we use a disabled person to feel better about ourselves, whether through pity or shame, we demean, devalue, and dehumanize their lives—and our own. *At least I'm not that*, we've all thought as we try not to stare at the schizophrenic homeless man peeing on himself in the subway. We gawk at a meme on social media: "He has no legs and ran a marathon—what's your excuse?" And for a moment we ride a wave of inspiration on the objectification of another. Pity, shame, and the use of others for inspiration are the gateway drugs to dehumanization and segregation.

On the other end of the inspo-porn spectrum are the Stephen Hawkings and Temple Grandins—disabled people doing truly extraordinary things with their exceptional minds. Or Stephen Wiltshire, the "savant" (we no longer say "idiot savant") autistic artist who can draw a city in minute detail simply by flying over it. Rather than overcoming their disabilities, their unusual minds are the basis for their extraordinary intellects. Who isn't inspired by their exceptional contributions? I certainly am. But geniuses are rare—and exceptional people doing extraordinary work are as rare among the disabled population as they are in the general population.[4] Nobody should have to be a genius in order to justify their existence on this planet. Nobody's challenges should be used to shame or inspire anyone else; nobody's accomplishments should be glorified because they happen to be disabled.

The most radical act of all may be to treat a disabled person as valuable despite their ordinariness. Our choices about beginning, designing, ending, and otherwise manipulating lives would look radically different if we valued all disabled lives equally. If the "we" doing the valuing included disabled people and their families.

Imagine an average person with Down syndrome, who, with a loving family and supports, is able to enjoy his family, participate in sports, and ultimately hold a job. He might have challenges along the way, and his adult life might look a bit different from a neurotypical person's. As Michael Bérubé says of Jamie, his son with Down syndrome, "Like billions of other people, Jamie would like to have a life partner, a companion who loves him and wants to spend her life with him," and has some challenges accomplishing that—much like many young men, disabled or not![5] Certainly his disability shapes this struggle, but it is a human struggle we all share. However, these ordinary human struggles are continually defined by a binary between the normate and "the disabled." We displace our anxieties onto disabled bodyminds, marking, sorting, and marring these lives as abnormal in ways that are profoundly ableist—and racist.

Google searches reveal so much about our culture's anxieties. Type in "Can a person with Down syndrome . . ." and the top hit is "Can a person with Down syndrome look normal?" What does it mean to "look normal"—normal to whom? The notion that people with Down syndrome do not look "normal" is breathtakingly racist, since they were originally called Mongoloid because the eyes typical of people with Down syndrome were thought to look Asian. So, "normal" here is defined as white. Some parents claim that they simply wish their child to resemble them. They are upset by the idea that people with Down syndrome resemble one another more than their own parents. The degree to which any child physically resembles either parent ranges wildly and cannot be predicted. Adopted children do not generally resemble their parents physically. Why is it so disturbing to people that a disabled person would look like another disabled person—that their disability might be a visible form of identity and community, a shared physiognomy? A collective identity as disabled seems to be one of the primary forces that ableist science attempts to eradicate. I am not arguing against reducing pain—I am all for eradicating suffering—but the very identity of being disabled itself is the target of much of science, for such an identity threatens the regime of normativity it is producing. We see that most clearly in our current discourses about disability and genetics.

JUNK GENETICS: VALUING THE MUTATIONAL

Genetics has become a sort of fetish object in our ableist discourse, following the "I know very well, but just the same" structure of fetishism identified by psychoanalysis.[6] We know very well that genetics are complex, that most disabilities are not inherited, and that those that are, are far more likely to be the result of a spontaneous mutation than a direct inheritance. Yet just the same, we speak obsessively of good genes and bad. If only we could eugenically sort, eliminate, abort, we would be free of disease, discomfort, disability, and yes, the ultimate *d* word—death. Those whose bodyminds differ the most from our society's norms are the biggest targets of this obsession. As Armand Leroi argues, "We are all mutants. But some of us are more mutant than others."[7] Genetic testing creates a paradigm in which some mutations are acceptable, while others are deemed "too mutant." These tests are created specifically to target those mutations that lead to bodymind differences.

With the advent of CRISPR technology, the genie is out of the test tube. Genetic engineering of human babies is no longer hypothetical, and no longer restricted to Down syndrome. Invented by Jennifer Doudna, CRISPR technology allows us to manipulate genes in utero. The acronym CRISP-Cas9 stands for a mouthful: clusters of regularly interspaced short palindromic repeats.[8] It's a particular stretch of DNA, a specific pattern, if you will. Cas9 is the important part: it's an enzyme that acts like a pair of molecular scissors, cutting DNA strands.

In both scientific journals and popular news reports, CRISPR is often referred to as "editing" our DNA. This crisp and clean, textual language of editing is actually a bit misleading. As George Estreich argues, "Every new technology is accompanied by a persuasive story, one that minimizes the downsides and promises enormous benefits. And the story of the clean edit, with its promise of crisply rewritten bodyminds, is just such a false, persuasive narrative"[9] A person is not a text; a body is not a script to be rewritten and perfected. Clean edits are impossible. Bodies are dynamic, messy systems.

CRISPR is actually *not* extracting the "bad" DNA, cleanly deleting the errant word, but breaking it. As scientist Ellen Jorgensen reminds us, "If you're trying to CRISPR a genome, the first thing you have to do is damage the DNA." Damage, not edit. The next step is to repair what you've damaged. Jorgensen notes, "After you break a double-strand through the double helix, then you can alter the gene through the repair process."[10] While this is a promising technology for some mutations, note that it involves rupture, at least initially. With CRISPR technology, we convince the repair processes to make the "edit" that we want. Unlike the natural "edits" that sometimes occur in genes, this requires a trauma, break, and intrusion into the genetic material. So arguably you are disabling the genome in order to supposedly fix it! Yet despite scientific evidence to the contrary, the CRISPR narrative insists, as Estreich notes, on a crisp rewrite.

Flagging features prominently in the language used to describe the way this editing would work: gRNA "flags" indicate where the cut—which is actually a rupturing, damaging break—is to occur. The solution to the problem of precision, of knowing where to cut the mutation and "stitch the gene back together," according to Dongsheng Duan, a researcher at the University of Missouri School of Medicine working on the use of CRISPR to "edit" the genes that create the mutation leading to muscular dystrophy, is to increase the number of such flags: "We were surprised to find," he reports, "that by increasing the quantity of flags, we could extend the effectiveness of the therapy from three months to 18 months in our mouse model."[11] More flags, more tests, more marking, cutting, "editing": this is always the solution. Rather than a unifying, mutating freak flag, these flags demarcate, damage, de-lineate.

Since the initial triumphant heralding of the brave new world of "clean edits" that CRISPR would inaugurate, more research has been done that suggests CRISPR, rather than being a neat cut-and-paste, out-with-the-bad, in-with-the-good system, in fact causes unintended changes to DNA. In a spate of reports with titles like "Study Suggests CRISPR Gene Editing Could Have Unanticipated Side Effects," scientists noted that this damage to the genome was unpredictable and uncontainable, far more systemic and imprecise a process than the initial rhetoric had promised. "In some cases," researchers reported, "the changes introduced were fairly large, with both deletions and insertions, possibly leading to DNA being either switched on or off at inappropriate times as a result of the edits."[12] Inappropriate! Suddenly the curative is rendered as exorbitant, uncontainable. Mutational.

So much of the language of genetics—and the contemporary medical discourse to which it is applied—is deeply rooted in an ableist rhetorical system. There are good DNA and "junk" DNA. Clean edits and bad ones. Flags demarcating that clean cut where the damage should be done. However, organisms function much more holistically than this cut-and-paste, delete-and-cure language imagines. It turns out the so-called junk DNA may actually be more complex—and necessary to the formation of RNA from protein—than anyone anticipated.[13] And while science strives for objectivity and believes itself to be purely evidence based and neutral, the lenses that human scientists bring to examine that evidence are colored by cultural ideas about disability. About what bodies "should" be and which bodies should be allowed to be at all.

These notions, bioethicists and medical anthropologists have been arguing for decades, shape not only how we view the evidence and data we create but also what we research in the first place. Let me be clear: I am not opposing innovation, science, choice, and all the rest, or trying to make suffering and challenges noble. But if we were able to value disability in its most ordinary forms, see variation as valuable, we might tell different stories—messier, more nuanced, with fuzzier edges—about what science can do, how, and for whom. Changing the story about CRISPR might help us think critically about how we use this amazing tool.

If we are ruled by the unscientific fiction that every human fetus is a normate-in-waiting, ready to be CRISPR-ed into perfection, we will make one set of choices about the science of genetic engineering, testing, and treatment. If we value biological diversity, see our bodies as mutational and dynamic rather than texts to be edited into supposed normative perfection, we might make different choices. And if the full range of humans—including those targeted for fixing and curing—were included in the decision-making process of how such technologies are to be applied, we surely would see those choices differently. As Sandy Sufian and Rosemarie Garland-Thomson argued in a *Scientific American* essay on CRISPR and its complex implications, "We are whole beings, with our genetic conditions forming a fundamental part of who we are." Their use of "we" is not merely a rhetorical flourish: Sufian and Garland-Thomson are both trailblazing, renowned scholars who are also people with sometimes debilitating conditions caused by genetic mutations. They note pointedly to their audience of scientists, "But CRISPR's tantalizing offer to achieve the supposedly 'best' kind of people at the genetic level is an uneasy alert to those who are often judged to be biologically inferior— one we know all too well. People like us whose being is inseparable from our genetic condition would be the first to go."[14]

There is no clean cut. We are all mutants, on the most scientific and foundational level of our chromosomes, the recipe for life we inherit from our parents. Our changing and changeable DNA offers us opportunities for transformation through CRISPR and other innovative technologies. But many disabilities—including innate ones—occur in the process of becoming. *De novo*: from the beginning. Anew, as the dictionary also defines it, through the miracle of becoming. Many disabilities occur not from the initial egg and sperm and pairing of same but later in the game. So they are not "inherited" per se.

Increasingly, autism researchers suggest that autism is not a matter of inheriting faulty genes but rather occurs as a spontaneous de novo mutation—or perhaps we might prefer to call it a transformation—in the early gestation process.[15] Other forms of bodymind difference like Down syndrome are clearly linked to specific genes, differences, mutations. And these transformations are an inherent and valuable part of our human story, of how we grow and change as a people. Just as we must value biodiversity over monocrops in our ecological thinking if our planet is to survive, we must value these diverse variations in phenotype and genotype for our culture to thrive.

As Steve Silberman argues in *Neurotribes*, his popular account of the emerging science of neurodiversity, neurological differences are not aberrations "but are rooted in very old genes that are shared widely in the general population."[16] He argues that these differences should be valued, viewed as diversifying gifts to the genetic pool, rather than as puzzles to be solved: tested, segregated, eliminated. But although the language of neurodiversity has been popularized by Silberman and others, and disability has increasingly entered popular public representations in the media—even included in an ongoing series of first-person essays by that venerable arbiter of American liberal culture the *New York Times*[17]—our discourse on interceding in prenatal disabled bodyminds remains stuck in a phobic eradication mode. The "birth defect" remains as a bogeyman through which, as Eli Clare argues, "defectiveness holds such power because ableism builds and maintains the very notion that defective bodyminds are bad, undesirable, disposable."[18]

This has led us to an increasingly paradoxical relationship to disability. Even as, on the one hand, the importance and value of diverse bodyminds is acknowledged with greater frequency in the public sphere, on the other, we continue to aim our science at eradicating them. Disabled people are consulted for information about what it's like to be disabled but not about what they would like from the tools of genetic testing and engineering, from treatment, care, and cure. Those conversations instead tend to objectify and otherize living disabled people, bringing them in as question marks, as lives to be debated about rather than as living experts as to what it means to be disabled, how to combat the ableism that makes such lives challenging, and how best to use the tools of science to enhance them. They are novelty acts: freak shows brought in from the outside, rather than rich resources each of us can find in our own families.

Part of the problem is that disabled people are too often only the objects of research; science education remains inaccessible to diverse bodyminds. Making the practice of science more accessible to people with disabilities is a key part of the equation. Disabled scientists like Stephen Hawking, Temple Grandin, and Aaron Schaal have argued for a greater focus on support for the needs of disabled scientists once they're in the field and for increased accessibility in earlier stages of their education. Schaal argues, "In my experience, there are too many obstacles in academia for people who have physical or mental-health conditions—and who have much to offer to science."[19] Grandin suggests that there is disability gain available to science from the unique perspectives of disabled people such as herself, pointing to how her autistic mind was better able than a neurotypical brain to think about certain aspects of anxiety and fear in other species. Even the American Association for the Advancement of Science has started questioning why "when new technologies emerge, too often the concept of accessibility is considered an afterthought or used in ways that do not improve the lives of the people who need assistance" and is exploring ways to center sci-tech on disabled lives and needs.[20]

Even more fundamentally, the basic assumptions underlying scientific research regarding cure and treatment, about whose genes are "normal" and whose need a little CRISPR-ing, would be transformed if disabled people—as scientists, patients, doctors, and parents—were at the center of the practices that seek to operate upon them. Such a reckoning with the de-lineating, eugenicist fascism at the foundation of so much of science's rhetoric and practices could radically shift the whole paradigm.

The incredible potential of CRISPR and other emerging technologies to manipulate our species—and the dangers of it resulting in a kind of eugenics on speed—is much debated in popular media and scientific circles. But it is not the technology that is the problem. Nor the choices it creates. It's something more fundamental. The ableist ideas that govern both the creation and the use of such technologies and that underlie how we think about, conceive of, make, and use these tools are what make them so dangerously, fascistically genocidal. They are directly traceable to the German Nazis and American racist segregationists. As with abortion, we need not reject these new tools designed to give us more choice and agency over our lives. But we must confront the old ableism that saturates how we use these potentially genocidal tools. We must value the diversity of our genome, which, like the biodiversity of our planet, is integral to our survival.

Because we have such thin and phobic knowledge of the rich, complex disabled lives of our ancestors who have been excised from the story, when we encounter the disabled lives of our families, it is largely only as an absence, an erasure. No wonder we are so keen on having science literally eradicate them. Our debates about how we value life, and how we might change it, have formed around the absences, aporias, and erasures of the actual lives of disabled people from our families.

The eugenicist bias of genetics remains foundational to how we imagine our inheritances—especially those we pass along when we choose to reproduce. If we understood that our children's genes mutate and diversify of their own accord, we would perhaps have less "genetic guilt"—fear of passing down an errant genetic trait. If we understood that the normative bodymind is a phantasmic one, we would not let it regulate our choices. Our genetic testing, as well as our treatments, would be ruled by a different logic. Imagine a genetics aimed at diversifying the human genome!

What keeps us from developing these powerful tools in a framework that would allow for human biodiversity is the pernicious, persistent modeling of an ideal human—free of "defects"—as the goal for such research. This model, strutting down the runway of our collective imaginations, rules who can and can't be in a family.

Whether we're hiding disabled people in sheltered workplaces, shuttling them off to segregated schools, warehousing them in institutions, or testing, CRISPR-ing, and aborting them before they're even born in the perpetual fiction that living people with perfectly "normal" genes won't end up disabled, the fear of disability both produces and is produced by the normate. If only ideal bodyminds are permissible in our families, our science becomes centered around eliminating all others, as if that were possible. As if that were desirable.

THE REIGN OF THE NORMATE

Rosemarie Garland-Thomson argues that the normate is the regulating, impossible figure against which disability is constructed. The perfectly normal bodymind that has no differences is a fiction, one necessary to produce a disabled bodymind in need of fixing. This idealized bodymind is nearly impossible to occupy: "If one attempts," she suggests, "to define the normate position by peeling away all the marked traits within the social order at this historical moment, what emerges is a very narrowly defined profile that describes only a minority of actual people."[21] The idealized normate exists precisely to produce and regulate disability. Moreover, from a scientific and genetic point of view, all bodies are deviant: the condition of cells is to mutate. The normal body is nonexistent. We are not exact copies of one another, partly because of these variations.

Nor can achievement or success be predetermined by ability. Increasingly, many people with Down syndrome go to college. Approximately two hundred fifty colleges and universities intentionally include students with Down syndrome.[22] And many people—the majority of adult Americans—who do *not* have Down syndrome do not go to college. In fact, only about 35 percent finish a four-year degree.[23] Should the rest be aborted? What an absurd thought. Yet our Google anxieties suggest that parents expect a specific outcome, underwritten by prenatal testing, and that disability is predictive of success and happiness.

I shared these two anxieties when my daughter was diagnosed with autism. Would my kid look "normal"? When she was little, her disability was invisible. This posed its own challenges, as her autistic behavior was read as bratty, the result of inadequate parenting rather than an innate condition. Other adults would glare at us, hoping to cow her into submission and me into—improved parenting? I'm not sure what the goal of those angry stares and occasional outrageous comments was. I started using sign language, even though Nadia has perfect hearing, and 100 percent comprehension of language, to signal disability to the angry onlookers. This helped protect us and hopefully shame them a bit into perhaps next time thinking before they glared. I wanted them to see that this sidewalk, that shopping mall, their Starbucks was populated by disabled people who had as much a right to be there as they did.

Now, she looks beautiful—and disabled. Her brilliant imperfection can be read off her face. Her yelpy speech. Her joyous skipping. The staring is different. Pity and fear, instead of rage and judgment, are more common. We balance our need to protect Nadia from these stares with the power of showing up, integrating spaces that are not used to having a stimming, singing, twirling kid in their midst. Stims—repetitive actions and sounds some autistic people make—harm no one and are no more disruptive than other sounds and behaviors neurotypical people make, yet they elicit contempt and rage, and mark us as visibly disabled. I know I am quick to compensate: to tell strangers, friends, anyone who will listen about her exceptional ability in math, her extraordinary poetry, her college-level work in chemistry. But what if she had nothing exceptional to "balance out" her supposed deficits?

I have been speaking as if selecting for certain traits—deciding certain genetic profiles make a life not worth living—is all hypothetical. However, in Iceland, the official policy is to encourage all women to test for Down syndrome prenatally and to recommend abortion to *all* whose test results suggest that they are likely to have a child with Down syndrome. This is sold as a feminist policy. Women are told that they have a right to a child without all the difficulties that supposedly inevitably come with Down syndrome. They are not told of the many parents who experience their children as a joy, of the rich lives of people with Down syndrome, of the profound difference social factors, education, and deinstitutionalization have made by objective measures such as lifespan in the lives of people with that extra chromosome. The results are a high abortion rate—and isolation and discrimination against those who are still born with Down syndrome.[24]

What the Iceland experiment exposes is one cultural fantasy about what we should do with disabled people: why, let's just not have them at all! This is problematic for many reasons. First of all, the vast majority of disabilities are acquired, not innate. According to the National Disability Alliance, it is estimated that 85 percent of working-age people with disabilities acquired their disability over a lifetime. Only about 4 percent are congenital.[25] One might argue that nonetheless, we should try to minimize or eradicate those that can be minimized or eradicated. But minimizing suffering and eradicating disabled people are not the same thing. This viewpoint assumes that disability is only and always a form of difficulty—negative, to be avoided. The value of disability to human diversity remains unexamined.

I also see in the embrace of selective genocide (for that is what it really is) a shrugging off of the true feminist conversation we need to have about interdependence and care work. Most cishet (cis-gendered, heterosexual) feminists that I've met would rather abort their way out of care work than hold their straight male partners to a standard of true equality, real accountability for participating in equal care labor. As long as women are given the lion's share of the unpaid, undervalued work of caring for elders, children, and disabled folks, it is no wonder that they rely on abortion as a means of minimizing this unfair distribution of labor. Rather than insist that men participate equally in care, and that this care be valued culturally and economically, women simply demand that they be permitted to eliminate the "problem" of care itself—with tragic consequences for all.

I know this is a harsh assessment of mainstream cishet feminist "choice" rhetoric, but the ableism and sexism undergirding the discourse of choice must be exposed. As D. A. Caeton notes, "The prevailing understanding is that feminism, both as activism and theory, harmoniously overlaps with disability studies. . . . [However,] the rhetoric surrounding reproductive rights frequently focuses on choice, health, and control. Such terms function according to different valences when thought through from the vantage of disability."[26] While most cishet feminists I know would certainly see themselves as "for" disability rights, if perhaps only vaguely as part of a general humanist commitment to equality, their rhetoric in actuality presumes that disabled fetuses are less valuable than those without disabilities. They view disability only through the lens of its burden to a presumed-female caretaker. As Caeton further suggests, "Until we embrace disability non-prejudicially, it will prove impossible to protect fetuses that exhibit traits of physical and cognitive alterity. This, of course, entails tremendous changes both at discursive and policy levels." I would add to that list of tremendous changes the affective level: the level of feeling.

If you don't value the differences that disability entails, only see disabled people as a care burden to a female body, and aren't willing to engage a revaluation of disabled people *and* the fight for valuing care and equally distributing it across genders, then your abortion politics are going to necessarily remain genocidal. Yet creating the kind of deep-tissue discursive change that Caeton rightly identifies as necessary for shifting our polarized abortion conversation seems unfeasible, considering our static, stuck discourse on prenatal life. To challenge the bedrock of choice, health, and control on which mainstream feminism is predicated feels impossible. To challenge the bedrock discourse that life begins at conception on which the pro-life movement is predicated feels equally impossible.

Two concepts from disability studies and activism are helpful here. They do not "solve" anything, but perhaps can help us think in less ableist, genocidal terms about the lives we begin and end, the people we care for and live with. Both connect profoundly to disability lineage.

The first is simply found in the *application* of the social model. If it is not the impairment but the barriers to inclusion that make a given impairment disabling, what happens when those barriers are removed? We have the test case! It's Down syndrome. According to research conducted by the Global Down Syndrome Foundation, people with Down syndrome were institutionalized close to 100 percent of the time until the late 1980s; their average lifespan was only twenty-eight years in 1985. In the 1990s, deinstitutionalization slowly became the norm, so now the vast majority live in families. According to a 2017 study, the average lifespan of a person with Down syndrome has increased to sixty, and the average IQ has increased twenty points. Twenty points and more than thirty years. That is a profound change. There is still no medical intervention available, but world experts who have extensively analyzed the data ascribe these gains primarily to deinstitutionalization.[27]

So, *without any sort of medical breakthrough, treatment, or cure,* a sea change in the quality and quantity of life for people with Down syndrome has occurred—to such a profound degree that Michelle Si Whitten, the leader of the Global Down Syndrome Foundation, refers to it as two syndromes: Down syndrome before deinstitutionalization and Down syndrome now. "By and large people with Down syndrome now live at home. . . . Most are attending public school and some are graduating with a typical degree. There are a handful who have gone on to achieve college degrees. More and more are holding down jobs," she notes.[28] Moreover, it is not society's investment in medication and cure that has enacted this profound transformation; as Si Whitten emphasizes, it is *families,* who connected with activists to work to eradicate barriers to inclusion. By no longer segregating people with Down syndrome from their families, they have been integrated fully into their schools, workplaces, and communities. Those families, along with the self-advocates who themselves have Down syndrome, have been motivated to work to eradicate the barriers people with this particular impairment face—and this has led to objectively longer, healthier, richer lives!

People with disabilities like Down syndrome often need support throughout their lives; however, these can be delivered primarily in a real community, in the person's own home and family, or in apartments with supports—not institutions. In fact, because of this, the US Rehabilitation Act of 1973 recognizes "the right of individuals to live independently, enjoy self-determination, make choices, contribute to society, pursue meaningful careers and enjoy full inclusion and integration in the economic, political, social, cultural and educational mainstream of American society."[29] Similar acts, such as the Disability Act of 2010,[30] have recognized this right in the UK, and the UN Committee on the Rights of Persons with Disabilities explicitly places self-determination and full participation in society at the very center of its statement.

Yet despite the existence of such laws and statements of principles, and despite all medical evidence to the contrary, the myth persists that disabled people, or at least the "severely" disabled, are better off not existing at all. Hearts, minds, and social practices are not changed overnight: not by fiat, decree, or human rights councils. They are changed by families.

It was inclusion in families—deinstitutionalization—that enabled the lives of people with Down syndrome to be so transformed. We now have a generation of people with Down syndrome who have successful, healthy lives; even in a recent mainstream article in *The Atlantic*, the terms of the debate have shifted because such families are part of the living equation. The valuing of lives purely for achievement, rather than their intrinsic and indeterminable value, smells vaguely fascist even to mainstream *Atlantic* reporter Sara Zhang, who notes that "jobs and college are achievements worth celebrating—like any kid's milestones—but I've wondered why we so often need to point to achievements for evidence that the lives of people with Down syndrome are meaningful."[31] That is because the sorting systems we've inherited from the Nazis and US racists have taught us to view such lives as valueless and to construct the value of "normative" lives against them.

In the wake of the renewed focus on civil rights and racial inequality that emerged in the summer of 2020, perhaps our society is now better prepared to focus on the barriers to inclusion. Instead of continuing to put its money on genocidal sorting systems and technologies, perhaps we can invest in eliminating obstacles to full lives for all people. If we examine the ways we devalue Black lives, and the barriers we've imposed to valuing them equally (or at all), we are hopefully more in a frame of mind to examine how we devalue other kinds of lives marked as other and to question this whole othering, devaluing process. We might also notice how racism and ableism coproduce one another.

The second concept helpful in rethinking how we value disability is that of *disability gain*. First developed in Deaf culture, disability gain points to the ways ordinary disabled people with no special abilities or talents may find benefit in their disabilities. Coined by artist Aaron Williamson in 1998, the term "deaf gain" offers a means of rethinking the whole notion of disability as deficit, beyond the specific case of hearing impairment. Instead of measuring against an impossible norm, bodyminds should be valued for their diversity—or the very differences and variety they carry. This is a biodiversity model: like biodiverse ecosystems that are valued for their diversity, social ecosystems' health should be measured by their linguistic, cultural, intellectual, and creative diversity. As psychologists Dirksen Bauman and Joseph Murray argue, "In this light, what might normally be seen as a biological loss can actually be seen as individual and social gain in guarding against the perils of monocultural vulnerability."[32]

Autism advocates have adopted this model to speak of the value of cognitive and intellectual differences, offering a model of "neurodiversity" in which autism and other forms of neurological difference are valued as part of nature's (or God's, if you prefer) endless variations, with specific benefits not just to autistic people themselves but also to the larger society.[33] The monofocus of autistics, for example, has led to many engineering and other scientific innovations, such as those in the field of cattle management by the well-known autistic scientist Temple Grandin. Climate activist Greta Thunberg argues that she was able to be such an international game changer about the climate crisis precisely because her autism doesn't allow her the forms of denial and deferral that neurotypical people engage in.[34] Her "deficits"—her inability to compartmentalize, her moral absolutism, her disregard for social norms and peer acceptance—may yet save the world.

Of course, not every disabled person can or should make such exceptional, world-transforming contributions. Few of us, disabled or not, can make such exceptional, world-transforming contributions! However, even the most ordinary disabled person gains a kind of fluency in thinking and working outside the box, in having to make work-arounds to the expectations and norms of society. Average people with disabilities and those involved in their care are often more adaptable and creative because they have to be.

This is quite a nuanced concept. "What is to be gained from disability cannot be easily delineated," notes disability writer-activist Barker. "Disability gain . . . is what good comes of a person's disability and impairment, that would have been unlikely or impossible otherwise. This can be as little as finding a new friend from a doctor's appointment, or as great as finding a new community and way of life that you would not otherwise have access to."[35] She also notes how access accommodations such as ramps benefit all of society—a phenomenon known as the curb cut effect. A modification such as a curb cut, designed for wheelchair users, may benefit nondisabled people such as parents trying to negotiate a curb with a stroller. As a mother with a newborn in a stroller, I gained new appreciation for a very literal curb cut effect! The curb cut effect of disability lineage is that we would all be less fearful of potential differences, mutations, and "defects" when we contemplated having children if we had lived experiences of disability in our family lives and stories.

Russell Harvard exemplifies what disability lineage can change and challenge: how an embrace of such lineage free of shame and stigma can transform a life, a family, and an entire field— and lead to disability gain *for the whole culture.* Harvard identifies as a third-generation Deaf person, raised by two Deaf parents, and though he has some hearing, lip-reads, and speaks, he primarily uses sign language and considers ASL his first language. He is capital *D* Deaf: Deaf culturally as well as physically. Harvard is an accomplished actor who has starred in productions on Broadway, on television, and in Deaf theater across the US. He also teaches Deaf children, is married, and makes amazing ASL music videos. Instead of "overcoming" his disability and assimilating into the mainstream performance world, Harvard has embraced it, viewing Deaf culture as his home culture and taking pride in his Deaf lineage. At the same time, Harvard has insisted on not being segregated into Deaf-only productions.[36]

This insistence on *both* identity and integration is rooted in his family's disability lineage—and their struggles to claim it. Harvard has written movingly of how his Deaf parents were pressured to mainstream him since he had some hearing, unlike them. As Harvard recounts, "I went to an oral school at first—I had residual hearing and my mom thought it was the best decision. But I was not a happy child at that time. I remember just crying every day, and my mom decided to bring me to a deaf school and I was very happy there [at the Texas School for the Deaf]."[37] Unlike other deaf actors who have crossed over to the mainstream, Harvard brings his Deafness—his disability lineage and culture—with him. Instead of assimilating to the mainstream, hiding his Deafness, Harvard brings it to roles like the Duke of Cornwall in a recent Broadway production of *King Lear*.[38] Appearing onstage with an ASL interpreter, signing to him and speaking most of his lines while he sign-acted them back, this performance made Deafness a fully integrated part of Shakespeare's world—and ours. Instead of seeming forced or awkward, the inclusion of a single Deaf actor made the world onstage feel more real, more connected to the lives we lead now.

Deaf gain is usually used to describe the benefits of Deafness for Deaf people: the culture and language one gains when Deaf. But my experience of Shakespeare's play—one I confess I've always found a bit confusing and melodramatic, from a distant time and place hard for me to access—was enhanced by the inclusion of a Deaf performer. It wasn't just "nice" that a Deaf performer was included, *it was a better production because of Russell Harvard's Deaf presence.* Disability lineage allows for this sort of mass cultural disability gain. Our lives and families are enhanced by the multigenerational cultures and experiences of our disabled family members. We all benefit from Russell Harvard bringing his family's multigenerational Deaf performance culture to the Broadway stage, and from the integration of our disabled ancestors into our current lives. Harvard's sense of the value of his Deafness came directly from his parents—and then was shared by thousands of Broadway audiences.

In our attempts to abort, genocide, segregate, CRISPR, disappear, and otherwise engineer disability out of our families, we miss the ways we all gain by including disabled people in our lives and lineage. The normate we instead aspire to reproduce creates a sort of hateful, flawless ideal that no bodymind can occupy. Technology can't do the work of lineation, of valuing the complexities of disability and what it offers. Our families can.

CHAPTER 4

DISAPPEARING IN PUBLIC

MODELING MAGNIFICENCE

In late August of 2020, as families across America contemplated yet another semester of online homeschooling amid the coronavirus pandemic, a parent-created prank emerged on the social media app TikTok. Its innocuous name—the Meet Your New Teacher Challenge—belied its ableist rhetoric. In it, a parent—usually a white mom—is filmed appearing to FaceTime with a visibly disabled woman for an audience of the mom's visibly nondisabled kids, saying or captioning it with a statement along the lines of "Hi, kids! Meet your new teacher!" The kids react with screams of disgust and horror. The so-called joke was that the horror of online education would be compounded by a visibly disabled teacher. Echoing and inverting the do-goody rhetoric of the Ice Bucket Challenge of a few years past, which aimed to help raise money for people with ALS disorder, the challenge here was not to help anybody, but rather to survive the horror of encountering somebody with the "disability" of ugliness.

Just as quickly as the video—and the inevitable memes it generated—proliferated across social media came the critique of it. Most were simply bromides about the importance of being kind and not bullying, from parents and teachers who did not themselves identify as disabled. Shock was one of the most common responses of commentators: "I'm stunned a parent, an adult, would do such a cruel thing," commented one fellow parent.[1] Bullying and the immaturity of such cruelty was the focus of these sorts of comments.

Few of these responses examined the conflation of disability and "ugliness" in the "Meet Your New Teacher" videos. Nor did these critiques situate the underlying assumptions regarding the relationship between ugliness and disability in public space. None placed this in the context of the ugly laws and the long history of denying disabled people access to public space because they were deemed "ugly." Few challenged the logic of the meme, this equation of disability with ugliness: it was simply deemed unkind, immature, and cruel to make fun of a person so obviously disadvantaged by their appearance. That this disabled face must inevitably be read as ugly remained unquestioned.

The most powerful response, however, challenging the terms of this "challenge" came from one of the disabled women who was depicted in it: Melissa Blake. A seasoned disability activist, Blake emphasized the ordinariness of this appropriation of her image. She was *not* shocked by the trolls mocking her appearance or by the ableist terms of the challenge itself. "As a disabled woman," Blake noted, "people ridiculing and mocking my appearance is practically the most predictable thing about social media."[2] Rather than turn this into yet another invective by an adult against the dangers of social media for kiddies, Blake used the dubious, negative notoriety the Meet Your New Teacher Challenge had provided her to change the terms of the conversation about disability. She highlighted how ordinary this conflation of ugliness and disability was—"practically the most predictable thing"—and then, instead of focusing primarily on how it hurt her, the individual disabled person being mocked, she examined how it hurts all of us.

Blake emphasized two things: the ubiquity of the conflation of evil, disability, and ugliness in our society, and the way it damaged not merely herself and the obvious butts of the joke—visibly disabled people—but also the children who were made witnesses to their parents' cruelty:

> I can't help but feel sorry for their children. Imagine your mom filming a vulnerable moment, one where you can't help but burst into tears, and they actually post it for the whole world to see. How is humiliating your child, or watching other children go through that, a source of amusement?[3]

This focus on the suffering of others might seem merely to be an example of an act of empathy, demonstrating how experiences of discrimination and oppression sometimes make disabled people more sensitive to the vulnerabilities of everyone else. But Blake is doing something far more profound, with implications for the relationship between the domestic space of the family and that of the public. How ableism regulates these two spaces is foregrounded by Blake's empathetic critique.

Blake brilliantly connects the ordinariness of the conflation of ugliness, disability, and evil with this public staging of it for children. Moreover, her analysis refuses the public-private binary. It offers a means of examining how the fear of being caught disabled in public shapes the private space of the family. And it exposes how the de-lineation of disabled people within their families is not merely a private matter but is imbricated in ideas about public space and its regulation.

The Meet Your New Teacher Challenge stages the public space of the school inside the private space of the family. The child is the intended audience. In including the child's role, Blake suggests that our stigmatizing and shaming of disabled bodyminds, our policing of them in public and in shared representational spaces, is intimately connected to our private, domestic lives and lineage. The phobic response to disability in public is thereby intimately connected to the private, reproductive, lineal space of the family. Children are trained to be ableist by their parents in relation to the gaze of an imagined public. They fear not only the hated, abandoned, disabled other but, more disturbingly, that they, too, will be hated and abandoned even by their own families should they be disabled. What Blake observes in the Meet Your Teacher Challenge is this staging of disability as potential trauma for the children who both watch the video and then are included in it as part of the meme's public spectacle. Disability lineage isn't merely denied or repressed: in its place is a lineage of fear, stigma, and othering, staged in the public-private space of TikTok.

The parents who produced the Meet Your New Teacher Challenge are stigmatizing and shaming not only disabled adult bodyminds such as Blake's but potentially those of *their own children*. The intimate sphere of the family couples with the public sphere to police, marginalize, criminalize, and punish disabled bodyminds, conflating them with evil and ugliness. The school, the street, and the TikTok create a regulatory space that, in trying to eradicate disability from the public sphere, inevitably makes the private sphere of the family a site of stigma, shame, and fear for all family members—including those of the future. The segregating and regulating force of this public sphere has profound implications for bodyminds in private. In families. Across generations.

The shaming and stigmatizing of people with disabilities in the public sphere works to regulate how families understand and pass down that understanding of disability. Families inculcate their children with the notion that disability is traumatic, unprecedented, and inadmissible in public. This is why Blake foregrounds the children's reaction to their parents' ableist antics. The parents are passing down a lineage of phobia, stigma, and shame, using the public sphere of TikTok to regulate their family's private, domestic understanding of disability. Rather than functioning as separate spheres, the domestic and the public work together to make disability disappear in public.

Of course, by law, at least since 1990, public spaces are supposed to be accessible to people of all abilities—and appearances. In our enlightened post-ADA world, where equal access to public spaces is at least guaranteed on paper and enshrined in law, explicitly segregationist practices are no longer permitted. A public sphere where disability is unwelcome may then seem like some relic of our barbaric past. But despite the le-

gal transformation initiated by the ADA, the culture of segregation remains. Thus the stigmatizing (if not actual elimination) of disability in
public persists. The ableist phobia that demands a public sphere free of
disability remains. The legacy of privatizing, segregating, institutionalizing, mass murdering, and invisibilizing disability remains. The laws may
have changed, but the ableist culture fundamentally has not.

It's not a coincidence that the Meet Your New Teacher Challenge was
a product of pandemic culture. The COVID-19 pandemic brought to the
fore the persistent cultural obstacles disabled people routinely encounter
in order to attain their legally mandated accommodations. In article after
article, think piece after think piece, journalists reported with surprise
how difficult it was for disabled people to work, go to school, shop, and
do the other basic functions of life that engage the public sphere. "Accessibility dissonance" is what one astute reporter termed this: the law
guarantees equal access, but the ableist social structures of the public
sphere make it nearly impossible to gain the accommodations that would
enable meaningful access and inclusion. Accommodations such as distance learning and working, deemed too costly or difficult prior to the
pandemic, magically were implemented overnight once people without
disabilities needed them. "As universities around the world go online and
many workers shift from cubicles to dining tables, some people with disabilities are left wondering if ableism was the only thing standing in their
way of previously being granted such accessibility," one of many such articles observed.[4]

Including disabled people in the public spheres of work and school,
as well as the quotidian life of the street, shopping mall, and sports arena,
isn't merely a low priority. It is actively prevented through the shaming
and stigmatizing of "ugly" bodyminds. Though disabled people are the
largest minority in the world, the architecture not just of built spaces but
also of workplaces, schools, and families is constructed with idealized
bodyminds. As Mia Mingus argues, "Disabled people get told we must
shrink ourselves and our desires to settle for living in the wake of an able
bodied parade. And especially if we are part of other oppressed communities, we are expected to be grateful for whatever crumbs are thrown our

way."[5] Staring, presuming able-bodymindedness, and more literal violence to disabled bodyminds are some of the blunter instruments used to
shame and stigmatize disabled people in public.

Public spaces are intentionally built to exclude disabled people, and to
define them in opposition to civic beauty. *The Vessel*, a failed $200 million
New York public art project that depended on the use of stairs to participate in its beauty, thereby excluding wheelchair users from its aesthetic,
also failed to imagine how mentally disabled people might be driven to
suicide by its "beautiful" views. After multiple suicides *The Vessel* closed,
then reopened—though this supposedly public art project would now be
limited to those who could pay for it as well as those who could climb it,
with the strange additional requirement that only people in groups of two
or more would be permitted. So access was even more limited, to those
with partners or friends and the means to pay for access. After the suicide
of a fourteen-year-old boy, despite these new, improved regulations, *The
Vessel* closed indefinitely—its architects still refusing to install the fenc-
ing and barriers that mental health experts advised would prevent such
tragedies. This vessel of ableism exemplifies the dominant understanding
of public space, which posits disabled bodyminds as other to its vision of
civic beauty.[6]

This ableist eradication from the public sphere is also perpetuated by
cutting us off from our disability lineage and ancestry. Because we are discouraged from learning about our disabled ancestors and family members,
we have no context for imagining ourselves or our children as disabled.
Or imagining their adult teachers, who are of course former children, as
disabled. The public sphere of first the classroom and then the workplace
is imagined as free of disabled people in part because of their de-lineation
from our families. As the Meet Your New Teacher Challenge phenomenon suggests, not only do we fail to pass down a legacy of pride in our
disabled lineage; we are also actively working to shame and stigmatize disability. To treat it as something that happens to other people, irreducibly
and horrifically other. Children are, in this scenario, made to see disabled
people as ugly others, and to fear a future in which they might themselves
be disabled and thus so dehumanized.

The public sphere continues to only begrudgingly accommodate disabled bodyminds legally, while socially and culturally it instructs families that they must hide, stigmatize, abort, marginalize, and otherwise restrict and contain their disabled children while we wait for science to cure the horror of difference in some always-around-the-corner curative future. Rather than passing down a healthy sense of their disability lineage, parents, as the TikTok videos make clear, pass down an inheritance of phobic ableism. The terrorizing of disabled people in public, whether in public schools, on the streets, or across the internet, is the tool used to perpetuate and reproduce stigma and shame in the domestic sphere.

I should know. This was my only disability inheritance. Part of what I feared was being in public and experiencing shame and stigma based on my daughter's appearance and behavior. I was not wrong, though when she was little, I was usually the one who was target of strangers' wrath when my daughter displayed her disabled bodymind in public. The sounds and movements of her body—which were not harming anyone or interrupting anything—were treated as my fault: as an epic, public, parenting fail. From eye rolls and other signs of disgust with my parenting to direct statements like "Some people don't know how to discipline their own damn kids" to "That's disgusting, what a terrible mother, you ought to be ashamed!" my daughter's disability was viewed as a problem that I was failing to solve. A problem for whom? The public. Like the kids in the Meet Your New Teacher Challenge, I had been presented with the narrative of my disabled Cousin XY only as an instructive tool of fear to create a phobic response about the possibility of I myself being disabled—or of having a disabled child. With no knowledge of Rhona or other lived, integrated experiences of disability in my family lineage, I feared what it would mean to live in public with a disabled family member. Cousin XY was not merely an absence but a cautionary tale.

It is not only that we have excised disability from the family narrative—the shared public-private space of the extended family. Every family has its Meet Your Cousin horror story, a narrative the extended family tells about that disabled relative who has been cut out of the kinship cloth. These occluded, partially hidden stories of disability are presented as cautionary tales about what might happen if a disabled person tries to exist in a family. This narrative space, now existing between the private, lived world of the family and the public representational sphere of the internet, is where the regulatory stigma and shame are reproduced that make real accessibility and inclusion still out of reach, thirty-odd years after the ADA became the law of the land.

The familial fear of public shaming and stigma is not unwarranted. Even white, privileged wheelchair users face annoyance from people on buses, in lines, and other public spaces when the public must accommodate their bodyminds. People with visible disabilities face hostility in public space; despite the ADA, the right to be disabled in public remains contested. And the consequences of that contestation can range from stigmatizing and shaming to physical harm and even death. In 2015, disabled people were two-and-a-half times more likely than nondisabled people to experience violent victimization and three times as likely to be targets of "serious" violent crimes like sexual or aggravated assault.[7] Twenty percent of those crimes occurred in public spaces. Of the nearly fifty thousand US students who were physically restrained during the 2013–2014 school year in the public school system, more than 75 percent were disabled.

Statistics like these demonstrate how appearing in public as a disabled person is occasionally lethal and frequently humiliating. Though the laws no longer permit explicit exclusion of disabled people from the public sphere, the culture still does. This cultural bias is a relic of the legal framework, a palimpsest in the bodyminds of every disabled person who's been stared at, mocked, memed, TikTokked, and otherwise policed by ableism in public space, who's experienced the fear of that policing public in their own families. Understanding the legal framework we've inherited regarding disability in public can help disinter what the hell is being unconsciously acted out via TikToks like the Meet Your New Teacher Challenge and in our own families.

UGLY IN PUBLIC: DISABILITY, RACE, AND PUBLIC SPACE

By examining the laws prior to the American with Disabilities Act of 1990 regarding disability in public, much is revealed about the culture that produced them—and their living legacy today. Disability historian Susan Schweik, in her landmark study *The Ugly Laws: Disability in Public*, exhaustively traces how and why disability came to be conflated with "ugliness" and moral evil. She examines both the legal and the cultural structures that created this and goes on to examine how they essentially produced the category of "the disabled." Her focus is on the period in the late nineteenth and early twentieth century when beggar ordinances were enforced in such a fashion to make it difficult—even illegal—for disabled people to appear in public spaces. Though putatively designed to prevent vagrancy in nineteenth-century America, these laws helped produce the category of "the disabled" and created the logic by which such bodyminds needed to remain out of sight.

The language of these ordinances suggests the dehumanizing effects of this new notion of the ugly/evil/disabled as a category. For example, the Chicago Ordinance of 1881 refers to such people as "disgusting objects":

> Any person who is diseased, maimed, mutilated, or in any way deformed, so as to be an unsightly or disgusting object, or an improper person to be allowed in or on the streets, highways, thoroughfares, or public places in the city, shall not therein or thereon expose himself or herself [sic] to public view, under the penalty of a fine of $1 for each offense (Chicago City Code 1881).[8]

Disgusting objects. Inhuman. Impermissible in the public sphere. It's not too difficult to see how such laws produced stigma, shame, and segregation of those bodyminds perceived as ugly.

These are not just part of some dark, invidious past. While the earliest of such laws in the US can be traced to 1867, they were still on the books as recently as 1974. The ugly laws were not just technically "on the books" as vestiges of a horrifically ableist past but were actively and continuously used to control the presence of disabled people in public spaces. Arrests, according to Schweik, were recorded as recently as the 1970s for the crime of being disabled in public.

These laws both reflect cultural norms and help magnify and institutionalize them. They gave us our modern sense of whose bodyminds belong and whose don't. They created a powerful narrative that underwrote mass institutionalization of disabled bodyminds. "Biopower"—the power of assessing and ranking bodies, producing norms and ranking bodies and minds in relation to them—is a term philosopher Michel Foucault uses to mark the way both formal mechanisms of law and the supposedly subtler, softer power of culture create certain bodies as norms and then regulate other bodies in relation to those norms. Instead of explicitly punishing these nonnormative bodyminds, they are regulated, categorized, marked—often putatively for their own good. As Schweik notes, "The ugly law of biopower identifies an abnormal group in order to 'care for' them."[9] This "care" resulted in sterilization, segregation, and the elimination of disabled people from both the public and the private spheres. They also resulted in the surprising appearance of disabled bodyminds in one particular kind of public space: that of entertainment.

For while these ordinances excluded disabled people from ordinary public spaces like streets, shops, restaurants, schools, and workplaces, they did not exclude the exhibition of disabled bodyminds for entertainment. Such people could be made into spectacles, freak shows, and other for-profit entertainments for the nondisabled. The two phenomena were inextricably linked: in the very same period that the ugly laws were initiated, interest exploded in public displays and performances of disabled bodyminds. Rosemarie Garland-Thomson suggests that "the freak show validated curiosity and authorized public staring at bodies that departed from the ordinary by embellishing differences to make money."[10] From P. T. Barnum's spectacular traveling exhibits to smaller, more local venues, disabled bodies were exhibited for their exaggerated exorbitance—and for profit—to eager crowds. But who exactly profited from these occupations of public space by disabled bodyminds?

While these exhibits may now strike us as appallingly exploitative, disabled performers and scholars argue for a more complex understanding of this phenomenon. As disabled performer and scholar Petra Kuppers notes, "The freakshow, carnival or sideshow was the first sustained and organized dramatic institution for disabled people"[11] and often afforded disabled people a means of making a living, the ability to create a form of performance art out of their lives and bodies, and even the opportunity to create families and lineages with other disabled performers. Kuppers and other disabled artists argue for the use of this paradoxical art form for contemporary disabled performers.

Neither Kuppers nor other performance studies scholars studying freak shows and their reclamation make note of something that immediately struck me: part of the exaggeration of the difference of disability that is staged in these performances is an exaggeration of the disabled performer's isolation, singularity. These are largely solo acts. The freak has no mother. Though of course all people have parents, and the freak show itself provided a means of disabled people forming relationships, marriages, families, children, and community, the freak show *stages* the disabled person as alone, separated from the familial and reproductive. When disabled performers were exhibited as families (as "little people," for example), the fact of their reproductivity was itself viewed as freakish, a grotesque and absurd mirroring of the normate, and thus, by definition, extraordinary.

Either lineage-less or with their lineage pathologized and spectacularized, disabled performers are separated from the public sphere. The very delineation of the freak show space *as* a spectacular public performance marks it as outside the domestic sphere of the family or the "normal" quotidian space of the street, school, and workplace. The connective cloth of family is not wound around them. They are flagged as freakish others. And though individuals who were flagged as such used their profession to attain some level of agency and self-determination, they were not able to fly their freak flag, remaking and remarking on the individualized freak as a communal sharing of disability. Or if they did, internally or in communion with other disabled performers, the act remained unreadable by the larger culture.

Moreover, the end of the era of the freak show and the ugly laws did not mean the end of the flagging, stigmatizing, and marginalizing of disabled bodyminds. As Rosemarie Garland-Thomson notes, "Medicalization and the rise of sentimental culture in the 19th century took extraordinary bodies off the freak show stage by the mid-20th century for the most part, sequestering them in asylums and hospitals."[12] This was part and parcel of the move to segregate and institutionalize disabled people, further separating them from their families materially. Rhetorically, this move defined the family as separate from the freakish, disabled, ugly other. Thus the eradication of the freak show meant the elimination of one of the few public spaces in which disabled bodyminds could exist with some level of agency, community, and integration.

The legacy of the freak show is found not just in the places you'd expect—movies, films, and yes, TikTok memes—but also in the supposedly objective spaces of medicine and science. Garland-Thomson suggests that "even though science has eclipsed superstition, the laboratory and the telethon have replaced the freak show, and the pathological has superseded the monstrous, experts still read exceptional bodies to establish the supposed truth of the ordinary."[13] Disabled bodyminds still appear in public discourse primarily to produce and regulate the familial norm. While the Jerry's Kids national telethon thankfully died with Jerry Lewis, my local hospital continues at Christmastime to parade disabled and ill children decked out in over-the-top Christmas outfits as angels and reindeer, begging for donations on TV, so the presumably nondisabled family viewing this spectacle at home can donate to prevent their kids from being contaminated by such ugly, shameful bodyminds. The TikTok-ification of the freak show restages this sideshow inside the family while broadcasting it across the globe.

Recently, disabled performers have investigated the legacy of these "freak show" performers, exploring how both the positive and the negative aspects of this history resonate with their contemporary experiences of being disabled in public, whether on stage or in the streets. Disabled artists like Mat Fraser, Riva Lehrer, and many others have explored the complex legacies of freak show performance, centering their work on the subjectivities of the disabled performers themselves and the way disabled spectators—then and now—might receive this work. Lehrer notes that in

her Circle Stories portrait series, rather than objectifying disabled people
for an ableist gaze,

> the portraiture method is a circular and collaborative process, based on
> extensive interviews with each participant. We talked about their lives,
> work, and understanding of disability. The circle of the wheelchair is
> the nearly universal symbol of disability. The wheel transforms the or-
> dinary object of the chair into a mark of physical and social difference.
> "Circle Stories" charts the existence of a community of Disabled inno-
> vators who work to redefine disability in the 21st century.[14]

Such rethinkings offer, in tandem with Blake's response, a means of
exploring how disabled people can use these public discourses of ugliness
and freakishness to restage the terms of their appearance in public and
their disappearance in the public-private space of the family narrative.
They also have provided a powerful means of examining how race and
disability intersect in such narratives and their performances.

It's crucial to note how racialized these freak show performances
were—how white privilege intersected with ableism. While white performers were often able to gain some control and autonomy of this staging of their "freakish" bodies, especially if they had a special skill like
juggling, Black disabled performers were frequently exhibited without
clothing in grotesque, sexualized stagings that mimicked the slave block
and echoed blackface vaudeville performances of racist degradation.[15]
Though certainly individual Black disabled performers may have gained
some measure of autonomy in their lives as freak show performers, they
were often only allowed to appear *representationally* as objectified bodies,
in demeaning roles in which their race as well as their disability were the
main event. Contemporary multiracial performance group Sins Invalid
engages the complex erotics and politics of these racialized performances.
Central to their work, in their own words, is to offer "a vision of beauty
inclusive of all individuals and communities."[16]

Sins Invalid places beauty at the center of their project. Disabled performers play with "pretty" costumes, taking on the personas of chanteuses,

strippers, and other figures conventionally coded as performing beauty. With glamour and sass, they play with performing desirability. They include explicit discussions of definitions of beauty and ugliness in their explorations of disability and its intersections with gender, race, ableism, lookism, and public space. As Schweik's and other historians' work makes clear, troubling the beautiful-ugly binary is crucial to any meaningful rethinking of how disabled bodyminds occupy and disappear in public space. This binary is central to all the racialized, exploitative contours of the histories of that (dis)appearance. Like Blake, contemporary disabled BIPOC performers such as Sins Invalid complicate—and even reverse— the relationship between the disabled performer exhibited to the public as a horrific, ugly object and the audience of supposedly nondisabled people who exclude disabled bodyminds from their family and public lives *except* in the context of the freak show. Claiming the public space of disability performance—the "freak show"—as a space of beauty and connecting that space to the larger public sphere are key to undoing the violence of the ugly laws and the freak show performance.

For the ugly laws and the freak show performances were really one phenomenon: twinned aspects of the policing, constructing, revealing, concealing, and erasing of disabled bodies in public spaces. Under this regime, disabled bodyminds could be displayed as extraordinary and exorbitant, and in some cases even gain a measure of autonomy, at least off stage, but they could not occupy public space in more quotidian, autonomous ways.

Moreover, the rise of the freak show often explicitly provided moral ballast for the ugly laws. As Schweik notes, "The ugly law(s) sprang in part from protective impulses on the part of offended legislators that also spurred laws against freak 'exhibition.'"[17] It is crucial to understand that freak shows and ugly laws were not separate phenomena but rather worked together to regulate how, where, and under what terms disabled bodyminds could appear in public. Ugly laws were enacted purportedly for the benefit of disabled bodyminds, for their own good, to protect them from the exploitation of the freak show, but in practice the laws served only to further marginalize and otherize disabled people.

Some disability rights lawyers and activists have criticized Schweik's isolating of disability in this study, as during this period Black bodies were often policed under these same laws as part of the effort to pathologize and contain Black people post-Reconstruction. As TL Lewis argued during a public talk at Georgetown University, a truly intersectional understanding of this phenomenon and its implication for Black bodyminds would necessarily see the policing of Black bodies during Reconstruction as equally or even more central to how Black disabled lives were shaped by the ugly laws.[18] Certainly the relationship between racism, ableism, and the ugly laws bears closer examination.

Nonnormative, disabled behavior in public—even when it is completely harmless—is still often at best met with disgust and at worst, for Black autistic people, criminalized with fatal results.[19] Ableism and racism co-produce one another and are inseparable in the public sphere. The disproportionate over-policing and violence against Black people endemic in American society is even greater for Black disabled people. The recent film *The Forty-Year-Old Version* plays this as comedy: the Black female protagonist is late to work and harumphs and argues with the Black bus driver who takes care to accommodate BIPOC disabled people trying to access the bus.[20] We are invited to identify with the eye-rolling Black protagonist, not the BIPOC disabled people accessing their legal right to appear in public, nor their caregivers, nor the bus driver working to accommodate them. Like the Meet Your New Teacher Challenge, there is an implicit threat to our future selves, our future offspring: we too might be the mocked object of derision if we become disabled. While the film turns the experience of being Black and disabled in public into something laughable, those of us who have been confronted with the rage of white people in the public sphere who want to deny us access to public spaces like buses know how potentially violent these encounters can be—particularly for BIPOC people. Our social and cultural norms still make it difficult, dangerous, and downright scary to be disabled in public. For BIPOC disabled people, it can be lethal.

Schweik does note how these laws undergirded and were coproduced by the racist rhetoric regarding containing and excluding Asian bodyminds as "ugly" and quarantinable—a phenomenon of the nineteenth and twentieth centuries that is disturbingly resonant with the anti-Asian violence that escalated during the COVID-19 pandemic. Treating disease and disability as foreign, Orientalized contaminants is not a relic of some racist past. Disability, in Lewis's and Schweik's analyses, is not only shaped by race and racism but is fundamentally produced by ideas about race. Thinking disability, race, and gender together is key to understanding how these different vectors of pathologized identity created the shame and stigma around "ugly" bodyminds that led to the Meet Your New Teacher Challenge and all its stagings of ableism in and out of the family. The pivotal role of the domestic sphere in the dynamics of this public disappearing of disability in the public sphere—and its hypervisibility on the stage—demands examination if we are to understand how disability structures the family and the stories the family tells about itself.

STARING BACK

The biopower of the ugly laws coupled with the freak show made disabled people into a new, separate, subhuman category, and staged them in the segregated space of the freak show performance away from the rest of public space. This cordoning off of disabled people in public, and the concomitant relegating of them to the freak show, had consequences for the supposedly private space of the family—and how it is haunted by the *impossibility* of that segregation.

For despite these systems of erasure and oppression, of course disabled people did, do, and will appear in other public places besides those intended for them. The necessities of life—work, school, consumption, and so on—require existence in the public sphere. One primary way disabled people are produced as other to the public (even as they appear in it) is through staring. It is in the stare that the public and private, the familial and the impersonal, are staged.

"Throughout history," pronounces poet-scholar-activist Kenny Fries grandly in one of the earliest collections of creative writing by and for disabled people, "people with disabilities have been stared at. . . . Those who live with disabilities have been defined by the gaze and needs of the nondisabled world."[21] The dynamics of staring and being stared at are fundamental to how disabled people are stigmatized, shamed, and marginalized in public spaces. Even disabled people with invisible disabilities often feel fearful of and policed by the gaze. They worry that their mental or cognitive disabilities will be unmasked or that they are only contingently included as a false self. Peta Cox movingly explores how "passing as sane" can be a survival technique for mentally disabled people. She argues that often a mentally disabled person must mimic the gestures and behaviors of the undistressed. When feeling distressed, the person must not *appear* distressed: a stress-inducing performance if there ever was one! Passing in such instances, she notes, is not neutral: it "is particularly important for people diagnosed with mental illness, because the costs for not passing can be quite high—including, in some instances, nonconsensual treatment and involuntary hospitalization"[22] The failure to pass in public can instantly de-lineate one from one's family and community. Passing serves as a mechanism to police and erase disabled people's identity as disabled, both within and outside the family. As with the Meet Your New Teacher Challenge, the feared gaze of the public operates inside the home as well as out on the street, internalized and interiorized. Of course, passing is a privilege that many visibly disabled people do not have, in public or in private.

Disabled artists, activists, and scholars have analyzed the role of the stare in public spaces exhaustively, examining how disabled people create passing strategies when possible, as well as creating novel responses of staring back and challenging this controlling gaze.[23] Often this is foregrounded as a form of "aggressive ableism"—a form of ableism in which the nondisabled person intrusively acts upon the disabled person in public. The stare is in itself othering, sending the message that the disabled person is somehow doing something wrong simply by being disabled in public.[24] Inevitably, disabled people internalize the shame and stigma of this gaze. It is also the first step in potentially dangerous, even fatal encounters, especially for people of color in general and Black male disabled people in particular.

However, the ways staring controls the supposedly private space of the family has received less attention. Fear of the stare, of the public gaze, is where freak show and ugly law meet, collide on the pavement in the cold scowl of a stranger to a child and her mother. Only by examining this public-private encounter can we fully understand the stare and its policing, shaming, stigmatizing, marginalizing force—and its enormous implications for disability lineage.

As I've discussed, to deal with the upsetting, stigmatizing, and potentially dangerous stares when my daughter and I were in public, and to protect my daughter from this disgusting ableist rhetoric, I would use American Sign Language to respond. This helped reframe the situation for my ableist audience: This child isn't acting out, with an ineffectual parent to blame, but is (drum roll) . . . *disabled*. Presumed deaf if not dumb. To be safe in public, we resisted the fetishization of the freak show and the ostracization of the ugly laws, appearing as a family and not a solo act. But my use of sign language ironically produced a public performance of a disability my daughter *doesn't* have—deafness—in order to contain the potential verbal and physical violence against us for a disability she does! Such was the price of public space for us.

This strategy has its limitations. In situations where my daughter was even mildly melting down in public or acting in an unusual way that might draw unwanted attention, I learned to get us out of the situation as quickly as possible. To remove us physically from public space. Note that in those situations, she and I were perfectly capable of getting back to a calm place. We knew how to manage her breakdowns and anxiety, together. Nobody was ever in danger—not she, not I, certainly not the glaring passersby. But my fear was that someone would call security, cops, or otherwise escalate the situation in ways that were definitely humiliating and potentially lethal to us both.

Now that she is a teenager, she will likely be blamed and harmed for appearing disabled in public. Much as I know that we have every right—just as much a right as the people disparaging us—to be in public, I cannot risk our lives to prove that point. I still resort to ASL to reframe these encounters on occasion. I delineate the range of phobic responses I've experienced in public with my disabled daughter to demonstrate how serious and dangerous this is. But even the seemingly minor forms of bias and phobia we experience—microaggressions, according to the popular term—serve to make us fearful in public space.

Every stare, every shake of the head, every time . . . these small things accrete. They add up. And they escalate: I had to stop going to our local grocery store and instead go to one forty minutes farther away because there was one clerk who we seemed to always get who would sigh, shake her head, stare, and otherwise make me and my daughter uncomfortable every single time we checked out. I noticed her hand on the buzzer to call security more than once, even though my daughter was simply making repetitive noises and gestures and causing no potential danger to anyone. "Why don't you just *tell* them that she is disabled?" asks the cop in my head. Well, I did. I do. But it always seems only to make the person angrier. How dare we be disabled in public! Using sign language tends to be less threatening, because the viewer can believe that she is, on her own, coming to the conclusion that we are disabled, so she doesn't have to feel fury at me and my daughter for pointing it out. Instead, she can enjoy a pity party, a freak show performance in which we are objects of her gaze.

But explaining our disability is a problem for another reason, one that I care about the most: it conveys to my daughter that her presence needs explanation. That we must give an account of ourselves, one never required of nondisabled families. No wonder some parents sequester their disabled families in their homes. Negotiating public space can be terrifying, humiliating, shaming, and dangerous for disabled people and their families. But we have both the same right and the same need to be in public as everyone else.

Our families exist in public. No matter how much I empower my daughter, share her disability lineage with her, and connect her to a whole world of disabled relatives and friends, public stigmatizing and shaming of disabled people—and their parents—happens constantly. A legacy of the ugly laws, the freak show, and our whole genocidal history of pathologizing disability awaits us every time we leave the house. My attempts to contain, deflect, and manage the general public's attempts to stigmatize, shame, and eliminate us from the public sphere are profoundly problematic. Confronting this oppression directly as individuals in a store, on the street, in a doctor's waiting room can be dangerous and ineffective. Yet despite decades now of legal inclusion, the culture continues to police disabled bodyminds in public spaces—and shame the families of disabled people as well.

Undergirding this is the persistent belief that disabled people shouldn't appear in public, that their disabled bodyminds need to be controlled, contained, segregated. Social norms of how to behave or simply be in public exclude the world's largest minority. The larger effect of this discourse is to normalize the segregation of public space, rendering disabled minds and bodies unwelcome, "abnormal." These norms are always racist and misogynistic. They reinforce the notion of the impossible normate. As disability justice activist Mia Mingus notes, "Ableism dictates how bodies should function against a mythical norm."[25] Such norms must be dismantled, for all our families.

BROADCASTING DISABILITY

These norms and models police our lives even when they are repressed. As I was finishing writing this book, a strange document entered my consciousness that made me think about the relationship between the public and the private spheres, and how disability lineage is produced in the places where they converge. Though I had used every imaginable research and search tool at my disposal as a professor at Georgetown University to obtain information about Cousin XY, and thought that I had found whatever was findable about him, I woke up one morning during the quarantine of 2020 and for reasons that I cannot explain, Googled my aunt and uncle's names.

Up popped a public notice, required by law, published in the newspaper attempting to locate my aunt and uncle before turning Cousin XY into a ward of the state. "Petition for the commitment of the minor child of Samuel A. and Carol P. Fink of parts unknown." I'd done similar—and far more sophisticated—searches a million times, but never had this appeared. The reason for the petition to commit this child? "The minor child of the above named person is an uncared for, neglected child." I read it over and over. Precisely in the space where the public and private meet, my cousin is excised from the family. By law, my aunt and uncle are called out by name in case they want to extract their child from the public care system. Did my aunt and uncle know of this—perhaps even, as one legal authority I consulted suggested to me, *orchestrate* this erasure, this absorption into institutionalization of this "uncared for, neglected child"?

It gnaws at me, this description. In 1978, four years after the last ugly law was expunged, twelve years before the Americans with Disabilities Act became law, I was twelve. On the brink of puberty, cared for by my family because I didn't appear disabled in public. This document, floating around the internet, appearing and disappearing seemingly arbitrarily more than forty years after it was first published, brought home to me the way the public and private spheres intermingle to produce and stigmatize disability. To institutionalize and abandon, to eradicate Cousin XY from the private sphere of the family, a public notice had to proclaim it.

Every time I read that public notice, I feel sick to my stomach. What's remarkable to me is that my cousin's disability—the cause for this neglect, abandonment, and institutionalization by the state—is mentioned nowhere in the proclamation. It is as if the disability itself is too ugly to appear in this final public announcement of the disappearance of a human being from his family.

DARING TO BE DISABLED IN PUBLIC

The rhetoric of the ugly laws and freak show profoundly shapes how and why families exclude disability in their lineages and lives in twenti-eth- and twenty-first-century America. The very concept of "ugliness" has a central, spectacular, and powerfully regulating, shaming, and stigma-tizing role in what we think disability is and where we allow it to appear.

The dehumanizing rhetoric about who is "beautiful" enough to appear in public shapes how we imagine our families at home and in the world. It's easy to point to unrealistic, misogynistic, racist beauty standards as the source of "lookism," which terrorizes disabled people and relegates them to the butts of online jokes. We all know that the images of beauty influencers online are modified by filters, the models in magazines have been photoshopped, and that if Barbie were a living human female, she would topple over because her giant chest couldn't be supported by her wasp waist.[26] If we've dug a little deeper, we even know that our notions of beauty originate in eighteenth-century ideologies that equate whiteness with visible beauty and Blackness with ugliness and deformity.[27] We know that our models of beauty—and the models who exhibit them—are fake. We know they are racist, misogynistic, ableist, and all the rest. We know, we know. This is not news! Yet these pernicious concepts of beauty persist. They shape who is included in public and private. Who is in our families and our family stories.

Too often, critiques of beauty quickly become incorporated into part of the dominant beauty culture narrative: like classical fetishists, we know very well that beauty culture is fake and toxic and ableist and all the rest, but nonetheless we remain obsessed with it. We want to keep talking about all the problems with the model rather than change it. Diversity in models, like women's skirt lengths, goes in and out of fashion, working more perhaps to stabilize than transform the norms. So mere inclusion isn't the answer. How do we change the very notion of models and ideals that regulate norms? The answer has everything to do with disability lineage.

The story of Melissa Blake has a curious coda. Her response to the appropriation of her image and disability for the horrifically ableist Meet Your New Teacher Challenge went viral. Featured in news articles, essays, and even TikTok itself, Blake's nuanced articulation of the manifold problems with this trope proved as popular as the original video. Already a seasoned activist and self-advocate, as well as an excellent writer and polished public speaker, it is not surprising that she was able to make this invasion of her privacy and personhood a teachable moment for the larger culture. Blake used the democratic tools of social media to give a personality and story to the face that had in a sense been ripped from her and disseminated. Then, the mainstream media outlets picked it up and amplified it. Her story—and her critique of ableism—ultimately replaced the original Meet Your New Teacher Challenge in popularity and ubiquity.

But the story doesn't end there. Melissa Blake became a model. A fashion model. In 2020, Blake was invited to appear in the Runway of Dreams

fashion show, an annual event showcasing clothes for people with disabilities, as part of New York's Fashion Week, the pinnacle of the high
fashion industry. Started by the mom of a child with muscular dystrophy
in 2014, this event is a sort of high-fashion version of the Special Olympics: a parallel, segregated show that mirrors but does not challenge or
integrate with the ableist mainstream fashion shows. The coverage of this
event went almost as viral as the initial Meet Your New Teacher Challenge itself!

When asked why she chose to model, Blake invoked her teenage self.
She observed that as a fashion-savvy teen under four feet tall, she never
saw anyone who looked like her. To have seen someone like her on the
runway, she poignantly noted, "would have been a game-changer for
me."[28] It is for her younger self and the future Melissa Blakes—teenagers of all bodyminds who wish they saw themselves in fashion—that she
claims the territory of the fashion model. In this fashion, she relineates
both personal-past and public-future disabled selves.

The presence of disabled bodies in fashion is not new. Madeline Stuart, for example, is a largely silent young woman with Down syndrome
whose striking red hair and cheery saunter have regularly made appearances across the world's fashion runways since the early 2010s.[29] These are
usually predictable relics of the freak show staging of disabled minds and
bodies or inspo-porny, "Even this disabled person can make an effort to
look good—what's your excuse?" meme-ready images. Such "inclusion"
does little to change the terms of how we understand, produce, and sell
notions of beauty. These virtue-signaling uses of disabled bodyminds to
make the fashion industry feel good about its ableist self are almost laugh-
ably, obscenely problematic.

Models are the idealized versions of bodymind norms. We get our
ideas about what our bodies should be, how they should appear in public,
what kinds of minds and moods should emanate from our faces, from
extraordinary bodies far taller, thinner, whiter, and younger than the typical body. The models are the deviant—unusual—and odd bodies, not
everyone else's. Moreover, they are staged and shot in extraordinary ways.
Rosemarie Garland-Thomson's notion of the normate as an impossible

being is nowhere more apparent than in the fashion industry's model culture. Given this, it is not surprising that the flip side to the idealized body is often freakishly staged on the fashion runway, a direct descendent of the freak show performer. The disabled bodymind is the necessary counterpoint to the impossible model. This, like the broader critique of corporate beauty culture, is not entirely news.

What is different about Melissa Blake's appearances as a model on the fashion scene is how she explicitly critiques ableism and the very notion of beauty (and the conflation of disability with ugliness) in her struts and poses. Despite—or in a sense because of—the shocking and explicitly ableist use of her image that initially produced her fame, she is reappropriating and restaging our fundamental concepts of beauty and disability through her own very public, embodied performance. In a specifically disabled, activist fashion, she interrogates the conflation of beauty, ability, ideas, and ideals about bodyminds.

Agency is key here. She is both the model and the framer of the meaning of her modeling. Echoing the rhetoric of many minority empowerment discourses that boil down to "You can't be what you can't see," Blake articulates movingly how her teenage self might have been empowered by seeing bodyminds like hers in the fashion world, and how both present and future teenagers with disabilities might benefit from seeing her on the catwalk. Blake places this in the context of *all* teenage experience, as a desire typical of teenagers: "When you're a teenager—disabled or not—you deal with issues of self-confidence and self-esteem."[30] Her use of the second-person "you" to address the reader universalizes this experience. By so doing, she insists on the *ordinariness* of her teenage desire to be seen in the media images of glamour and fashion that most teenagers use as part of the reinvention of their child selves as burgeoning adults. It is absolutely ordinary, this desire. What is pathological is the lack of images that reflect the true diversity of teenage bodyminds.

Moreover, Blake challenges the fundamental conflation of beauty with the pageantry and glamour of fashion. She interrogates the conflation of disability with ugliness in a down-to-earth, accessible way that makes her disabled bodymind the model, the norm, as much as a conventionally beautiful high-fashion model's. More than fashion is at stake, Blake astutely notes: "These strict beauty standards dictate what is and isn't considered beautiful and, by default, acceptable."[31] The beautiful regulates not only what is considered aesthetically pleasing, but also what—and who—can be accepted and included in our society. She waves her freak flag glamorously and proudly in the face of the very notion of beauty and its ableist norms.

There is an important temporal dimension to Blake's reframing of her own image via modeling, one that has implications for how we conceive of disability lineage. Blake imagines what public images of disabled, nonnormative bodyminds like hers would have meant to her past teenage self. She also addresses the present and future in her closing comment in an editorial she wrote about her experiences as fashion model on CNN: "Indeed, seeing disability and fashion come together so beautifully tells us something pretty powerful: Disability inclusion is the ultimate fashion statement and forever on trend."[32] Refashioning the language of fashion itself here, she is arguing that disability inclusion, instead of being the latest freak fad to stabilize the norm, can change—permanently—the way public space works to represent disability.

This argument for a permanent, fundamental shift in how public space and its regulating models work is intimately tied up with how we imagine our own disability lineages. If disability were included and modeled in public space, "forever on trend," at the center of norms and models, the culture that has excluded them would profoundly shift. We would no longer need to segregate, institutionalize, murder, and marginalize our disabled family members, since we would no longer fear the internalized gaze of a disabling public that decrees who is beautiful, who is ugly. Who lives, who dies. Who is included in the family and the story it tells about itself.

Blake suggests that in occupying the public space of fashion, we could remake our familial relationship to access and inclusion. Our family photos, our social media feeds, our public stagings of our domestic lives—the fashion runways of the private sphere—would celebrate and include disabled relatives. Our kin's diverse bodyminds would help our kids see themselves, in all their shattering glamour. In all their gorgeous genetic diversity. In all their bodyminds. By reimagining both the spectators and the performers in the family fashion runway—and framing these roles as interchangeable rather than static—we can begin to incorporate all our family members into our lineage, as well as the larger public social fabric into which it is woven.

In remodeling the normate, Blake creates a space where disability and difference are normalized and shared by all. She takes the pedagogical power of the parents who instruct their children to fear disability and difference—in themselves as well as others—and positions herself as the model: the shaper of social norms, the instructor on how to include all bodyminds. Blake comes full circle by occupying the most public and idealized space of all, the virtual epicenter of the norm-production machine: the fashion industry. The model—who others adulate and copy. Who appears in public. Whose job is literally to be stared at. Who teenagers in particular look to as they form their ideas of belonging and exclusion. Meet your new teacher, indeed.

Temporally, Blake offers us a means of creating a lineage that neither fetishizes nor freakifies difference, but rather offers communion across generations. Since exploding on the national scene via her response to the Meet Your New Teacher Challenge, Blake has not only continued to model, she has also participated in the design of clothing for people with disabilities. Her young fans have turned her image into memes, cartoons, and stained glass ornaments, participating in this radical redefinition of whose image matters, who can model. Who can be sexual, and on whose terms. "I used to participate in other people's notions of beauty when it came to dating," she proclaims to her 116,000 Twitter followers. "If I could just walk, if I wasn't disabled, if I could cover up those scars, then I could be the woman who gets the guy. I could be the woman who is desired and wanted. Oh, how wrong I was . . ." She accompanies this post with an image proudly displaying her disability, captioning it, #MyBest-Selfie.[33] Flaunting, valuing, and sexualizing herself on her own terms is the message that her young online followers giddily repost.

Disability justice activist Mia Mingus takes this remodeling of the beauty-ugly binary one step further. She suggests that we dispense of the whole concept of beauty (and its fraternal twin, ugly). In her essay "Moving Toward the Ugly: A Politic Beyond Desirability," she encourages a valuing of all that has been labeled ugly (read: nonnormative) in one's bodymind as magnificent. Instead of arguing for a new model, she suggests refashioning the terms we already have. "Magnificence," Mingus argues, "has always been with us. Always been there in the freak shows—staring back at the gawking crowd. . . . magnificence was always there."[34] Like Kuppers and others recuperating the lineage of the freak show, Mingus rejects mere inclusion in the culture of beauty. She argues instead for embracing the "ugly"—the disabled difference of one's bodymind—and looks to her ancestry and disability lineage to imagine and value a new, magnificent model.

Melissa Blake embodies and imagines a politics of magnificent ordinariness in how she occupies public space. By including both her past disabled teenaged self and imagined future disabled teens in her runway performances, she claims full citizenship, insisting on her right—and the right of those before and after her—to be disabled in public. Blake intercedes in the internet's reproduction of her visage as the feared other of the public education system: the terrifying visibly disabled teacher.

It was in the context of public education that Melissa Blake first appeared in public. Public education is one of the fundamental spaces where citizenship is produced and enacted in modern democracies. The inclusion and exclusion of disabled bodyminds have been regulated there in ways that in turn define and determine what it means to be a citizen. Underlying debates about disability and education are "debates about the role of government and citizenship rights" for disabled people, as Kim Nielsen argues in her examination of education and disability in the American context.[35] Everything is notoriously and falsely private in the US. A brief examination of disability, citizenship, and education in UK society, in which the right to access public benefits and public spaces is viewed as central to citizenship, reveals an alternative model for our magnificent appearance in public.

I came upon this model by accident—or rather, by lineage—while interviewing Heather Grey, the current director of Cosgrove Care, the site of the disappearance and reemergence of Rhona from my family's disability lineage. In our interview, Grey spoke with pride about building partnerships with large employers like Target. She described how recreation for disabled people had expanded to include camping trips and other holiday excursions. This focus on autonomy, community, and independence evolved over many years, but Grey noted that the movement for Scottish independence, culminating in the vote in 2014, had opened up some new space to redefine disability rights in terms of full citizenship. "What would full Scottish citizenship look like for disabled people? What obstacles lie in the path of disabled people participating as citizens in every aspect of life? The 2014 Scottish vote for independence allowed us to ask these questions, and redefine disability rights independently of existing ableist English frameworks," Grey explained. Disabled people themselves, she noted, have primarily enacted this reframing.

Moreover, the Scottish Human Rights Commission, an official monitor of human rights in Scotland, used the 2017 United Nations Convention on the Rights of Persons with Disabilities to assess the strengths and weaknesses of the landscape for disabled people in Scotland, culminating in detailed reports with action items. The framing is explicitly that of rights and citizenship: "The reports set out a series of areas where disabled people's rights are not currently being fully protected and realized in Scotland."[36] It is not just protection of rights that is valued here but also the *realization* of those rights in full citizenship, including self-determination, access to work, social integration, and recreation. Such a realization involves valuing the ordinary ways disabled people might occupy public space in their everyday lives.

Cosgrove evolved along with the disability rights movement in Scotland, deploying the rhetoric of citizenship to create a cutting-edge model of support and care. Most of its services are now delivered to people living in their own families, or in supported group settings where they have maximum autonomy. In this regard, the rhetoric is similar to that of the contemporary US disability rights model of identity and autonomy. However, at least since 2014, the Scottish model has focused on the right to work, voting, and other hallmarks of participation in the national culture. In contrast, in the US, disability rights groups have primarily used the language of identity politics—of "identity, agency, and subjectivity," as cultural critic Anna Molow succinctly names the "familiar rallying cries of identity politics movements."[37] Disability rights activists in the US have worked for recognition of disability as a minority identity, often modeling their rhetoric and activism on the LGBTQ+ rights movement's notions of identity, pride, and inclusion. Even in disability justice conversations, which go beyond the rights model and center on the lived experiences and needs of disabled people themselves, disability tends to focus on identity, adding disability to the laundry list of minority identities claiming civil rights and cultural space.

This fundamental, structural difference in the model of disability rights in Scotland versus the US was evident in the very words Grey used; "full inclusion" and "full citizenship" were repeated often both in Grey's interview with me and in the documents related to disability rights published by Cosgrove and other progressive UK organizations. The material realization of that full citizenship went well beyond the civil right to vote or work; it included more informal, intangible rights: to shop, to hang out with friends of one's own choosing, to go camping. The reason these were understood as rights is because disabled people themselves were writing them: they were at the center of the conversation of what it might mean to be disabled in public. A disability politics of magnificent ordinariness emerged from my dialogue with Grey, embodied in the practices Cosgrove now implements that include everyday public activities.

For disabled people to be truly lineated—in public space and private families—such a joyful, magnificent ordinariness must be cultivated. Scotland rewrites disability rights to include camping: Blake places herself on the catwalk. These quotidian practices of ordinary, public fun may be as important to creating real inclusion as changes in laws.

Disabled people are reimagining beauty/ugliness, normate/disabled other, citizen/dependent, public/private, and all the false binaries that regulate our relationship to our own disability lineages. They are magnificently

sex selection demonstrates.[2] However, the public proclamation of this desire is currently socially unacceptable. As psychotherapist Anna Mathur notes, there is now a stigma, a secret shame to uttering a sex preference: "any hint of a gender [sic] preference gets cast as selfish and shameful."[3] Even the fabric hospitals swathe our newborns in is a studied mixture of pink and blue stripes.

Instead, parents now perform a ritual invocation in which they disavow any sex preference at all. To the question "Do you want a boy or a girl?" they are supposed to demur, "I don't care what it is . . . " followed by the specific assertion "as long as it's healthy." This is invoked like a chant, as if to ward off the bad fairies of illness, disability, and difference. The desire for a particular (male) sex has been replaced by the *disavowal* of that desire—I *don't* care about the sex of my child—coupled with an invocation of the supposedly more equitable desire for health.[4] This coupling is not incidental: the link between sex and health—and our fears about its opposite—is central to how both gender and disability are produced in our culture. The pairing indicates that gender and disability are woven together in a complex knot worth unraveling: one that is shaped by race in ways that remain unspeakable and unspoken.

It's hard to imagine that any parent would say, "I just hope my child is ill." Or even, as they do about sex, "I don't care what my newborn's health is." However, all infants and children get sick. What if the baby is healthy at birth, but then develops an illness or disability or is disabled in an accident? As Sarah Sahagian argues, "When your child is born, if they happen to have chronic ear infections or reduced vision, or fit into any of our other socially-constructed categories about what it means to be 'unhealthy,' would that make your baby less lovable or valuable?"[5] Surely not. Yet "as long as it's healthy" rhetoric persists.

"As long as it's healthy," I said over and over again when I was pregnant. As a pregnant person with "advanced maternal age"—when you're pregnant, being over thirty-five makes you basically diseased—I knew the risks of birth defects and disability were high.[6] I yearned for a girl, but was afraid to say so. I also wondered at all these earnest recitations of a disinvestment in gender, its defining power, by cishet women in the pregnancy support groups and casual acquaintanceships I encountered, whose lives seemed to me to be so entirely governed and constrained by gender norms. As a feminist and queer theorist who's spent her life marking and challenging the power of gender to define humans, it seemed odd for me to buy into this illogic, claiming no investment in "its" gender identity, chromosomal sex, or genital configuration. But I stayed silent and went along with the chant. Instead, I bargained with the (vague, nondenominational) gods for a nondisabled child of any genital configuration. "As long as it's healthy," I repeated nervously. I had the idea that the Universe understood I wasn't a particularly great person, so despite my advanced maternal age, I'd have a child free of disability, since I felt ill prepared to handle any sort of illness or difficulty. If I agreed to have a boy, then I would get a "healthy" one. This disturbing cluster of ableist and gendered thoughts were masked under the routine performance of "As long as it's healthy."

Healthy. A vague and innocuous-seeming term. But what do we mean, exactly, in this invocation? "Health" is often a surrogate for more specific, charged words: is disabled, has Down syndrome, looks visibly disabled, uses a wheelchair, is autistic. "Health" allows us to not work through what we really mean. Would we accept a child with a mild learning disability? One who is slow at math? How about one with the genetic markers for addiction? The BRCA genetic mutation that causes breast cancer? Where do we draw the line, exactly? And if it's not healthy, what are our plans—infanticide? Institutionalization? As biologist Ruth Hubbard notes, "Health and physical prowess are poor criteria of human worth."[7] "Healthy" is intentionally vague. "Healthy" sounds nice. But "healthy" obscures the eugenicist thinking undergirding this matrix of ableism.

Health is a vague concept that stands in for a wide range of conditions, including disability. Even seemingly objective medical definitions of a "healthy" baby are themselves socially constructed. At birth, my daughter received a perfect Apgar score: a supposedly objective measure that is used in hospitals to determine the health of an infant at birth based on their activity, pulse, grimace, appearance, and respiration. Yet even at birth, she had "abnormalities"—differences pointing to genetic variation that the Apgar didn't capture. At two and half, she was diagnosed with nonspeaking autism, though like many girls, it took a year to get that diagnosis because her autism presented differently from that of boys her age.[8] She was and is the picture of health: robust, happy, learning. She rarely gets viruses and has never once had a bacterial infection. Is my daughter healthy? It depends on how health is defined, and by whom.

Health is complex, changes over time, and is defined by social norms. The underpinnings of these norms must be interrogated to investigate why we are we replacing a misogynistic system with an ableist one. In fact, the misogyny has not been eradicated but rather displaced onto our highly gendered care system. Moreover, this misogyny intersects with structural racism in ways that make this displacement doubly violent for BIPOC disabled people and their caretakers.

This seemingly innocuous phrase "as long as it's healthy" provides a means of examining sexism, racism, and their displacement onto ableism. The normate, that impossible, nonexistent creature, is the only desirable child. This popular incantation, which would seem so progressive on first glance in its refutation of sex bias, naturalizes and perpetuates ableism. As Sahagian notes, "Symbolically, it ['as long as it's healthy'] enforces ableism by suggesting a good parent shouldn't care about things like sex . . . , but it's only natural to want an able-bodied baby with a good immune system and a naturally sunny disposition."[9] Yet *all* infants by this definition of health would fail the test—they all get sick and grumpy, and they are incredibly needy for at least the first two years of life. And sex difference is one of the most defining differences remaining in our culture—especially in relation to disability and care.

The wish for an impossible, perpetually healthy child is linked to rhetoric about sex preference because fear of disability is, fundamentally, a fear of care. And care work is organized around gender and race in profound, troubling ways. By denying the possibility (or inevitability) of a baby's care needs, and perpetuating fear and stigma of the "unwellness" that will necessarily be a part of every life, we defer an honest conversation about the racist and misogynistic organization of care in our society. By pretending eternal health and independence are possible for our children, we don't have to face the gendered and raced nature of how their care will be organized—and our own role within this system. It is no wonder birth rates are declining in societies where women have achieved the greatest degree of agency and equality; our misogynistic care system undoes all those gains. Mothers are required to do double duty as workers and caretakers.[10] A more honest grappling with the unequal, gendered organization of care work in the particular case of disability would help us confront the larger problem of inequality in care for all members of our society. After all, at some point, we are all dependent infants with "high care needs."

If we continue to deny the need for care, how can we possibly rethink it? Only by embracing our disability lineages, which necessarily include care and caretakers, can we hope to create less oppressive care structures.

CARE NARRATIVES AND THE NUCLEARIZATION OF THE FAMILY

My dad used to tell this mildly off-color joke whenever the subject of pets came up: "Wanted: a dog that never sheds, eats glass, and shits diamonds." We seem to expect a similarly impossible child, free of need or care. At the very least, we feel entitled to having a child whose care needs will follow a set developmental script: high care needs in infancy (met by a mother whose labor is unacknowledged and uncompensated); medium care needs during childhood waning into young adulthood; a flight from the nest around age eighteen; followed perhaps by a return in late adulthood to care for the aging parents (again, this late-in-life care work also falls disproportionately on daughters, not sons: between 70 and 80 percent of informal caregivers of the elderly around the world are women[11]). Such a narrative ignores that many children have care needs that mean they will always be dependent on their families and communities; that children who *don't* have disabilities often return to their families of origin in adulthood; that as elders, we will all need care from informal or professional caretakers. Indeed, since the economic crisis of 2007, it has become far more common for adult children to return to their homes in adulthood, regardless of ability: three in ten now do so, according to Pew.[12]

Despite the long-lived realities of interdependence and extended kinship systems, the nuclear family—a recent invention that has proved a miserable failure at caring for its elders, infants, and disabled members—is still envisioned as the norm, maintainable only as long as they're healthy, without needs. Only the rich can possibly make this sustainable. As *New York Times* columnist David Brooks bluntly puts it, "Affluent people have the resources to effectively buy extended family, in order to shore themselves up."[13] This is the dirty secret of white two-career couples. They buy the inevitable care work of parenting at obscenely low rates from BIPOC workers that used to be done by extended kinship systems. The disabled child is the scapegoat of this system: if the child proves to have high care needs, the system will be exposed, the hidden dependence of the nuclear family on BIPOC care workers rendered visible.

"As long as they're healthy." Even before a person is born, their care needs are wished away, repressed, feared. Forget eugenics, genetic testing, CRISPR, and the rest: the technology of parental desire is far more damaging than all that. Rather than challenging the ableist nuclear family system, parents invoke this incantation to ward away disability and the care needs that come with it. The care needs that come with being human.

The normative care narrative makes the lives of disabled people unthinkable and unlivable. Unimaginable in the developmental narrative, sustainable only through care rendered by BIPOC women, in the case of elites. Underneath the fear of disability is the fear that women—even white-collar white women—will have to sacrifice all their own career ambitions and subjectivity to provide care. In a broken system where care is delivered primarily by women both informally in their nuclear families and as underpaid workers, it is no wonder that ableism has wended its way into parenting culture. The real fear underlying the proclamation "as long as it's healthy" is that otherwise we, the mothers, will be consumed and subsumed by care needs.

While there is no simple way to undo this damaging system, embracing and understanding our disability lineage offers a means of rethinking the way individuals and their lifelong care needs are figured from conception to death. For if we began to include disabled people in our family narratives, their care needs and caretakers would also necessarily become part of the story. To make disability a part of the family story is to make care a part of the narrative as well.

If we had an understanding of our own disability lineage, we would see not only our disabled ancestors but also their caretakers—the family members and caregivers who aided them. The feminization and racialization of care would no longer be submerged. We would also make visible the labor of our own caregivers at the beginning and the end of every single life. Envisioning our own care needs, as well as those of our children (whether disabled or not), would mean destigmatizing and normalizing care. Perhaps we could then also see not only familial and individual (female) sacrifice but also the interdependence and deep, unique bonds that develop in care relationships.

Valuing care would also change our relationship to gender and race. Our disability lineage would no longer seem linear, a singular tree, but a complex system of interwoven roots and branches fed by an unequal, racist and sexist system. To transform that system and make it more equitable would involve seeing disability as communal and normal, not tragic and individual. As TL Lewis argues, this would involve a sharing of disability: a reconfiguring of disability as a collective experience rather than an individual problem for a nuclear family to solve (with the invisible labor of a bevy of underpaid BIPOC care workers in the background).[14] By making care and care work visible, in both its informal and professional dimensions, and by allowing that story into the family narrative, we would truly alter the racist, misogynistic structure of ableism.

To do care work is to be female. To be female is to do care work. Care work is what defines female gender as such. Mothers are charged with caring, defined as caregivers, valued for their caregiving, yet that care work is unpaid, marginalized, denied. The professional caregivers who are paid (poorly) to care in cases of disability, illness, and old age are expected to mirror that maternal effacement, both in affect and in gender performance. Eva Feder Kittay suggests that the maternal relation to the child is the originary paradigm in the patriarchal system, which all other care systems mirror.[15] Care work, like mothering, is marginalized, underpaid if paid at all, and not valued as essential, necessary, and inevitable. Who would want this role—and who would want their child then to be gendered as female, stuck caring?

"As long as it's healthy" performs the gendered, raced, and classed anxieties undergirding and enmeshed in care. We *do* care about sex and gender: the whole way we organize our families and their care is still assigned and sorted according to gender, with women doing the lion's share of the labor and/or outsourcing it to BIPOC women.[16] White, middle-class women deny both the gendering of care and its necessity, appealing to a fantasy of perpetual health and a masculinist model of independence underwritten on the backs of BIPOC women doing the bulk of care work, which is then rendered invisible.

The profound racism and sexism structuring care and its erasure must be interrogated as part of our disability lineage work. We need to make visible the labor of our ancestors' caregivers, both informal-parental and professional. In so doing, we will begin to undo the ableism woven into the fiber of the family. Race and racism underwrite the gendered care system in ways that disability exposes and the focus purely on "sex" elides. We *do* care about gender, precisely because of all the ways it—as well as race, sexuality, class, and other vectors of difference and power—is implicated in care work.

RACING AND ERASING CARE WORK

A primary, discomfiting reality erased in the "as long as it's healthy" narrative is that the vast majority of professional care workers are BIPOC women. This is neither accidental nor incidental: it is a legacy of our settler-colonialist, slaveholding past. Our modern American care system is a direct product of racism: it emerged in the antebellum South, where Black enslaved women took care of white families. Redefining them first as "domestic servants," "domestic workers," and now "home-care aides" and "group-home workers," civil rights legislation has consistently aimed to define these essential workers as *not workers at all*. The Fair Labor Standards Act (FLSA), part of the New Deal, which aimed to guarantee minimum fair wages and working conditions for all, explicitly made an exemption for (almost entirely Black and brown female) domestic laborers. With each iteration of labor reform laws, including the 1974 amendments to the FLSA, this exemption has persisted. Of the 2.3 million home-care workers in the US, 62 percent are women of color and between 80 and 90 percent are women. Their median annual wages of $16,200 remain among the lowest for any profession.

Care work has been legally and culturally defined as . . . not exactly work. When the feminized labor of care that all women are expected to do with their own children and elders is professionalized, it is farmed out to BIPOC women and devalued.[17] During the COVID-19 crisis, when home-care and group-home workers were at high risk for infection and often didn't receive PPE (personal protective equipment), countless articles were written about their plight, as well as that of women who had to leave their jobs to perform care work and homeschooling for their children. The media acted as if this were a new crisis, a problem born of the pandemic. But as home-care labor organizer April Verrett commented, "What has gone unsaid is that we, as a country, have treated home-care workers as decidedly inessential, due in large part to the profession's roots in slavery."[18] While care workers are no longer only, or in some regions of the US primarily, Black (though the majority are still primarily minoritized people of color), the legacy of slavery still defines the profession as inessential. This is systemic racism in a nutshell: the racist structure and value system remains regardless of who is doing the care work.

Given the devaluing of care work and its imbrication in a racist, misogynistic system, it's no wonder that I participated in the rhetoric of "as long as it's healthy" and feared having a disabled child. As a white, professional, liberal woman, the last thing I wanted was to participate in such a system, either as uncompensated, deprofessionalized caregiver to a high-needs child or as the employer of BIPOC women exploited in such roles. Yet I also knew that I would not abort, no matter what. Instead, I took my prenatal vitamins religiously, drank no coffee or alcohol, and chanted "as long as it's healthy" as if it were a magic spell. Such rhetoric avoids an honest engagement with care and care needs, with caretakers informal and professional, and with the intersections of race, gender, and ability in a racist, misogynistic, and ableist system. For white women to do care work is for them to be deprofessionalized. For white men to do care work is for them to be emasculated. For women of color to face the prospect of doing care work for a disabled family member is even more challenging. BIPOC women already face tremendous obstacles to being viewed as competent, professional, and powerful.

Moreover, BIPOC women rightfully worry about the treatment of their disabled child or family member at the hands of a racist system that has difficulty valuing BIPOC people as worthy of care. As the Black Lives Matter movement has highlighted, disabled Black people are doubly devalued, often with fatal consequences. Sandra Bland, Marcus Davis-Peters, Deborah Danner, Tanisha Anderson, Freddie Gray, and Eric Garner are just some of the Black people who have recently been murdered by the police essentially for the crime of being Black and disabled in public. While exact numbers about the rate of police brutality toward Black disabled people don't exist, researchers at the Ruderman Family Foundation have estimated that one-half to two-thirds of all Americans killed by the police have a disability.[19] Given that police violence is the leading cause of death for young Black men in the United States, and that over the course of their lives, about one in every one thousand Black men can expect to be killed by police, the calamitous consequences of being both Black and disabled are obvious.[20]

In a society where Black disabled people face the potential threat of police violence and where medical professionals also routinely underestimate the physical pain of their BIPOC patients, it is understandable that BIPOC women might fear having a child who is deemed "unhealthy."[21] Who might not only have high care needs but might also face extraordinary discrimination and violence from caregivers and police alike. But in fact, Black parents have been at the forefront of challenging the intersecting racism and ableism of our culture rather than perpetuating the fear-based white culture of "as long as it's healthy." Mothers like Camille Proctor, founder of the Color of Autism Foundation, points out that "when an African American person is disabled and can't process a police command—with any luck—he'll end up in handcuffs, but most of the time, it's fatal." Maria Davis-Pierre, creator of Autism in Black, notes that "our children having interactions with the police is a constant worry for us."[22]

These two Black mothers of Black children with disabilities are trying to change the racist, ableist culture that puts Black disabled people in constant danger. Their lived understanding of racism makes them agents of inclusion and change. They do not indulge in the denialism of care, the myth of the white normate, for they know that their children never conformed in the first place to the notion of the healthy, able white male bodymind with no needs. They articulate a fear not of disability but of police violence: of a state that criminalizes Black, disabled existence.

TL Lewis argues that "anti-Black ableism" is in fact redundant and contradictory simultaneously "because ableism and anti-Blackness are mutually inclusive and mutually dependent." Our care system and care fears are prime examples of how they coproduce one another. To truly dismantle ableism, we must engage its systemic racism and misogyny instead of evading and displacing it.[23]

CARE, COST, AND CLASS

The economic dimensions of care are profound. Because the inevitability of care needs is denied, they are underfunded, cut out of the social and economic fabric of our life and the systems governing it. As with all the other dimensions of ableism, this denial and marginalization affects people differently depending on race, class, gender, and sexuality. While professional-class women such as myself fear being redomesticated and deprofessionalized by the care needs of a disabled family member, working-class women living in precarity in our postindustrial society fear not being able to make any kind of living at all. Care needs of family members can cause a calamitous slide into poverty and underemployment. Often working-class women must provide care in the home while doing service work as contingent, nonunionized laborers in low-paying service industries. They risk being forced out of the paid labor market by a family care crisis into the unpaid, impoverished realm of subsisting on government benefits. This is the dire situation for so many working-class and poor women with disabled children and elders.

Moreover, as Ai-Jen Poo, Evelyn Nakano Glenn, and Grace Chang have demonstrated, the American anti-Black racist system of care is now entwined with a neocolonialist one in which underpaid BIPOC immigrant women are compelled to care for the bodyminds of primarily white nonrelatives.[24] Glenn characterizes this system as coercive. She traces how the deinstitutionalization of disabled and aging people, the end of welfare programs for mothers, and labor migration from the global south to the north have resulted in a system where "race, gender, and class have remained central organizing principles of care labor. As a result, care labor remains an arena where coercion holds sway, and where full freedom and citizenship are denied."[25] This results in oppressive working conditions for and the social inequality and marginalization of care workers.[26]

But it is not only the rich, white, and privileged who have disabled children and elders. What of those who can't afford our increasingly privatized, racist, exploitative system of care? In alarmingly titled studies such as *Expensive Children in Poor Families: The Intersection of Childhood Disabilities and Welfare*, sociologists lay out the costs of disabled children for poor women in our privatized culture of care: "Between 20 and 25 percent of the families [on welfare] had a disabled or ill mother or child, 10 to 12 percent had a disabled child, and 3 to 5 percent cared for children with severe limitations." According to this study, work was directly affected by a child's disability: "Families with disabled children also incurred indirect costs in the form of forgone earnings. Mothers with more than one moderately disabled child or with at least one severely disabled child were 20 to 30 percent less likely to have worked in the previous month than mothers with healthier children."[27] The study notes how racialized this all is: the vast majority—over 90 percent—of the study's subjects were BIPOC. But rather than indict the system that leads to these inequities, the disabled children are blamed, accused of being *expensive*.

It's also remarkable that the gendering of the caregiver as a woman—"mothers"—is assumed here. Nowhere does the study ask why mothers are expected to supply these care needs—why the state and local government do not provide this care or why fathers or other kin are not expected to be primary caretakers of their high-needs disabled children. Privatization and feminization are assumed. The mother is tasked with putting her child's care in competition with her ability to make a living.

Her experience of caregiving is figured only as a loss: of income, of work. That caregiving a loved one could be more rewarding than repetitive minimum-wage labor is not questioned. Of course the public costs of this system are the point of the study, but the gendered, private informal care system is never interrogated. Disability is the problem here!

The family—also known as the mother—is expected to provide care for disabled people at all stages of the life cycle. The blunt, gendered facts are startling: Women make up 75 percent of all family caregivers.[28] For the working poor, this returns mothers to the public welfare systems that have been systematically defunded since the 1980s—and to low-paying care work that extracts care for others while rendering them unable to care for their own families. Grace Chang analyzes the consequences of this extractive, racist neoliberal system for the immigrant women who provide this care. "Ironically," she notes, "these women's labor—caring for the young, elderly, and the disabled—makes possible the maintenance and reproduction of the American labor force at virtually no cost to the U.S. government. At the same time, this labor is extracted in such a way as to make immigrant women's sustenance of their own families nearly impossible."[29] It is horrifically ironic that care workers are rendered unable to care for their own families in this exploitative system.

For wealthier families, this privatized system deprofessionalizes women, returning them to patriarchal gender roles and systemic sexism that they had supposedly "solved" on an individual level through egalitarian marriages. Kate Washington, a privileged, professional-class cishet white woman, chronicles the unmanageable care burdens she faced when her husband became ill. Her husband's disabling cancer led to her total deprofessionalization and burnout. Washington suggests that only by exposing the gendered nature of care and the privatization of care systems can we begin to ameliorate this. "The challenges of caregiving arise not because individual families have foolishly failed to set themselves up better to do it. They exist because our society consistently devalues care and does little or nothing to support it,"[30] she argues, in part because it is seen as "women's work." However, Washington never addresses the ableism at the heart of our dysfunctional relationship to care—and kinship.

The entwining of care work in racist, anti-immigrant, classist, and misogynistic systems of oppression is the result of the dismantling of the institutionalized care system without a similar dismantling of the ableism that underwrote it. Deinstitutionalization of disabled people, which happened on a massive scale in the late 1970s in the US, privatizes care, making families rely on the unpaid labor of mothers and, in the case of privileged white families, underpaid and exploited care workers, most of whom are BIPOC women.

While deinstitutionalization is in my view an unalloyed moral good, the patchwork system that has replaced it, consisting of home care, "special" education, and public services of varying quality, has left mothers in the role of caretaker. As Kim E. Nielson notes, "One reality of deinstitutionalization was that neither the federal government, states, or cities developed enough structures to provide sufficient support for people who needed it to live on their own—even when doing so was far cheaper than institutional living."[31] Mothers are expected to step in and step up—and step away from their own careers. Since self-directed supports and mutual aid are largely unavailable, it is mothers who must sacrifice their own needs and professional goals to try to meet their family's care needs. It's the care crisis all working mothers in the US face, but on steroids. Reinforcing outdated gender roles, neoliberal extractive labor and immigration practices, and antebellum racism, our care "system" really isn't a system at all. It's a regression.

When my daughter received her diagnosis, my unspeakable fear was that this would just connect me to a long, depressing history of female caregivers. Self-effacing, with no identity besides caring for their child, these women were then hated by their other children—and sometimes by the cared-for child themselves. I had struggled my entire life to redefine gender roles. To live a life free of the heteronormative and sexist expectations that define and limit women. That relegate women to supporting, care-giving roles while the men get to be independent, swashbuckling achievers. To be carefree. I chose to have only one child, late in life, in order to minimize the impact of care on my independent, feminist life. And I chose a gender-nonconforming female partner who would be an equal caregiver, ensuring that despite my being the birth mother, we would share the minimal burdens of our needs-free child. Like Washington, I naively thought that I could individually solve the systemic problems of care by having an egalitarian marriage—queer gender-nonconforming edition. All that was missing in this needs-free fantasy was the diamond poop. I had no models, no lineages of caregiving that demonstrated the *value* of giving care to a disabled person in a nonsexist fashion. I had no lineages of caregiving at all.

"Behind every successful disabled kid is a bedraggled mother," quipped one cishet "autism mom" friend. We met in the parent group I dutifully attended for the parents of kids with disabilities when my daughter was first diagnosed. "Parents," it turned out, meant moms; my partner and I were the only couple to attend, and there was not a single dad in sight. Nor were there any single-parent families represented. Most of us were middle to upper-middle class, and three-fourths were white, with the rest being mostly Asian and South Asian, despite living in a county where 15 percent of the population are African American and 12 percent are Latinx.[32] We certainly were a bedraggled lot. Sacrifice seemed to be the theme. Accepting your child's limitations. Submerging yourself to your child's "special" needs. A kind of hyperfeminine Christian martyrdom was valorized. Oy veh! My queer, Jewish self wondered how she got here.

I wanted to escape: not from my daughter and her disability but from the system that seemed intent on denying the reality and ubiquity of ableism, instead sequestering disabled lives away in a privatized system of racist, sexist care. I found enormous value in the unique experience of caring for my daughter—and in forcing the system, from my position of extreme privilege as a white, tenured professor of English at an elite university, to adapt to my caretaking needs rather than deprofessionalize me.

My Asian American partner and I balked at entering the racist care system where BIPOC women were delegated the hardest, supposedly low-skilled, lowest-paid care work while a bevy of white female professionals handled the speech, occupational, and other high-skilled therapies. We were able instead to share the care work in an ungendered way, due to the flexibility of our white-collar jobs and our shared socialization as women. But we struggled to find a way to engage paid care-work systems that didn't feel like a perpetuation of racism intersecting with sexism. We still struggle to find parent groups that don't perpetuate sexism and heterosexism.

While our peers were baffled by our seeming embrace of lowly care work, and praised our DIY indie spirit and apparent adoption of maternal self-sacrifice, we didn't recognize ourselves. Our own positionality felt unprecedented and unrecognizable. Where were we in this deeply racist, misogynist, and heterosexist story? Utterly cut off from our lineage as caregivers, which is as inherent a part of the story of disability as disabled people themselves.

JOYFUL CARE: TOWARD A FEMINIST CARE ETHIC

In the Deaf community, it is common to talk about "deaf gain"—how the physical fact of deafness can lead to capital *D* Deafness: to gaining access to a rich, unique community; to acquiring a new language of communication that is embodied and complex; to a new way of being in the world. As I suggested earlier, disability gain extends beyond deafness to the larger community. The so-called disability we call deafness has benefited the larger non-Deaf society. For example, the distinctive ways sign language relies on nonverbal communication has expanded neurology, linguistics, and brain science, leading scientists to a greater understanding of the nonverbal dimensions of speech.

The coronavirus pandemic revealed some of the ways disability gain could benefit caregivers, and demonstrated how caregivers of disabled people can help make all of society more accessible and flexible. As one insurance company noted in an optimistically titled article on its website, "How a Post COVID-19 Workplace Can Embrace Accessibility—for Everyone," the coronavirus was in some respects easier to adapt to for some disabled people because "for those with disabilities . . . having limited access can be the norm. The disabled community is well-equipped to offer knowledge about navigating this new normal."[33] This general claim was certainly proven true in my own family. My daughter already did much of her learning remotely because of her disability; our community of teachers and caretakers already knew how to build community and teach effectively in virtual learning spaces.

I, too, as a caregiver had some gains to share. I found myself helping my neurotypical professor colleagues at Georgetown rethink their pedagogy; I already knew how to teach remotely effectively and inclusively precisely because of my work as my daughter's caregiver. As the connective tissue between her and her teachers, I had gained the ability to learn and teach in a more accessible, fluid fashion than those without this experience. "We know how to stay in touch remotely, be socially connected while physically distant, make limited resources work in tight situations, make plans and adjust on the spot, build care webs that support each other, and work through challenging circumstances," observes Elizabeth McClain, who is both a disabled activist and an instructor of musicology at Virginia Tech.[34]

Disabled people themselves have a depth of knowledge and expertise about care that all can draw upon, yet this is frequently unacknowledged or marginalized. As Leah Lakshmi Piepzna-Samarasinha bluntly notes, "In the face of systems that want us dead, sick and disabled people have been finding ways to care for ourselves and each other for a long time."[35] To value care, we need to value the unique forms of knowledge that come with diverse bodyminds. We need to value the experience of caring for disabled kin, and look to disabled people themselves for the most dynamic, vital models of care.

I do not mean to minimize the challenges of care work. Nor do I want to romanticize caregivers as saintly, self-sacrificing, feminized figures without needs of their own. Ugh! But my own experience suggests that doing care work can and does transform the lives of caretakers in positive ways. There is "care gain" just as there is disability gain. If care were integrated fully and equally into our lived realities of kinship, rather than outsourced or privatized in misogynistic, racist systems, its value would be visible. If disability were part of our collective kinship histories, rather than produced as an individual trauma for both the disabled person and the mother who has to figure out how to meet that person's care needs alone, we would be in a better position to reimagine caretaking beyond its current racist and sexist configurations.

Too often, instead of challenging or transforming the problematic systemic dimensions of caregiving, we aspire to the false independence of masculine subjectivity, complete with that diamond-shitting dog. Our devaluing of care, of interdependence, of disability gain, and our lack of any sense of disability caregiving lineage lead not to freedom but rather to denial and ableism. This results in the perpetuation of unequal systems of care. If we deny the very need for care and care work as a natural and inevitable—and potentially positive—aspect of life, how can we possibly challenge the structural racism and sexism of care systems?

The fear of being burdened by the care of another, of having one's hard-fought feminist freedom curtailed, and of ultimately being a burden to another shapes the fear and stigma underlying ableism. This enables white women like me to ignore and disidentify with the caregiver lineages from which we came. Missing from this is any specific history of caregiving. Instead, care looks like the abject plight of the great sea of (race unmarked) women. When faced with the care needs of family members, white cishet women are encouraged to "outsource" to BIPOC women rather than challenge their male partners to participate equally. Instead of challenging the public systems of school, work, and healthcare to include disabled people at the center rather than the margins of their funding and care structures, we retreat into the fantasy that we are somehow immune to disability. To aging. Dependency.

"As long as it's healthy" is a fiction that pastes over the reality that no child is completely healthy for long. Instead of clinging to this ableist fantasy, we need to face the complexity and inevitability of care work and challenge our assumptions about who provides care and under what conditions. Only then can the costs—and joys—of care work be more equitably examined and shared.

Feminist disability studies has worked to expose this gendered distribution and devaluing of care, critiquing the false models of independence that perpetuate this order. Its implications, like those of disability gain, are not just for those with disabilities in their families but for all of us, as we all will face care needs of some sort for ourselves or others at some point in the life cycle. The racism and sexism of the entire care system—and the deep stigma and shame surrounding the very fact of care needs—are simply more acute in relation to disability.

White women's privilege is defined by outsourcing care and by denying the value of caregiving or the lessons (positive and negative) to be gained from placing one's own experience in the context of one's family caregiving lineage. Eva Feder Kittay brilliantly explores the misogynistic dynamics of this system of valuing and devaluing care work. Feder Kittay, a professional philosopher and parent of a disabled adult, frames valuing care as part of a feminist ethic in which the interdependence and care needs of all humans are acknowledged, absolute independence is exposed as a patriarchal lie, and society works to create a more gender-equitable and honest relationship to care and interdependence. This involves normalizing care, and letting our values and practice derive from meeting the needs of the *most* dependent. "An ethics of care," Feder Kittay proclaims, "derives from the best practices of care for vulnerable dependent persons."[36]

One of the most compelling aspects of Feder Kittay's argument is its articulation of joy. She speaks of her joy in simply being with her daughter, rather than in regard to anything her daughter does or produces. She examines the complex experience of physically caring for and being with her daughter, celebrating the routine intimacies and pleasures of such a relationship. Those positive, joyous aspects of care and interdependency are key to valuing caregiving—and assuring that it is done in the most ethical manner. Feder Kittay suggests there are "extraordinary possibilities inherent in relationships created in caring for someone like her [daughter Sesha], someone who reciprocates but not in a like coin (say, by caring physically for another), but by bestowing her warmth and love."[37] Seeing care relationships as reciprocal is key to Feder Kittay's valuing of care—even if the exchange is not "in like coin."

It is not incidental that the metaphor of exchange is coin: for compensating care workers properly is a crucial part of the equation. In

Feder's reconception of care, professional caretakers are compensated better, trained better, and respected more for the important labor they are doing. She optimistically assumes that this increase in respect and compensation will decrease abuse. Besides this instrumental effect, she argues that an "ethics of care" depends on such valuation of care and caregivers. Feder views valuing care as a twofold process: of valuing and reorganizing the gender dynamics of informal care inside the family, and valuing the work of professional caregivers through the more formal mechanisms of labor (compensation, training, prestige). Given the racist and misogynistic history of caregiving, coupled with the neoliberal capitalist imperatives of the marketplace, this is not an easy task. Nor is the reorganization of gender roles in informal caregiving. And, of course, these are not separate issues.

However, while in some families disability leads to a reification of raced gender norms, in others, new models are emerging. Necessity is the mother of the reinvention of motherhood, care, and the raced gender roles that surround it. While many families with children or elders with high care needs defer to the narrative of the self-sacrificing mother, the poorly compensated BIPOC, female care worker, and the absent wage-earning dad who funds the whole enterprise, some families have found in the joys and challenges of care the opportunity to rewrite the gendered, raced narrative of care entirely.

Fathers like Michael Bérubé, George Estreich, and Ralph Savarese have not only taken primary roles as caretakers of their disabled children but also found in the experience a radical challenge to the gender norms in which they were raised. Their accounts tend to be optimistic, stressing the disability gain rather than the caregiving challenges of parenting a disabled child. As Bérubé comments, "[My disabled son] taught me more than I ever thought I would know about people with Down syndrome, and about intellectual disability and intraspecies variation in general. You could call that an opportunity. Some might even call it a blessing. I call it an adventure in lifelong learning."[38] They use their cultural power as white, cishet male authorities to question the gendered and raced assumptions about caretaking and dependence. They chronicle how they share equally the burdens and joys of caretaking their disabled children with their female spouses, but are the primary narrators of the family story in their public accounts. Their work has been truly transformative; Savarese in particular has, in collaboration with his son David James "Deej" Savarese, created films, scholarly books, and memoirs that amount to a sea change in how people with communication disorders are viewed. His *Reasonable People: A Memoir of Autism and Adoption* is one of the most compelling, thoughtful, and ethical accounts of neurodiversity and family.[39] But despite their deeply egalitarian and feminist values, such stories are heralded as exceptional by the media. It is still exceptional—book-worthy, even—when men take on caretaking roles in relation to disability.

Meanwhile, the alarmist "autism moms" are rightly disparaged for their ableist narratives. "Autism Ruined My Life!" and "Most People Don't Want to Hear the Ugly Details: Our Struggle to Raise Our Autistic Son!" scream the headlines of these popular accounts by women who are the primary caregivers of their disabled children.[40] Instead of the unfair distribution of care work, it is the source of the care—the disabled child—who is to blame in these sensationalized accounts. This displacement perpetuates a misogynistic, ableist system in which mothers are set up to fail at impossible care work unevenly distributed. In reality, parents of all genders in families of all compositions have often not just stepped up but also changed the course of entire communities, challenging the ableism of the self-appointed experts, as Clara Park did in her advocacy for her autistic daughter. In the mid-twentieth century, Park challenged the notion of the "refrigerator mother" as autism's cause.[41] Today, many mothers continue her legacy in fighting for their disabled children's rights to access school, work, and recreation.

There is a rich, deep history of mothers advocating successfully for disability rights; this work has led to some of the major structural changes in our society. Yet when a parent faces the challenge of arranging the care needs of their disabled child, the legacies of caretakers among their relatives, ancestors, and other family members—both informal and professional—often remain invisible. Those of mothers are effaced and those of fathers are heroized. The paid caregivers remain anonymous, marginalized in the family narrative, if they appear at all.

If we knew and valued our own family's disability lineage, we would also know and value a lineage of care. However, one obvious danger of focusing on caregivers is that they can easily become the *primary* focus of conversations on disability and care. A slogan of the disability rights movement—"Nothing About Us Without Us"—reminds us of how easily a focus on interdependence and care can slide back to an ableist, narcissistic focus on caregivers. Centering disabled people in any discussion of their care is crucial. This is particularly crucial—and tricky—in cases where disabled people do not have adequate communication tools.

Feder Kittay points to this conundrum of her inability to include her daughter's views on care and caregiving; because her daughter has no communication system, "I am in the awkward position of speaking of an individual with a disability—needing to speak not only *about* her but, contra the disability dictum [of centering disability discourse in the words of those who are themselves disabled] *for* her."[42] It is easy to project simplicity and absence to a nonspeaking person who may in fact have a complex, highly verbal inner life. Before I found a communication system that worked for my daughter, I found myself doing this. It is precisely because of this understandable tendency that many in the disability justice movement have adopted the slogan "Presume Competence."

Moreover, it is not the job of a person with high care needs to be joyful. Or to preserve a childlike bond with their caregiver. Stacy Clifford Simplican observes that the dyadic parent-child model of care often denies both caretaker and caretaken real agency and subjectivity, or any capacity for the dynamics of this relationship changing over time. "We need a model of care that tells us how to cope and respond to conflict and complexity," Simplican concludes, "not how to make ourselves transparent or vulnerable."[43] "Cope" still suggests that care is always an abnormality, aberrant, a crisis: not a normal part of everyday family life.

It is also problematic and infantilizing for disabled adult children to be solely reliant on their parents (and by "parents," we often mean mothers!). Nothing has been more important to my daughter than finding—

and often having to forge in its absence—a community of peers who share her disability. This has connected her to a larger sense of identity as a disabled person, as well as a community in which she is centered. It enables her to have peer, age-appropriate relationships and vitiates against the controlling, infantilizing tendencies of the dyadic mother-child relationship.

The need for new models of caregiving that are not racist, heteronormative, or subtly sexist is beyond self-evident. One reason we cannot seem to find those new models is because we have nothing on which to model, neither for nor against. Caregivers have been as thoroughly erased from our family narratives as those who have been cared for. Disability lineage can be fully figured only with the inclusion of the caregiver. Otherwise, our pictures of our disabled kin are incomplete: we perpetuate the fiction of the nuclear family as the proper site of care. Yet the caregiver cannot be the center of the story, the primary authority over the lives and narratives of disabled people. Indeed, by including caregivers in our disability lineages, stories of caregivers' abuse and mistreatment, as well as the heartwarming stories of caregivers' joy and dedication, would be made visible. The racism, sexism, and other structural inequalities in care work—as well as the unique joys of disability caregiving—would likewise be seen in all their complexity.

LINEATING THE HIDDEN CAREGIVER

Disability lineage helps us see, value, and accept not only the disabled people in our family histories but also their caregivers. This lineation might help us move beyond fantasies of autonomy and "self-care." It would also complicate our narratives of selfless caregiving to include the realities of exploitative labor practices, and the shameful abuse and neglect of our disabled kin.

My own experience exemplifies the subtle yet radical shifts that occur when caregivers are included in the story. For without them our disability lineages are incomplete. And if fear of care work—and the sexist, racist organization of this hidden labor—is the fuel feeding the wildfire of ableism, then we must make visible the care lineages of our families, in all their unfair, uneven, sexist, and racist dimensions.

When I learned about Rhona, one bell went off. In talking to Rhona's sister and niece, I got one view of how my family lineage had been rewoven to include a disabled member with high care needs. Of the successes and failures of that integration. How institutionalization and segregation had shaped even this loving, forward-thinking family. But I needed to understand more. I asked the director of Cosgrove, Heather Grey, to introduce me to anyone who had had direct contact with Rhona during her time there. "Ah, that'll be Kathy. She knew Rhona the best."

And so I arrived on a Glasgow-foggy afternoon at Cosgrove's suburban congregrate-care house. I rang the buzzer and wondered who this Kathy person might be. The door opened, and there she was. Kathy: a middle-aged, white, working-class Scotswoman with a quick laugh and thick Glaswegian burr. She greeted me warmly and took me into her office.

"So you want to know about Rhona. She was a character, was she. Rhona! A bundle of life. A typical Down's lady, you know—very sweet and warm. A lot like Vera, really. And Vera and her mother visited all the time. All the females in the family did. And if anyone gave her any trouble, she'd say, 'You know my mum started this whole place.' Typical Down's lady!" Kathy laughed warmly, her affection for Rhona evident. I remembered how I would say practically the identical words when I was a child at my grandparents' summer camp. I'd brag to the other campers, with zero self-consciousness, that my grandparents owned the whole place! I thought about how we tend to ascribe every characteristic of a disabled person to their disability. "Typical Down's lady!" But disabled people have unique characteristics unrelated to their disabilities—and sometimes inherited from their families. Clearly, these were the words of a Fink.

"What else do you remember about her? What did she like to do with her days?"

"Ah, she loved to color: she'd go to sleep with her colored pencils and paper all lined up in the bed beside her. Tidy was she." I tried to picture the girl from Vera's photos in bed with her colored pencils. I pressed Kathy further. "She loved being Jewish. Loved to say the prayers, though she couldn't get them quite right. We'd light the candles, say the prayers every Shabbat, and Rhona would lead the service."

I rustled through my notes. "Did she get out much? She didn't work, right?" I had that feeling that I wasn't asking quite the right question—the one that would tell me what I didn't already know. That maybe I didn't want to know.

"No, none of them worked back then. Right shame. But Rhona: Rhona loved to be out in the world, at the shops, the synagogue, the cinema—she loved movies!—all around town. Oh, she loved the homey atmosphere here. She loved to bake—it's a shame though." Kathy teared up. I pictured Rhona baking with my daughter, our family's baker-in-chief. "She only got to enjoy this place a year. The old place on St. John's wasn't half as nice. No kitchen—more of an institutional feel. Rhona loved it here, was so happy when we moved. But then, not a year later, got sick she did. Senile, confused. So sudden. Now we know Down's people often get it. She went quick."

I was confused. "So she couldn't stay here at Cosgrove when she was sick?"

"Oh no. We weren't equipped, you see. None of the hospice places would take her, because of the Down's, so she died in hospital. Spent the last few months there with dementia, disoriented, sick, and upset. Terrible, really."

I wanted to know more about this terrible end. Why wouldn't any other institution take her? Why couldn't she stay at Cosgrove—or in her parents' home?

I asked, but Kathy was determined to breeze past this. "Can't tell you much more than that. Now we know dementia is common with Down's people. But she was a happy sort up until then. She loved to be out and about. At the shops, the park. Her mum and Vera took her out all the time. A lovely person—a lot like Vera."

"And how about her brother, Myron, and her dad?"

"I hardly knew them to recognize on the street. Never visited, really." I felt like there was more to this, but I could tell Kathy was wary of airing family secrets. And why should she? But she'd given me plenty: she'd exposed the gendered nature of disability care in my own family.

While we were talking, a middle-aged man entered repeatedly. "Can we go, eh?" he asked anxiously.

"It's not time yet, John," Kathy told him several times. "I have a visitor. Give me a moment and then we'll go." To me, she said apologetically, "Sorry, but he's just really keen on going to town."

I felt in that moment the care and understanding between Kathy and her disabled clients. She didn't lock her office door, implicitly asking me to accommodate his need to interrupt. After all, it was his house, not mine.

I asked if she had any other photos of Rhona. Kathy didn't think so, but promised she'd look. I somehow knew there weren't any. Kathy was a paid worker in an institution, however caring she might be. It wasn't her job to produce the public record of our family, to tend to this fallen branch of my family tree. As I left, I felt like a long-buried root had just pushed through the ground.

When I talked to Rhona's caregiver, all the bells rang. I saw a much fuller, more complete picture of my disability lineage. The sexist dimensions of her father and brother's disengagement came into sharp focus. The way gender norms shaped and limited caregiving, and shaped Rhona's life both in her family and in this seemingly benign institution, only was evident once I encountered a narrator outside the family. Seeing Kathy's deep compassion and intimacy with the current residents of Cosgrove gave me a palpable sense of Rhona's life there, in all its joys and limitations.

Talking to the person who spent the most time with her in her adult life, and who was *outside* the family system, gave me a better sense of Rhona's everyday life—and a more sharply focused lens on the family that nurtured her. It also put in stark relief the ways institutionalization de-lineated her, both during and, most tragically, at the end of her life.

This encounter helped me place my own caregiving experience in context and see both Rhona more clearly, in all her funny, vivid, and joyous quirks, and the caregiving systems that isolated her from the male members of her family while placing unacknowledged care expectations on the female ones. The links I saw between Rhona and my daughter felt profound: the bragging, the baking. These small, humanizing personality quirks were surprisingly powerful. Primal. They connected us, in a deep-rooted way.

Meeting Kathy gave me a context for my own experience of caregiving, in my family and outside of it. Inspiration? Cautionary tale? Neither. It was more surprising, deep, and complex than that. I felt like I found the forest for the trees. All these hidden roots encircling us. Meeting Rhona's caregiver was as moving and profound—and unsettling—as meeting her family. My family.

I will never know my cousin XY's caregivers. His caregiving history is erased. I know him only through court records and family whispers. Through an absence of a story of care. That absence is a fundamental, structuring part of my disability lineage.

To truly normalize and integrate disability into our notion of a family, the caregivers, paid and informal, have to enter the picture as well. What we know—and don't know—about the individuals and institutions that took care of our disabled relatives matters, in all its inequitable, raced, classed, and gendered specificity.

Concepts of disability lineage and the lineages of care cannot change policies and practices overnight. The deep-veined systemic racism, ableism, and sexism of our cultural views will change only with transformations in policies, laws, and healthcare systems. Activists, lawyers, union organizers, care workers, and others are already working hard to create such deep structural change. But while patriarchy and racism are formidable forces, so is the family narrative. The stories we tell about our families, our ancestors, our kin—the bodies and minds we include and exclude, the care needs and caregivers we erase—shape how we imagine disability and its relationship to our own lives.

To create more inclusive families, we must tell fuller family stories. Disability lineage must be part of that. But such a lineage is incomplete unless care and caregiving are a central part of the narrative. Perhaps, then, saying "As long as they're healthy"—along with the larger racist, sexist, and ableist system this sentiment so pungently reflects—can become as socially unacceptable as expressing a sex preference. Here's a new response to the old what-sex-do-you-secretly-want question: "I don't care what sex or care needs my child has. I just look forward to meeting and caring for whoever they might be!"

CHAPTER 6

REIMAGINING CARE

LINEATING MUTUAL AID

Too often, disabled people still face delineation, separation from their families, and even institutionalization, as Rhona did at the end of her life and Cousin XY did throughout his. Transforming our care structures, inside and beyond the family, means transforming both institutions and kinship structures. What it really means is reimagining our relations with one another at the individual, familial, communal, and structural levels.

Just such a reimagining is already occurring in the disability justice movement. Disability justice activists, care workers, families, cultural workers, and self-advocates are reimagining paradigms of care with unprecedented energy and imagination. The mutual aid movement that began in the twentieth century is flourishing amid the crises of the twenty-first. It offers compelling models for how disabled people can take charge of their own care and care work in a more humane, equitable, and communal fashion. BIPOC disability justice activists like Stacey Milbern and Leah Lakshmi Piepzna-Samarasinha have embraced and refashioned this mutual aid model in ways that serve the specific needs of disabled people, creating organizations like the Disability Culture Club and Fireweed Collective.

These mutual aid organizations often position themselves in opposition to family and institutional care. Such a binary may unintentionally perpetuate the notion of the family as a static purveyor of ableism. The concept—and practice—of disability lineage offers one possible means of deepening the mutual aid movement, using its principles to transform the family and end its ableist regime. Disability lineage may also help make these innovative movements more sustainable and deeply rooted. Conversely, mutual aid can help connect the individual family disability narrative to a richer, more communal sense of kinship and lineage.

Activists in social justice movements—including the disability justice movement—have popularized the term "mutual aid" to describe ways that social movements can provide care and support for people who are marginalized. According to veteran activist, organizer, and lawyer Dean Spade, "Mutual aid is collective coordination to meet each other's needs, usually from an awareness that the systems we have in place are not going to meet them."[1] This paradigm emphasizes how ordinary people with no specialized training can care for each other outside the official state and family systems of care. It's nothing new; the lesbian healthcare workers—some completely outside the medical system—who cared for their gay male friends during the AIDS crisis of the 1980s and '90s are just one example of how this has informally worked in marginalized communities for decades. The Black Panthers' free breakfast program is another. More recently, as Spade recounts, the same activists who were protesting the antidemocratic rulers of Hong Kong quickly mobilized to create apps to track the COVID-19 virus, distribute PPE, and promote other life-saving health information measures that successfully contained the virus in Hong Kong. Spade highlights the importance of self-determination in the creation of these new systems and methods of care, echoing many of the principles of the disability justice movement.

Though utopic in its vision, mutual aid is, in practice, incredibly practical—as basic as providing breakfast to needy kids or changing the catheter of an HIV-positive gay man. The idea is that larger structural change and solidarity will emerge from this small-scale aid. Mutuality is key: instead of waiting for external saviors from nonprofits, charities, the government, or other outside entities, the community itself builds its own expertise and power. "Solidarity not charity!" is one of the mutual aid movement's rallying cries.[2]

Mutual aid groups are born in crisis, and during the COVID-19 pandemic, numerous such groups sprouted. Even as staid a cultural institution as the *New Yorker* took note in an optimistically titled article, "What Mutual Aid Can Do During a Pandemic." Reporter Jia Tolentino details this proliferation of mutual aid groups and chronicles her own participation in such a group loosely organized online. She notes how members of mutual aid groups emerging to address unmet material and health needs in the pandemic were often formerly part of social-justice mass movements that had been similarly organized along lateral, collective, and nonhierarchical principles: "As I called individuals around the country who were setting up coronavirus-relief efforts, I kept encountering people who had participated in anti-globalization protests in the early two-thousands, or joined the Occupy movement, or organized grassroots campaigns in the aftermath of the 2016 Presidential election."[3] Indeed, many COVID-19 mutual aid principles came from Occupy. It's worth considering what made this movement so powerful—and ultimately unsustainable, though its principles have disseminated into mutual aid groups and the larger coalition of the left.

Lateral in structure, the Occupy movement was developed along mutual aid principles. Leaderless, open to anyone, bottom-up, deploying an amazingly inclusive decision-making process, it served as a powerful critique of globalized late capitalism. But it was not sustainable. After a few months, when the state brought in its full force to vanquish it, Occupy vanished almost overnight.[4] The very lack of structure that made Occupy so radically inclusive and compelling made it difficult to sustain. Burnout is another factor: the crisis that often initiates mutual aid saps everybody's energy to the point that, once the crisis is over (or at least ameliorated), the community formed in its wake dissolves. Nothing else besides the crisis connects the community, or ultimately keeps it rooted.

Moreover, mutual aid is not inherently progressive—and in some ways reflects and refracts neoconservative hyperindividualism. As Joanna

Wuest notes, the antiestablishment, decentralized elements of the mutual aid care model are as much a product of the right as the left: "For decades now—and especially since the pandemic started—libertarians and conservatives from organizations like the Heritage Foundation and writers for *National Review* have commended care provided by those other than the state. Like their counterparts on the left, these groups have advanced an understanding of mutual aid not as a tactic alone but as a vision for remaking society."[5] Wuest point to elements of mutual aid in the anti-abortion movement's crisis pregnancy centers. Anecdotal evidence supports this claim. One friend of mine, who is staunchly pro-choice, found herself at an anti-choice pregnancy center because, when she was a pregnant teen, it was the only place where someone was willing to really listen (for free) to her conflicted feelings about her pregnancy at any hour. This listening wasn't neutral, as she was dissuaded from abortion and encouraged only to consider adoption. Nor was it nonhierarchical or truly mutual, though the women on the other crisis pregnancy hotlines all claimed to have been in similar situations, but it *felt* like it. This feeling of mutuality is key. So is the collective nature of the enterprise.

The focus on collective action can sound like Marxism in hipster drag, but as Dean Spade and others suggest, it is not the state-sponsored failed collectivism of the twentieth-century Soviets or the market-based totalitarianism of the current Chinese communist system, but rather a term to capture the collective work that women serving church suppers, caring for elders in their community, and leaving their jobs to care for disabled children *are already doing*, which is often rendered invisible in our patriarchal, individualistic society. There is a conservative (in the ecological sense of conservatism as conservationist) dimension to the original concept of mutual aid as conceived of by Peter Kropotkin, its inventor. He observed how species such as swallows and marmots cooperated in order to flourish, and how in preindustrial human societies, cooperation and interdependency were crucial. Kropotkin viewed mutual aid as a necessary part of human evolution that could get us out of the destructive, competitive imperatives of industrial capitalism.[6] In our postindustrial society, on the brink of ecological and economic collapse, this point resonates more powerfully than ever. *Both* evolutionary and conservationist, mutual aid goes beyond the collectivism of the left or the preservationism of the right. In this sense, it is truly progressive.

In the disability justice world, amid the multiple crises of populism, ableism, COVID-19, economic and ecological collapse, mutual aid has flourished. In some ways, it shares key principles and paradigms of the disability justice movement. Rather than merely arguing for equality and inclusion in the nondisabled world, disability justice focuses its politics and practices on the lived experiences of disabled people themselves. Disabled people are centered, their lives and desires viewed as intrinsically worthy, rather than in need of cure, fixing, or solving.

This is a seismic shift in the focus and purpose of activism. As disability justice activist Nomy Lamm argues, "Disability justice challenges the idea that our worth as individuals has to do with our ability to perform as productive members of society. It insists that our worth is inherent and tied to the liberation of all beings."[7] Centering disabled people in the discourse produces profound changes. Mia Mingus links this to "access intimacy," which she defines as "the ease in relationships that happens when disabled people don't have to continually push for basic needs."[8] Mutual aid based on disability justice recenters its discourse and practices. It shifts from a rights-based focus on including and gaining access to ableist society, to self-determination and valuing of the differences, needs, and social experiences of disabled people living and communing with other disabled people. It stresses the creation of an alternative culture as a fundamental part of care.

The Disability Justice Culture Club exemplifies this ethos. With no infrastructure, no fancy board of rich funders, no nonprofit administrators, barely even a website, the DJCC has modeled a fantastically diverse, dynamic community-building model of mutual care. Creating culture as well as providing access to care by disabled people for disabled people, the DJCC is not a fly-by-night concept: it is an actual place, an activist house providing space particularly for BIPOC disabled queer people to aid one another in housing, healthcare, and more. Along with the nimble, contingent, online aspect of mutual aid, organizations like the Disability Justice

Culture Club are providing a literal home for their members. The name "culture club" winks at the '80s rock band Culture Club. Being a fan of the gender-bending Boy George was a sort of sonic secret gay handshake in those homophobic times. It also gestures toward a serious desire to create culture: to value crip culture and space as a fundamental element of mutual aid and care.

The Autistic Women and Nonbinary Network (AWN) is another such organization that advocates, networks, and funds work by and for autistic women and nonbinary people. They similarly do the work of culture making and building, listing "autism acceptance events, seminars, book reading/discussions, coffee shop meetups, picnics, dinners, movies, arts & crafts, etc."[9] as just a few of their diverse activities. As with the Disability Justice Culture Club, the social and cultural dimensions of aid are emphasized as much as the political and material. Self-care, originally a radical concept Audre Lorde developed regarding how to value and care for oneself in the face of systemic racism, is here recuperated from its (much-critiqued) white consumerist banality. Instead of buying expensive products to care for one's individual self, sustainable, communal practices of healing and culture making are supported.[10] Rather than relying on ableist notions of wellness and health, and pursuing an idealized bodymind that is always in need of another product to correct its flaws, acceptance is at the center of these communal care practices.[11] AWN is leading the movement for true acceptance and support of autistic people through its organizational activities not only for autistic women and nonbinary people but also for their families. Their groundbreaking anthology, *Sincerely, Your Autistic Child: What People on the Autism Spectrum Wish Their Parents Knew About Growing Up, Acceptance, and Identity*, edited by three of its member-leaders and first self-published as *What Every Autistic Girl Wishes Her Parents Knew*, offers frank, diverse first-person accounts aimed at helping parents better understand their autistic children's needs from a nonpathologizing, social justice–oriented, feminist perspective.[12] Such work shows how much the mutual-aid, disability-justice movement has to offer families and parents of disabled people (as well as disabled people themselves) in transforming and depathologizing all disabilities.

The Fireweed Collective similarly models what mutual aid can look like, but in the context of mental disability. They provide peer-to-peer counseling as well as referrals, resources, workshops, and trainings. People with mental disabilities are empowered to help one another, disrupting the binary between caregiver and patient. When members of the Fireweed Collective spoke at Georgetown, they spoke of how important it was for those with mental disabilities to aid one another. They emphasized that elements such as racism and poverty, while not necessarily causal, fundamentally shape both the experience and the treatment of mental disability.[13]

More important than what they do perhaps is *how* these mutual aid organizations do this work. "Healing justice" (HJ) is the framework through which Firewood Collective conducts all its activities, because it "provides us with tools we can use to interrupt the systems of oppression that impact our mental health. Fireweed Collective uses HJ as a guide to help redefine what medicine is, and increase who has access to it."[14] They emphasize structural analyses of oppression rather than individual pathologies. Instead of merely asking for inclusion and rights, these grassroots, bottom-up mass movements value justice and equity. Healing and justice, not cure and rights, are key here. Even conservative, mainstream organizations like Autism Speaks are feeling pressure to change their structures to mirror the nonhierarchical, disabled-centered rhetoric of the disability-justice, mutual-aid movement, adding autistic board members and centering more services on care rather than cure.[15]

There is much to celebrate in this grassroots turn in the disability rights movement to mutual aid, justice, and healing. My own little *mishpacha*, an informal mutual aid group of letter-boarding autistics and their families, has provided me with my first experience of access intimacy, where our families' needs are implicitly understood and accommodated. What I notice, however, as a middle-aged queer female veteran of the AIDS crisis, is that these organizations are populated primarily—though not exclusively—by relatively young people without strong ties to their families of origin and who are almost entirely themselves childless. These mutual aid organizations generally provide neither child- nor elder care. There is often no deep intergenerational connection, no appeal to existing elders, and no transformation of the family of origin. The stress is on lateral interdependence and self-determination—both of which are extremely important but deny the power of families and their primacy for all humans, at least at some stages of life. Moreover, it's hard to imagine how those who are dependent on family members or professional caregivers to communicate, to breathe, to survive could access these communities. Slogans popular in disability-justice, mutual-aid communities, like "We are the ones we are waiting for," powerfully resist the white savior complex so often at the center of disability care work but deny the need for professional caregivers.

People with intellectual disabilities who cannot fully articulate their needs or live independently may be left out of this equation. People with physical support needs who require highly skilled caregiving may also be left out. Infants and children need care and cannot—and should not—be expected to care for others. Elders need care. If we live so long, we will all be elderly—and disabled. Many of us will need extensive supports and may require institutional care. Mutual aid too often leaves out these people from their equation, and relies on individualistic solutions to structural problems.

If we truly do not want disabled people to be abandoned and mistreated by institutions, de-lineated as Cousin Rhona and Cousin XY were, we need to rethink institutional care too. Though often disability studies historians write about the age of institutionalization as something from the past, congregate care in institutions remains a fact of life for about one-quarter of disabled people at some point in their life cycle. Rhona's death between two institutions was a twenty-first century one; the continuing problem of systemic abuses at numerous state institutions for mentally disabled people in New York State were exposed as recently as 2016.[16] Congregate care in institutional settings is still sometimes necessary at some point in the life cycle and need not be inevitability de-lineating, isolating, noncommunal, or abusive.

The Autism Self-Advocacy Network (ASAN) has been a leader in articulating what real self-determination means for disabled people, particularly in institutional contexts. As ASAN argues in its landmark document,

Keeping the Promise: Self Advocates Defining the Meaning of Community Living, institutions must take seriously the language about integration and access to community of the Developmental Disabilities Act, which promises "access to needed community services, individualized supports, and other forms of assistance that promote self-determination, independence, productivity, and integration and inclusion in all facets of community life."[17] But whose community—that of the institution, now rebranded as an "assisted living community," controlled by caregivers, or its disabled residents?

ASAN suggests that independent living in apartments rather than in group homes is one key element in enabling disabled people to truly be the decision makers in their lives, in their care. In ASAN's guidelines, they extend this focus on integration into all facets of life: work, home life, interpersonal relationships (including sex and romance), and healthcare. The disabled person decides where and with whom they will work, get healthcare, and, ultimately, pass away. The disabled person's living situation is the center from which these other facets of self-determination flow. Notably, ASAN demands this standard of self-determination for *all* people throughout their life cycle, regardless of the severity of their impairment, rejecting curability as a sorting device.

To truly transform our care systems we need, along with institutional reform and mutual aid, large, scalable systemic changes in the formulation and administration of care by our government. Critics of the mutual aid movement have focused on how it lets government off the hook, as well as its inability to scale up effectively. It leaves the existing flawed and ableist care systems intact, while perpetuating myths of self-reliance and community as band-aids for deep structural inequalities. "We would do well," Wuest cautions, "to guard against this despotic individualism—the natural condition of the social without the state—and to be sober about what spurred this renaissance of mutual aid and what it portends."[18] Though "despotic individualism" is the furthest thing from the stated aims of mutual-aid, disability-justice groups, they may unintentionally perpetuate it by accepting and normalizing the disaffiliation and rejection of the ableist family.

There is a familiar cycle to the mutual aid movement: amid a crisis, a group of energized young people mobilize. Cut off from our disabled elders, we create temporary families out of our comrades, only to eventually burn out. Then we disengage from collective movements, go our separate ways, and sometimes even have children. Almost all of us will be called to elder care. All of us will be disabled if we live long enough. Most of us came from families, and many of us will create, return to, or be haunted by them. Disability lineage offers a critique of the current construction of the family's ableism, exposes its norms as fictional, and offers new possibilities for connecting disability-justice, mutual-aid practices with those of the family, radically redefined.

RADICALLY REDEFINING FAMILY: FROM ABLEISM TO LINEATION

From poet Philip Larkin's notorious definition of family as what "fucks you up" to *Modern Family*'s contemporary American ménage of malaise played for sitcom laughs, the family continues to be imagined as a force of dysfunction. Family in this formulation is inherently conservative, alienating, and borderline abusive. It is a static, unchangeable, defining force. Moreover, it is universalized: the specific ways race and gender shape kinship are effaced, erased. Families are static, sadistic, staid, and all the same. Lineage is only an oppressive burden. Such a view perpetuates the notion of the family as an inevitable manufacturer of trauma and ableism.

It also presumes implicitly a particular kind of family: a white, non-disabled, middle-class, heteronormative nuclear family defined by biological ties, rather than the extended kinship system of Black communities described by Carol Stack, E. Patrick Johnson, and many others. Queer parents, disabled parents, step- and foster parents . . . all are flattened by the dull reproductive logic of family inheritances. The care work of mothers is invisibilized, reduced to pathology. In this dominant cultural story, the family is both oppressive and inevitable, its form and rhetoric white, heteronormative, and nuclear.

However, BIPOC families often are not only fluid and extended kinship systems but also rich sources of sustenance and radical praxis. Black families often form strong, complex kinship systems that weave together grandparents, exes, and friends. Carol Stack and numerous other scholars and activists have explored the strength and power of such kinship systems and illuminated the ways they can be more dynamic and inclusive than traditional nuclear families. "Black families . . . and the non-kin they regard as kin have evolved patterns of co-residence, kinship-based exchange networks . . . ," Stack argues, "that comprise a resilient response to the conditions of structural racism that they face."[19] As E. Patrick Johnson argues, for Black communities, the family and kinship system is a sustaining, nonnuclear site of critique and empowerment in relation to the dominant racist white culture. He uses bell hooks's term "homeplace" to denote this expanded familial space. "It is from homeplace that people of color live out the contradictions of our lives," he suggests. "Cutting across the lines of class and gender, homeplace provides a place from which to critique oppression ."[20] Rather than reproducing oppression, the homeplace fosters its critique.

"Kinship," "family," and "lineage": these terms are entangled with one another, but are not identical. They point to the complicated ways we find family, both biologically and through other means, in the homeplaces we forge. The ways simple biological inheritance tells only half the story. The way blood lies. "Blood supremacy is the notion that blood ties are paramount, even at the expense of one's own well-being," notes Amita Swadhin; it is used to underwrite patriarchy and every possible form of oppression.[21]

Queer families complicate the relationship between blood and kinship; we often form family systems where no one, or only a few people external to the family unit, is biologically linked. Biology itself is reimagined; for example, the writer Michelle Tea carried the child of a known sperm donor coupled with her partner's egg. As she delivers her baby boy, she poignantly speaks to the universal magic of meeting her new baby, the "us" of a new family forming. But "us was also her, my wife, that prince," she notes, gender jamming the usual narrative. Queer author, parent, and theorist Maggie Nelson suggests that the notion of the family as merely a site of oppression for queers ignores the ways LGBTQ+ parents queer the notion of family and reifies "the tired binary that places femininity, reproduction, and normativity on one side and masculinity, sexuality, and queer resistance on the other."[22] She argues for a dismantling of this false binary and an acknowledgment of the ways queers are transforming how families form and function. Nelson's alternative model of the queer family as an argonaut, a mobile ship whose pieces are constantly rearranging, challenges the static models of family prevalent on both the left and the right.[23]

Cultural anthropologists Faye Ginsberg and Rayna Rapp suggest a "kinship imaginary" to describe the ways disabled people are reconceptualizing family, similar to the homeplace outlined by Johnson and the mutable argonaut by Nelson. This would foreground "that families are both flesh-and-blood collaborations and always acts of cultural imagination."[24] Disability, they suggest, itself is one of the key cultural conditions under which family and kinship are being imagined. But disability's continued de-lineation from the family imaginary doesn't figure into their optimistic assessment of this expanded sense of kinship.

Queer, BIPOC, and other kinship systems contain vast, underutilized repositories of knowledge for the re-lineating of disability. There is a wealth of knowledge about how extended families born of poverty and systemic racism, sexism, and heterosexism have forged innovative, sustainable, resilient, and inclusive kinship systems.[25] As Mia Birdsong suggests, "Reinventing family, friends, and community is a process we do *with our family, friends, and community*."[26] We already have resources for such reinvention. An expanded sense of family and kinship can draw on these forms of knowledge, this communal wealth, to forge a resilient, anti-ableist, more inclusive sense of lineage.

There is a deep yearning in disability justice movements for precisely this rooted, multigenerational sense of disability lineage, family, and kinship. Yet de-lineation from family often makes it difficult to achieve. As disability/crip justice activist Stacey Milbern observes in a moving dialogue with Leah Lakshmi Piepzna-Samarasinha in *Care Work*, "We may be the only one like us in our given and chosen family stories,"[27] which, given the de-lineation of disabled people from family and kinship narratives, is often the case. She suggests alternative forms of affiliation and care along the lines of disability justice and mutual aid to repair the damage done by these exclusionary family stories. Milbern argues for an expanded sense of disability kinship, locating it in ancestorship for disabled people. She notes that disabled people often have lives shortened not by their disabilities but by "social determinants of health," such as inadequate care. "People sometimes assume ancestorship is reserved for those who are biologically related, but a queered or cripped understanding," she contends, "holds that our deepest relationships are with people we choose to be connected to and honor day after day."[28] The expanded sense of lineage and ancestry that Milbern provides makes us not mere victims of chance: of who and how our nuclear family members happen to be. It allows for the active, chosen, extended sense of kinship to fight ableism and racism that Johnson describes.

To form such a chosen family, Milbern suggests a crip doula to help shepherd the birth of a disabled identity—a seasoned disabled person helping a newly disabled or newly coming-into-the-identity-of-disability person. This is necessary, she argues, because disabled people frequently don't have other disabled people in their families to mentor or guide them. Milbern explains that "I was the only disabled person in my immediate family, and they loved me but didn't have tools for conceptualizing my life outside of brokenness needing healing or a bootstrap mentality about 'overcoming.'"[29] Instead, she suggests self-birthing and doulaing one's new identity as disabled: a rich metaphor of gestation and parenting with a disabled family of choice.

Milbern believes that there were literally no disabled people in her family of origin. While that may *seem* true, it is because the lineage of disability in any given family is repressed, stigmatized, erased. The power of that erasure is real, traumatic, and wrong. It is not only morally wrong—it is also objectively false. Disabled people are already a part of our families. They are our parents, grandparents, great aunts. Cousins. Even if they have been cut out of the story, they exist. They are ours. But we need to reimagine what family was and what kinship can be to rewrite these stories.

The absence of actual disabled elders in our families is one problem in reimagining our disability lineage. Rhona was only half a generation older than me, yet I discovered her existence only after her death. Both Piepzna-Samarasinha and Milbern speak longingly of the need for disabled elders: "Young people are always like, where are our disabled elders? . . . I both do and do not have disabled QTBIPOC elders in my life. Ancestors, yes. Elders, not so much,"[30] Piepzna-Samarasinha comments. Rhona was my ancestor, but not my elder. We need disabled elders in our families and immediate, inherited kinship systems as much as we need them in our ancestral lineations. Their actuality as well as their stories. This will also help our immediate, nuclear family—our parents—imagine us not as broken but as part of a whole culture, with an ancestry reaching back many generations.

While we all need community, the need for familial acceptance, integration, and lineation cannot be "fixed" by community. I have a chosen disability community—as do Milbern and Piepzna-Samarasinha, who are community leaders—yet I yearn to know my family's disabled elders, for my daughter to know her disabled family, see herself in their faces. The two are never truly separate: the public sphere and private are co-constructed, as Melissa Blake and the Meet Your New Teacher Challenge demonstrate. Our families of origin are twisted around the communities that engaged or abandoned them, pathologized or fetishized them, in public and private. Intergenerational community is intrinsic to the homeplace.

The reasons one might want and need a sense of disability lineage *beyond* one's biological or nuclear family are as pressing as they are obvious. What if your family is intractably ableist, as Milbern suggests hers was? What if you can't find any information about your disability lineage? What if you are estranged from your biological family? What if your family abused you? What if your elders are no longer alive and you are childless? What if you are adopted? The majority of us likely experience some of these forms of alienation and lineage rupture in our contemporary American culture of rootlessness. Forces such as genocide, war, colonialism, capitalism, economic migration, and immigration serve to sever ancestral ties. So many less dramatic, more banal aspects of American contemporary culture also sever these ties: a late capitalist society in which people disconnect with their families after they reach adulthood, live in nuclear suburban isolation, divorce frequently, and move often for work doesn't lend itself to deep, rich, multigenerational family ties.

Milbern's focus on choice is not arbitrary: so often, disabled people are forced to spend time with caretakers, therapists, and other professional caregivers not of their own choosing. She suggests that in addition to the people we choose to be with in our present lives, we can select disabled ancestors who have passed, from the "ancestral plane," people we may never have even met, as part of our expanded sense of ancestry and, I would argue, family lineage. This expanded plane of ancestry is both a substitute for and an expansion of a lived, known relationship to one's own disabled family and lineage. Milbern powerfully articulates the ways an extended sense of ancestry beyond the biological family can be reclaimed. Her intervention is an important one, as she suggests how we can connect beyond our individual family narratives to a larger sense of disability ancestry. However, she leaves behind the family itself as a source of only alienation and disconnection from disability ancestry. We all come from some sort of family system, however buried, displaced, ruptured, or fucked-up. And within those systems are disabled ancestors ripe for reclamation.

RE-LINEATING CHOSEN FAMILY: KITHING OUR KIN

Chosen family is such a dynamic concept. Though practiced by African American families as part of expanded kinship systems for generations and by Indigenous communities for centuries, the term was popularized by the LGBTQ+ movement in the wake of the AIDS crisis, when nonbiological kin became caretakers in mutual aid arrangements. As the SAGE encyclopedia defines it, "Chosen families are nonbiological kinship bonds, whether legally recognized or not, deliberately chosen for the purpose of mutual support and love."[31]

While chosen family can be a powerful form of affiliation, it is something we can really only create as adults. Moreover, it doesn't speak to the multigenerational sense of connection that is the foundation of a truly integrated sense of identity. Identity, as Louis Althusser argued, is not only what we fashion, choose, and select, but also what we inherit, are called by, and marked as by others.[32] He calls this process interpellation—how we make sense internally of how the outside world sees and names us. Identity—familial, disability, ancestral—also chooses *us*. The chosen family tends to be available to certain kinds of bodyminds, at certain times in life. Infants and elders can't rely on this volitional creation. And we all are our inheritances—and will leave traces of our embodied stories embedded in our family narratives, whether or not we have children ourselves.

Though it seems like a radical critique, the "chosen family" model views the family of origin as an inherently static, conservative structure, and cedes its power to abuse and exclude disabled people. It makes little room for long-haul dependency. As Eva Feder Kittay and others have noted, the "we are the ones we're waiting for, nothing about us without us" rhetoric emerges from the same culture of self-reliance as the dominant narrative it critiques.[33] The dependence some disabled people require to survive is effaced by this. People with intellectual disabilities— innate and acquired—are particularly poorly served by this rhetoric. "Of all disabled people," Kittay notes, "those labeled 'severely intellectually disabled' have least benefited from the inclusion fought for by a disability community that is dominated by people who are able to speak for themselves."[34] What of people with Alzheimer's? Do we again delimit "us," the worthy disabled who can assert their will without assistance and give as well as receive care and aid? This seems incredibly ableist. It *is* incredibly ableist.

In suggesting that we reclaim disability lineage, I am inviting us to draw on an expanded sense of kinship, and to redefine it to include disabled relatives—blood and beyond, all entangled in our *mishpacha*— whom we have never met. Who were cut out from our family's myths. I am not interested in recuperating or centering a conservative, white cis-hetero-patriarchal model of the nuclear biological family here, and then begging it to accept its disabled members. Acceptance and tolerance marginalize under the guise of inclusion, preserving the ableist, nuclear family at the center. Instead, I am proposing we lineate collective disability ancestry writ large to the familial. I am using the terms "family" and "lineage" to denote an expanded sense of family, one that might include nonbiological, distant, or other forms of kinship. But I don't want to conflate this with the "chosen family" that adults create out of their peers.

The family, understood as an extended kinship system, can connect both nonbiological and biological kin. As Joshua Chambers-Letson argues about nonbiological kinship in Black queer communities, "While the performance of queer or nonbiological kinship might open up possibilities of 'family' for queers, . . . it can also remake the notion of kinship such that your biological mothers have a place at the table next to your queer mothers. These overlapping forms of family can be of critical importance: the queer of color child needs all the help she can get if she's going to survive this world. The same goes for her mothers."[35] Chambers-Letson's notion that these forms of "overlapping" family could help both the extended kinship system *and* the biological one suggests that we could connect the chosen family to the family of origin in ways that transform both. For disabled people, this overlapping of kinships could be similarly transformative, remaking the homeplace as a source of inclusive care and sustenance. To truly, radically reimagine care, we need to reimagine family, drawing on the practices in BIPOC, disabled, and queer communities that already connect the chosen and given families. Mutual aid and family care could then sit together at the table.

This also means rethinking professional caregiving. Families with children with complex medical conditions and high, specialized support needs don't have the luxury of disengaging from professional caregivers; to do so would be an illegal—not to mention profoundly immoral—form of child neglect and/or abuse. Instead, families can model and infuse the clinical world with disability justice and anti-ableist values. This is not a neoliberal defense of institutions or an argument for incrementalism. Radical, systemic change is necessary *now* in how disability is constructed and cared for. But systemic change necessarily involves engaging systems, rather than merely critiquing them and providing small-scale alternatives for those who are privileged and independent enough to be able to access them. It also involves honoring and compensating care work and the expertise it involves at all levels, treating care like the skilled profession it is, viewing emotional labor as labor. Racist, misogynistic, and

lineages, reclaiming and reimagining them, I also connected to this wider, wilder world of imagined, collective crip ancestry. Cousin XY led me to Rhona, which led me to the larger unknown spirit world of all the disabled people in and beyond my family, and ultimately to a sense of being part of something larger. Though I'm an atheist, this feels deeply, authentically spiritual.

Such a reimagining of kinship would connect the ancestral and the familial. It would replace the static, fixed binary between family of origin and chosen family with a more fluid sense of kin. Mutual, familial, and state systems of aid could then be connected. Such a transformation sounds rather epic! It is beyond the scope of this book—or of any book—to provide a blueprint for such a redesign. Rather than focus on how to perfectly unite these disparate systems, discourses, lives, and stories, I want to push back on the very notion that we *can* perfectly design it.

UNIVERSAL DESIGN AND CRIP KINSHIP

The concept of universal design has gained popularity as a way of approaching how to design all sorts of things—public spaces, buildings, pedagogy—for maximum accessibility. Instead of trying to imagine all bodyminds and design a static, perfect building, only to find that it then has to be retrofitted to accommodate needs it didn't anticipate, universal design starts from the premise that one *can't* anticipate all bodyminds and their needs, and therefore flexibility, openness, and the capacity to change are vital.

Coined by Ronald Mace in 1985,[39] universal design was founded on the principle of "flexibility in use": it attempts to build in flexibility so it can be modified. "In use" is key here—the needs of actual users, instead of imagined normates and their disabled counterparts. This centers users, not builders. So, while I am advocating for redesigning our understanding of the relationship between chosen and inherited family, I want to leave the exact structure of that connection to the individual users to imagine. Since our families and our ancestries, as well as our access and connection to them, are so diverse, it makes no sense to suggest a static model to connect them all. One size will fit none.

Another of universal design's seven principles is "tolerance for error." In the architectural context from which universal design was derived, this means that instead of expecting the user to occupy the space in the "right" way, the builders should anticipate mistakes by users. "The design minimizes hazards and the adverse consequences of accidental or unintended actions," the principles suggest. But I read this another way: our attempts to connect are messy, rife with miscommunication, errors, mistakes. When we dig into our disability lineage, there may indeed be "hazards and adverse consequences." When we invite our chosen family and family of origin to the table, they may not get along.

Tolerating the challenges, minimizing the damage . . . This is the only blueprint for disability lineage I can honestly offer. I've made many in my own family uncomfortable with my insistence on including in our *mishpacha* my queer, disabled, interracial family, my diversely gendered chosen family. By digging into the family archive and disinterring my cousins, adding their traumatic disability lineage to the family myth, I've made my share of errors. Lineation and repair demand a spirit of forgiveness, generosity, and tolerance that I find challenging, but ultimately, our family is the richer for it.

Of course, universal design doesn't necessarily lead to more integrated, equitable kinship relationships. Disability studies scholar Aimie Hamrie offers a trenchant critique of universal design's enmeshment in existing forms of oppression. They argue that universal design is laden with unequal power relationships, particularly in relation to the users the designers imagine: "What designers, users, and advocates mean by this term can be as varied as their conceptions of and relations to the idea of disability. . . . Promises of Universal Design for 'everyone' materialized in relation to particular types of users. When the goal is to design for 'everyone,' I ask, who counts as everyone and how do designers know?"[40]

We can ask the same about disability lineage: who counts as "everyone" in our *mishpacha*, and how do families know? Who defines kinship? How can we transform our family narratives, redesign them for "future users," our yet-to-be-born future kin? I leave these charged questions open. Engaging such provocations in the personal realm of our own families, communities, and the stories we make of them seems far more important to me than arriving at any categorical answers.

Instead, I'll tell you a story.

When it became apparent a few years after her diagnosis that my daughter was not just autistic but a nonspeaking autistic, I felt at first like we were part of a very small club of which, to paraphrase Groucho Marx, nobody wanted to be a member. As Nadia continued not to speak, while several kids in our autistic family peer group *did* start talking, we found ourselves no longer invited to birthday parties. No longer welcome. We were sorted into a specific pile: the parents of the severely disabled. Those parents of autistic kids who started speaking couldn't get away from us fast enough! I still have some of their names in my phone, first names whose surnames I've happily forgotten.

It was only when I began to seek community for my daughter with other families with nonspeaking autistic kids who use letter boards to communicate, that I was able to find real, material support, disability community, and aid. This was a very bottom-up project; at first, we just started hanging out informally at the houses of two other families, alternating loosely who hosted; then my partner started a monthly hiking group for local families, some who we barely knew; then she began a book club for nonspeaking autistics online that attracted a national following. My daughter loved these opportunities for community, identity, and age-appropriate peers; we appreciated the aid and support of families like ours, without the hierarchies we found in other "autism moms" groups.

When we had our first Thanksgiving at one of their households, it occurred to me that these strangers were now our kin. No apologies were necessary for the stimming between (or in the middle of) courses. For perhaps the first time, I experienced the joy of real access intimacy—of not having to explain or apologize for our family's disabilities. We felt truly welcomed and included, in a way that was both fun and relaxing.

As we continued to develop a community of nonspeaking autistic letter-board users, we made tons of mistakes along the way. We encountered many "users" we hadn't considered in our unplanned, haphazard design. We had to modify our format to include the needs of nondisabled siblings as well as those of nonspeaking autistic kids who were also wheelchair users. This community-building work connected us to larger issues and communities related to disability and access, beyond those specific to nonspeaking autistic kids. Both my partner and I began to incorporate disability justice activism and mutual aid practices into our professional lives.

The more our small family of three forged our own disability community, the more, like Milbern and Samarasinha, we felt the need for multiple generations. I discovered Rhona and disinterred Cousin XY. Our circle started to include grandparents—our daughter's and her friends'—many of whom were themselves experiencing the disabilities that come with aging. I was moved to write this book as part of that act of lineating and, as Milbern movingly suggests, to leave traces. I wanted to ensure our family would be on the record for the next generation of Nadias and Rhonas—named, claimed, and honored.

I don't have a formula or a recipe, but starting small, right where you are, with the people who are already in your life who support and connect to your family in all its diverse abilities seems key. That table full of stuffing and stimming was a start. As Mia Birdsong reminds us, we already have all the ingredients to reinvent family, friendship, and community: "the remedies are in our kitchens."[41] We just have to make more room at the table.

CHAPTER 7

SEWING THE ANCESTRAL CLOTH

WEAVING US TOGETHER

I wear my grandmother's ring on my fourth finger. It's an intricately carved, quirky little garnet, precious only to me. "I'm married to my grandmother," I say to anyone who asks. It's a queer form of irony that marks my longest, deepest love: Adina Chaleff Lewis. A tiny, eccentric leftist who adored me, Jewish folk dancing, and Adele Davis's health food regime, possibly in that order. Though she was a terrific student who tutored all the other kids, her father made her drop out of high school because she was a girl. Adina found a way out of poverty through a Jewish socialist community in New York, where she met and married my grandfather, Harold "Hal" Lewis, an educator and artist.

Adina never worked outside the home, couldn't drive, and never wrote a check in her entire life. My grandfather managed everything. Even by the standards of their generation's strictly defined gender roles, my grandparents were extreme. Yet they had one of the most loving partnerships I've ever witnessed. In their retirement home, the staff dubbed them "the lovers" because they were always holding hands or walking, with the arm of my tall, handsome grandfather wrapped around my tiny grandmother's fragile frame. Only after they passed did I consider the way disability shaped this incredible partnership.

Adina Chaleff Lewis was deaf. She hated her hearing aids and couldn't really lip-read. She was hard of hearing from birth: I'm not sure exactly when she became "officially" deaf. My grandmother spoke of disability only with disgust. She saw disabled children as disposable tragedies. I can see the face she made when disability was mentioned. Tragic, but also disgusting. Was that how she felt about her own hearing impairment?

Grandma Adina spoke in a near shout, in heavily Yiddish-inflected Brooklynese. Fearful of the outside world, she was seemingly content to be a *balubustah*, a super-housewife with left-wing leanings, who insisted that feminism meant the right to stay home. Completely cut off from any notion of disability as a positive identity or culture, Adina Chaleff Lewis was the most ebullient, loving presence in my life. She found everything I did worthy of celebration and made light of any annoying character traits I revealed.

My mother inherited her impaired hearing, but not her shame. My mother lip-reads, purchases every possible gadget to access or amplify sound and language, and religiously wears the latest and greatest hearing aids. Whereas Grandma Adina appeared to have little ambition, my mother went from a working-class Brooklyn childhood to a marriage to a prominent scientist to a career as a high-school special ed teacher to, at fifty, a PhD from Harvard and a second career as a college professor. She has published three books and has dedicated her life to training special education teachers and researching dyslexia. She could not be more interested in the outside world. Her hearing impairment has increased steadily over the course of this noteworthy career.

Yet only as I was finishing writing this book did I think of including two of the people closest to me—the women who formed me, who loved me the most, one whose ring I wear on my finger and the other whose smile I wear on my face—in my disability lineage. Shame and stigma about disability are so great that I had internalized them, unconsciously refusing to acknowledge that my very own mother and grandmother were disabled. For I would have to confront another facet of my ableism: my own fear of deafness.

In developing a disability lineage, we not only uncover lost, hidden, disappeared family members who were institutionalized, abandoned, murdered, or otherwise cut off from the family tree. We may also discover that the family members who we never thought of as disabled—who perhaps never thought of themselves as such—were and are disabled. By valuing the diversity of bodyminds among our kin, we rediscover the disability lineage right in front of our eyes, their deaf ears listening intently right across the dinner table from us. We also confront their erasure: how marginalized or otherwise mistreated they were because of their disabilities. It's not that disability lineage is always hidden away: it was right there in front of us, but shame and stigma kept us from seeing it as our inheritance.

Jennifer Pastiloff makes an important point about the deaf gain of having to pay attention to others and be a good listener—and the radical empathy this develops. "Even though I had either no hearing aids or crappy ones, people were saying that I was the best listener they had ever experienced," she observes. "I had taught myself to listen without my ears."[1] It took a friend of mine to recognize this earless listening in my own family. My friend pointed out that my mother, the family empath and outstanding listener, was shaped by having to be the ears for her deaf mother her whole life, and now, like Pastiloff, must read lips to understand others. Pastiloff is the last person to sugarcoat the challenges of having a degenerative hearing impairment. She discusses at length in her "No Bullshit Motherhood" posts on social media to her thousands of followers how upsetting it is when she can't hear her own son. Nor does she identify as part of Deaf culture, the world of sign language users who have created a strong, distinctive identity and culture. Nonetheless, Pastiloff ascribes her extraordinary career to her need to truly "listen hard" because of her hearing loss. We needn't minimize the challenges of impairment in order to value the gifts they give us. "I love that I am hard of hearing," she wryly notes, "and have made a career out of listening."

Our impairments, Pastiloff suggests, can help us not only gain unusual skills such as "listening hard," but also be self-advocates. She enumerates how it took the coronavirus pandemic to fully name and claim her disability, as she had to advocate for herself, since she couldn't read lips whenever others were wearing masks. Pastiloff learned how to ask people to unmask at safe distances or use other forms of communication and, for the first time, fully claimed her disability and insisted on accommodation. Ever the great communicator, she exhorts, "Each of us—disability or not—needs to communicate clearly what we need to feel safe, heard, seen, or accommodated. This often requires a level of vulnerability and energy that's hard to muster. But if we let go of the shame surrounding our needs, if we simply state what it is we are dealing with without attaching a story of unworthiness to it, this will all become easier."[2] Pastiloff's point here is indeed true for all of us: It's the shame narrative, not the disability, that leads to self-silencing. The impairment itself often teaches us to be flexible, and even has side effects such as learning another language or being part of a community. And it is the story we—and the larger culture—make of our impairment that is either disabling or potentially, revolutionarily empowering.

Pastiloff also writes about something more fundamental: the power of stories. She talks about the "bullshit stories" we tell ourselves that keep us stuck, passive, and at the mercy of others. While this doesn't address how systemic ableist oppression is, it does powerfully articulate how as individuals we internalize and perpetuate it. The bullshit story I told myself about my grandmother is that she was a bit of an eccentric shut-in because of her deafness, not because of the ableism of our community, of my family, of myself. We never thought of my grandmother as potentially part of a community of Deaf people or imagined how her legacy of disability might be a powerful form of identification for her disabled heirs. An inheritance more valuable than that garnet ring.

Instead, Adina was encouraged to hide herself in the home when she couldn't "overcome" her disability. By viewing her story as only hers, and not part of a larger lineage—a family story of disability—we marginalized her. The bullshit story we told ourselves about my grandmother was that she was alone in her disability, that it had nothing to teach us, no potential gains. That we should fear inheriting her genetic predisposition to hearing loss, and that she should be shamed for not successfully overcoming it.

While my grandmother retreated, my mother instead pursued the "overcoming" narrative, which I, along with the rest of my family, perpetuated. In this narrative, the disabled person needs to somehow magically transcend their objective impairment and mask that they aren't cured. It's part of the inspo-porn phenomenon: the meaning of their disability lies in their ability to inspire nondisabled people. It has value only to the extent that it is disappeared through their will. Individual will is viewed as the "solution" to disability rather than structural legal and social changes that would accommodate the disabled person *and their disability*. It reduces the disabled person to their disability—they are defined by this overcoming. As disabled Paralympian Elizabeth Wright notes, "There is such a reductionist quality about the term 'overcoming.' By reducing disabled people to some kind of ableist miracle fantasy, you are completely eliminating every other aspect of their identity."[3] This pairs nicely with the genocidal narrative: implicitly, those who can't transcend and overcome their disability with will or magic or science don't deserve inclusion, respect, life. "You're talking too loudly," I said to my mother on more occasions than I care to admit, demanding she overcome her loud, deaf speech.

In rethinking the crip kinship of my grandmother's deafness in light of my daughter's disability, I've reclaimed that lineage. I use it to imagine a less ableist, more just future for my daughter. For my mother. For myself.

CRIP *MISHPACHA*: THE FUTURE OF DISABILITY LINEAGE

By embracing our disability lineages, we can connect these individual family narratives to a larger tapestry of disability legacy. This not only is transformative for us but also has radical material consequences for our children, grandchildren, and extended communities to come. As I've come to understand disability as a powerful, positive, and, above all, normal aspect of life, I've grown to understand the importance of extending that sense of family disability to a larger web. To the present and future of disabled biological and nonbiological kindred spirits. My grandmother would have used exactly the right word for this. *Mishpacha*. Your people.

Your family that isn't your family, *bubbeleh*, as my grandmother explained in her Deaf Yinglish.

For disabled people, a clear recounting and reclaiming of the family disability lineage can be a powerful means of naming and claiming one's own identity with pride. But it's easy to get stuck in the normative model of family. In seeing disability lineage in purely personal, individual, and familial terms. Such lineages fan out into communal narratives about disability lineage, identity, community, and ancestry.

Stacey Milbern writes movingly about "crip ancestries." She suggests that we need not only personal, family lineages, but also require a larger legacy of "crip elders." In her signal essay, "On the Ancestral Plane: Crip Hand-Me-Downs and the Legacy of Our Movements," she uses a literal hand-me-down—the "crip socks" another disability activist-writer gave her—to concretize the way we use our disability inheritances, lineages, and ancestries. Noting that many disabled people's lives are shortened because of the effects of ableism, Milbern argues for a spiritual legacy and kinship not contingent on earthly presence or family relation: "People sometimes assume ancestorship is reserved only for those who are biologically related, but a queered or cripped understanding of ancestorship holds that our deepest relationships are with people we choose to be connected to and honor day after day."[4] This queering and cripping means attending to how disabled and LGBTQ+ people have long complicated the sense of relation and time of normative (ableist and homophobic) culture. It also means expanding our sense of family, ancestry, and time.

Jack Halberstam, José Esteban Muñoz, and other queer theorists have argued that LGBTQ+ people cannot rely on a linear sense of history and time because so much of our history is buried, destroyed, or misrepresented. Moments from the queer past can touch the present and future, erupting in a nonlinear fashion as we look at a photo of two sailors embracing suggestively, their relationship unknowable, yet speaking loudly and powerfully to us across time, space, and the social construction of sexuality. We can't know what their erotic connection meant to them, but we can use this fragmented, somewhat unknowable past to make sense of our present, and to imagine a more progressive and inclusive queer future.

Since queer identity is not reproduced vertically by families, the meaning of inheritance, family, and lineage is reorganized and opened up by queers. Therefore, temporality—the way past, present, and future are organized—is "queered," rendered open and fluid. This queer time is not merely a loss or absence: it potentially provides a less linear, more dynamic relation to both past and future. How we remember and organize our queer lineages, as Muñoz argues, is not only constructed and political, but "our remembrances and their ritualized tellings . . . have world-making possibilities."[5] The implications of this extend beyond people who happen to be LGBTQ+. Halberstam suggests, "Part of what has made queerness compelling as a form of self-description . . . has to do with the way it has the potential to open up *new life narratives* and alternative relations to time and space" (emphasis mine).[6] Note how life narratives, "ritualized tellings"—the stories we tell about our lives, our worlds, given power through repetition and ritualization—are central in this opening up and queering of time. Queer time shares with universal design a capaciousness: a nonlinear, flexible sense of form and structure.

Feminist disability studies scholar Alison Kafer builds on and extends this notion of queer time. She suggests that "crip time," like queer time, imagines a relation to time, narrative, and space—fundamental elements of life for all people—that creates a more flexible, less frantic and impossible one than that of normative culture. "Rather than bend disabled bodies and minds to meet the clock," she argues, "crip time bends the clock to meet disabled bodies and minds."[7]

Crip time places humans, in all their diversity of body and mind, at the center, instead of forcing them to shape themselves around the demands of a clock oriented to an impossible schedule that no human can meet. This crip time is profoundly linked to how we imagine the future and past in relation to disability. Kafer challenges even queer feminist utopian views that imagine a future without disabilities, and links this to mainstream rhetoric about cure and transcendence in campaigns to fund research for this or that disorder. "The time of the 'future' is portrayed as a time of cures, genetic and otherwise," Kafer suggests, arguing that this imagined future time is both impossible and ableist, and posits that

we need crip time to imagine a future that includes disability and difference.[8] Kafer refuses the notion of an idealized past "before" a disability,
but says little about how valuing and knowing our disability lineages—
our familial and collective disabled pasts—might inform this queer- and
crip-inclusive future.

To arrive at this new understanding of the future of disability, our
disability lineage must be recuperated so that crip time is not suspended
between an impossible curative future and a feared, repressed past, but
rather celebrated and incorporated. Crip time acknowledges that much of
the individual lives and identities of our disabled ancestors is unrecoverable but can still be celebrated, imagined, and lived in the present. The incomplete, sometimes misrepresented and obstructed lives of our disabled
ancestors are crucial in helping us create sustainable, disability-inclusive
futures. The benefit of such reimaginings of how we construct and value
family, how the past and future relate to our present, are, as Halberstam, Muñoz, and Kafer suggest, not limited to people who happen to
be LGBTQIA+ or disabled. They are potentially transformative for everyone, as they offer new, expansive possibilities beyond the social scripts
and constraints of the heteronormative, ableist paradigm of a narrowly,
biologically defined family.

Yet the family remains the fetishized, hated, norm-producing factory
that both queer and crip theorists inveigh against. As I demonstrated in
the previous chapter, it's a convention of leftist organizers in both queer
communities and disability communities (and queer crip communities)
to speak of "chosen family" as self-evidently superior to one's family of
origin. In invoking the power of crip ancestorship, Stacey Milbern argues,
"ancestorship, like love, is expansive and breaks man-made boundaries
cast upon it, like the nuclear family."[9] Such a dismissal of the family presumes an oppressive, closed nuclear family structure quite different from
the complex extended-kinship formations of many Black and Indigenous
communities. So much of queer and crip theorists' sense of family as re-
pressive, closed, nuclear, capitalist, homophobic, and ableist depends on
white, heteronormative, middle-class notions of family. Indigenous communities in North America often organize ancestry, time, family, and

disability in a radically inclusive fashion. Black families' kinship systems, though pathologized from the notorious Moynihan report to Obama's scolding address to Black men at My Brother's Keeper events,[10] have historically been organized quite differently from the white cishet nuclear model, in ways that are more inclusive of disabled bodyminds.

Carol Stack, in her landmark study *All Our Kin*, explores how in the midwestern community of The Flats, "Black families and the non-kin they regard as kin have evolved patterns of co-residence, kinship-based exchange networks linking multiple domestic units, elastic household boundaries, lifelong bonds to three-generation households," and numerous other flexible, inventive structures that contrast with the patriarchal male-dominated nuclear family unit.[11] Her study offers more expansive notions of kinship, wherein a single family's lineage isn't limited to just one family at all. This expanded sense of lineage is profoundly linked to how disability is viewed as shared, normal, and part of the weave of life in Black communities.

A quite different history has shaped the integration of disability into North American Indigenous communities. Kim E. Nielsen notes that while Indigenous individuals have always had physical, cognitive, and mental differences, these differences were understood as normal, and valued relationally. Prior to genocidal, violent settler colonialism, she observes that "most indigenous communities had no word or concept for what in American English today we might call 'disability.'" None was needed. An integrated sense of the mental, physical, and spiritual, combined with the worship of ancestors as living presences, made for an inclusive world of bodymindsouls.[12]

It is not for nothing that Stacey Milbern invokes her Korean heritage to delineate the power of crip ancestorship: "My crip queer Korean life makes me believe that our earthly bodymind is but a fraction, and not considering our ancestors is electing to see only a glimpse of who we are."[13] Indeed, it was precisely because I already experienced family, time, and lineage as a queer person who had created a BIPOC family that I was able to move beyond the initial crisis and tragedy model soon after my daughter's diagnosis. I already had a critique of the "normate" and the normative from living as a queer person my entire life. I had already created family and kinship in inventive and nonbiological ways that incorporated my Korean American relatives, my queer friends who functioned in place of my biological family, my Korean Jewish daughter, my Korean American queer partner. The fantasy of normativity—of the white, cis-het bubble of nuclear relation and linear time—was never fully available to me, despite my enormous levels of race and class privilege. Time and family, relation and its inheritance, were already queered for me; their cripping was perhaps easier for me to access than for those who live the lie of the normative nuclear family.

Precisely because I have experienced this queering and subsequent cripping of family lineage, I see its incredible power as well as its limitations. Instead of rejecting the personal and familial aspects of lineage as hopelessly ableist, heteronormative, and oppressive, I want to reclaim these individual stories and legacies ghosting our families as part of the collective lineages we as queer and disabled people construct. The ancestral, the familial. The chosen, the inherited. We need both. They are woven together, inseparable, disparate threads creating one cloth.

Moreover, any real sense of disability justice needs to connect the biological, the familial, and the personal to the ancestral. Link the personal and familial to the larger collective sense of lineage, heritage, and identity. Milbern and other activists presume an experience within the (presumed) nuclear family as one of alienation and misrecognition at best, if not abandonment and abuse. The crip community and the wider ancestorship it can provide become the curative to this, the reparative force countervailing the familiar familial dysfunction. But the family of origin is left intact as the reproductive agent of trauma and ableism. Its particular, concrete disability lineage is unexamined. The potential of queers and crips to reimagine that primal and primary family, to discover its specific disability ancestry, is left untapped.

Unless disability is re-lineated to the family of origin, it will *retain* its singular force in replicating ableism, reproducing the family as inevitably traumatizing and de-lineating. Without such a re-lineation, the collective narrative of disabled ancestors remains abstracted and separated from the families we come from, the families we create, and the families we return to as elders. These individual family stories need to be connected to that larger narrative of communal eldership on the familial, lived level as well as in the afterlife's ancestral plane!

Milbern herself suggests not only that disabled people benefit from relationships with such communal elders, both living and not living, but that these are places of longing: "All of my ancestors know longing. Longing is often our connecting place."[14] Can the longing for family, for knowing and honoring its lineage, be part of that crip ancestorship? Would that longing be satiated by connecting the familial narrative—fully including its disabled members—to the ancestral communal one? How can we weave the two together?

Milbern suggests, Milbern argues, Milbern notes. The present-tense conventions of expository writing resurrect Milbern to the present moment of my writing, and to the future moment of you reading this. Stacey Milbern is dead. Yet she lives on in my writing. She is my ancestor. And perhaps I am, in some queer crip sense, yours as you read these pages. For whether I am alive or dead at the time of your reading, I am alive in this text, my ideas and stories animated, just as Milbern lives as I read hers.

Ancestry is living knowledge. Not just of history and culture, but of self. We know and define ourselves through learning about our own family's ancestors, and by learning the larger story of others who share our identities. For those with disabilities, who in schema like Andrew Solomon's are often viewed as having horizontal identities, it is crucial that they also gain a vertical sense of identity by learning about their people—those who came before them who shared their disability status. But by embracing our people, we change who they are, who they were, what their lives meant.

Milbern makes a startling claim about the temporality of this learning: "I believe they [the ancestors] learn as we are learning, just as we learn from them.... When we become ancestors, we will also continue to learn."[15] She suggests that this is a two-way street, transforming our sense of linear time. This might seem a little "woo woo," contingent on a belief in an afterlife. But I don't think this learning requires any such belief.

Though Milbern is dead, I am following the convention of putting her words in the present tense here. Her words are alive, and the meaning we make of who she was and what those words mean is changed by how we use them. The past lives and changes as we shape its meaning. Perhaps this is the most powerful and important aspect of reclaiming our disability lineages, both within and beyond our families.

My own disability lineage has led me to reconcile my familial and collective sense of ancestry. By exploring the work of Rhona and her family to create care institutions modeled on inclusive, Jewish justice principles and examining the very Scottish notion of disability rights as full citizenship and participation in the public sphere, I've come to see some of the limits of hyper-individualistic, privatized mutual-aid models—as well as their generative, radical potential. My disabled ancestor teaches me new ways of thinking about disability inclusion, while also allowing me to think critically and creatively about the models Rhona's family and society proposed. It was *through* my family's disability lineage that I was led to a larger sense of disability culture and community. As Milbern suggests, I learn from my disabled ancestors, and perhaps as we utilize their stories in all their visionary and appalling aspects to create a better future, they learn from us.

I hope I have not only recuperated Rhona's story, including it in the larger family narrative, but also transformed a life cut out of my lineage. Restored its complexity and dignity. Honored it. By including my grandmother's disability in my memory of her, I've changed who she was, and who she is in the living present where her spirit lives in my heart. In my daughter's laugh, so Adina-ish. I have found nothing more powerful in my family's disability journey than this reanimating of my family's disabled ancestors, in the present, as Milbern hopes to do through her writing. Hoped.

It is hard not to be moved when reading Milbern's words. Knowing that Milbern herself left the earthly plane and joined the ancestors shortly after she wrote them in 2020 makes her words that much powerful and poignant. This expansive, two-way street of ancestorship is envisioned as much larger than individual familial lineage: "Ancestorship, like love, is expansive and breaks man-made boundaries cast upon it, like the nuclear family model," Milbern argues.[16] However, it is hard to reach this ancestral, astral plane of disability lineage if you do not first have your own sense of familial lineage. Queers today often want inclusion in *both* a family of origin (including ones they themselves create and procreate) and an extended family of choice. Instead of either-or, let's insist on both. I honor my personal disabled elders, family members such as Rhona and Cousin XY, as part of a larger imagined community of disabled ancestors. I rewrite the lived disability narrative of my immediate elders: my mother and my grandmother, reevaluating their repressed deafness, giving it a vivid afterlife.

I don't know how many other disabled people in my family were simply written out of the story by the ableist narrators of the family drama. That's why expanding the story to include the larger narrative of all the disabled as our ancestors, our collective elders, is so powerful. By thinking of us as part of a larger web of disabled ancestors, their families, and caregivers, we share disability. Disability becomes woven into the fabric of the larger cultural story of what it is to be human. This also connects us to the vast universe of forgotten disabled people who died institutionalized, their names and lives unknown to their descendants, in a great unmarked grave. The concept of crip ancestry allows us to honor and imagine them. And it allows us to do so for those individuals who ghost the margin of our own family narratives, whose lives and stories cannot be recovered, like Cousin XY.

While Jews do not believe in any certain afterlife, we do honor our ancestors in our life cycle rituals and at other specified times with the phrase "of blessed memory," *zichrona livrachah*, which is also a kind of prayer: may their memory be a blessing. This suggests that our memory of our ancestors points in two directions: to the past, as a memory we bless, make holy, honor, and keep alive; and to the future, to serve as a blessing of the living as we move into our future—which will inevitably involve our own death.

Within the invocation *zichrona livrachah* lives a compelling contradiction that speaks to the queering and cripping of time. There is evidence that in biblical times this phrase was used to bless the living, the veil between living and dead conceived as permeable.[17] Living people are encouraged in this invocation to think of themselves as future spirits, as Milbern does in her writing that we read in the present but is the product of her living past. Today, queer and feminist Jewish activists have retooled this phrase as "May their memory be a revolution!" To which I imagine Stacey Milbern would lift a glass.[18]

Such a concept as that of the dead living in us through our memories is similar to those in other religions; it provides a way of practicing our crip ancestry and disability lineage in a living, spirited, and spiritual fashion. Though I am firmly on the side of valuing every life in the here and now over some promised, amorphous, uncertain afterlife, the notion that our legacies extend beyond our time on earth, beyond the limits of our biological families, is powerful and moving. Moreover, the queer-crip insight that we can remake the meaning of those legacies in how we incorporate them into our present lives is a powerful antidote to queer and crip erasure.

Still missing from this conversation, however, are our personal, familial lineages and heritages. This can be difficult in North American culture, where so many of us have had our lineages uprooted by enslavement, immigration, and the genocidal wars of the twentieth and twenty-first centuries. Other elements of postmodern culture—dysfunctional, distant families moving across a sprawling continent for work or other reasons— can make it difficult to find and claim one's disabled ancestors. I am the third generation of my family born in the US, while many of my grandparents' cousins, such as Rhona's parents, remained in the "old country." We are cut off from my partner's Korean extended family by distance and language. My generation of queers were thoroughly de-lineated (if not literally disinherited) from our heteronormative families. Homophobia excised our queer predecessors from the family myth. We had so little access to our queer-crip ancestry.

Even if we are the first generation to proudly pass on our disability stories to our children and grandchildren (or other next-gen family members if we ourselves don't have children), we can forge our family's disability lineage. So, search for the hidden story where you can. And if none emerges, be the beginning of a new narrative of inclusive disability and caregiving in your family for generations to come. If you find no disabled people in your immediate family, the larger "family of choice" that disability activists create can provide narrative threads. Weave it, sew it, discover and rewrite a new story.

RENDING AND MENDING THE FABRIC OF THE UNIVERSE

Though we planned for two years, COVID-19 made us turn my daughter Nadia's bat mitzvah into a gil mitzvah, a sort of preamble to the main event (to be held in a COVID-free future). Nadia prepared Torah commentary. I prepared to cry. We chose her dress together; we went online to Bloomingdales, Grandma Adina's favorite store. She adored the discounts and the unsweetened soft-serve yogurt. Nadia adored all the dresses.

"I can't choose!" she typed.

"Pick two," I suggested. She chose three. We ordered and hoped for the best.

The purple plaid one with the unlikely metallic pink accents she finally chose to wear was gorgeously blingy and fit perfectly. Grandma Adina loved such unlikely color combinations. The gil mitzvah was more moving than I imagined anything on Zoom could ever be. Nadia's words, Nadia's prayers, Nadia's thoughts. Nadia's passion for Torah, for questions of God and speech and silence. Only when I was looking at the haphazard iPhone pics I took of us afterward did I notice how Nadia's woven plaid echoed Rhona's taffeta. Same pattern, same confidence.

The term "lineage" itself gestures toward this expanded sense of belonging, meaning a collective as well as individual ancestry. This double sense of heritage is precisely where disability lineage and ancestry meet. Where our personal family histories and personages join with the larger ancestral memory. I pray to my deaf grandmother and remember all our disabled grandmothers.

A sense of belonging to a greater story is integral to all humans. In imagining a future in which I will certainly be disabled if I am so lucky as to be alive, I have my deaf grandmother to guide me. Grandma Adina can show me how to live joyously with a disability that she disowned during her life. I have Rhona now, reclaimed in all her sass, to help me better understand and care for my daughter. And I have Cousin XY, whose absence still haunts me, but whom I feel more deeply connected with after this deep dive into our disability lineage. In my dreams, he plays cards with me in my grandfather's basement.

The concept of disability lineage points both to the past, to the disabled ancestral *mishpacha* in whom we seek to find ourselves, and to the future, to the disabled great-great-great grandchildren for whom we leave our legacy. Instead of buying into the damaging ableist myth that in some bright, imaginary future, disability will no longer be part of human experience, I instead want to consider a future in which disability lineage is passed down with the same pride and joy—as well as honesty about challenges—that my Jewish heritage has been. That is why leaving evidence of our existence as disabled people, as disabled families, is so crucial. The writer and activist Mia Mingus eloquently argues for precisely this on the mission statement for her blog *Leaving Evidence*:

> We must leave evidence. Evidence that we were here, that we existed, that we survived and loved and ached. Evidence of the wholeness we never felt and the immense sense of fullness we gave to each other. Evidence of who we were, who we thought we were, who we never should have been. Evidence for each other that there are other ways to live—past survival; past isolation.[19]

My grandmother's ring as I twist it around my finger, the pattern of Rhona's dress that my daughter chose to wear for her coming-of-age ceremony, the feel of the leather of Harriet McBryde Johnson and Laura Hershey's sock-boots on Milbern's feet as she struggles on the tile. We wrap ourselves in these disability artifacts. The image of the inherited crip boots that Milbern explores is a complicated one, for she notes that those same cherished boots of the ancestor betrayed her, made her slip and fall. Yet she still wears them sometimes. It's an interesting detail: if Milbern just wanted to celebrate her crip ancestry, she might leave it out.

Our lineage and ancestry are filled with difficult realities. Physical and mental challenges. Imperfect ancestors all. This suggests to me that we must embrace the full complexity of this inheritance. That our ambivalence—and theirs—must be woven into disability lineage. That we have things to teach our disabled ancestors. That we are all part of a story that is constantly being rewritten.

As Martin Luther King Jr. proclaimed in his "Letter from Birmingham Jail": "All men are caught in an inescapable network of mutuality, tied in a single garment of destiny."[20] A garment of destiny: what a brilliant metaphor. And like all powerful metaphors, it is not arbitrary. Garments are tangible. They mark the space between body and world, self and other. Clothes function as stand-ins for bodies, skin, people. But unlike our bodies, we can take them on and off. Tailor them to our needs.

Tom Shakespeare describes a literal tailoring of his disability lineage. After his father's death, he took to wearing his tailored bespoke suits, embracing the formal father's style, which he'd rejected as a young man who was besotted with punk. Shakespeare's father also had achondroplasia, the genetic variation that he has inherited, and viewed such preppy clothing as the best bet for fitting in. Though he shared his father's disability, he didn't want to share his shame: "I wasn't my father. To me, clothes and haircuts were statements of difference, not opportunities for conformity." However, after his father's death, like Milbern, Shakespeare finds himself refashioning his relationship to his disability lineage feet first, literally stepping into the clothes of his father: "His suits had been specially tailored so that no one else [except someone with his disability] could wear them. And my mother hates to waste anything. Which is why one day, I realized that I was standing in a dead man's shoes. Not just his shoes, but his jacket, trousers, tie, and overcoat as well."[21]

Shakespeare reclaims this look, refashioning in terms both literal and metaphoric his disability lineage, literally wearing it on his sleeve. "These clothes represented my history," he explains, "and my father's history before me. I wanted them to live on . . . continuity matters."[22] He alters this formal clothing a bit to suit his own frame and tastes, as a form of embracing and honoring his disability lineage, the disability ancestry he inherited from his father along with the genetic trait they share, while unraveling the normativity and shame that were part and parcel of these vestments for his dad. Moreover, in wearing them with pride, he subverts expectations of freakishness that accompany disabled bodyminds.

Like Milbern and Mingus, Shakespeare is similarly redressing how he wears his disability lineage. Tailoring that inherited cloth to better suit him, shaping his father's memory, viewed only as a genetic curse by his father, into a blessing. He then turns himself into a living blessing to his grandchild, who shares his disability. Like the freak flag made out of genocidal ableist nationalism, this cloth is soaked in blood. In trauma. And in joy. The survival of these garments of destiny that bind us together and connect us to our past and future are testimonies to the fact of our survival, the persistence of our being, against all ableist odds. They are strong precisely because they are here, ours, now. How will we reweave them, how will we wear them? How will we pass them on?

As I clean my deaf grandmother's ring every day, I embrace this lineage, circle my ring finger with it, and imagine how it might shape my future disabled bodymind. When I give my grandmother's ring to my daughter, I will connect her to her deaf grandmother and great-grandmother, as well as Cousin XY and Rhona. I have woven their stories into the complex family narrative I've been telling her since she was born. I have also had to mark their absence, mourn their erasure. We are our stories, and ours is one of multiple, broken strands woven together to create our disability lineage. When I pass, I hope my daughter will wear my ring—and the stories of disability it encircles.

Observant Jews wear a *tallit*, a prayer shawl with strings that give it a raggedy, unfinished appearance. There are many interpretations of why, but the one I like best was told to me by Grandma Adina: We are held together by a cloth that is unfinished. Each of us must unravel the story we inherit and sew a new garment. This book—and the lives it describes, redresses, rings with new possibilities—is one such unraveling.

CLAIM YOUR DISABILITY LINEAGE

However you define family—whoever you are or were, and whoever might be your kin—I hope you will take the opportunity to do the sometimes profound, occasionally tedious, and ultimately world-making work of claiming your disability lineage. Here are some tips for how to approach finding your disability lineage. They are just a beginning to what I hope is a tidal wave of work in naming and reclaiming our disability lineages for all of us, for all our families.

Not all disability lineages are recoverable. Some are lost, erased, destroyed. But hopefully the act of lineating—of researching and creating a living disability lineage—will itself be healing. This is a gift to yourself, and to all your kin. Do it to honor your ancestors and as a gift to your descendants.

- **Be Out**
  The more you talk about your or your family's experiences of disability, the more others—including living family members—will share about their own. If you talk about disability as a neutral, normal part of life, that will make others feel comfortable sharing their disability family stories without fear, shame, and stigma.

Talk up your disability and those of other family members, and out will come the stories, photo albums, and testimonies.

• **Expand Your Concept of Disability**
Include invisible and mental disabilities as well as visible, physical, and cognitive disabilities.

Often, ableism leads families to define invisible disabilities, like learning disabilities, as . . . not really disabilities! And only recently have "mad pride" activists reclaimed mental illnesses as disabilities. The wider net you cast, the more you'll gain, as you learn about the wild and wooly diversity of your family's bodyminds.

• **Consult (Skeptically) the Internet**
The internet is an amazing archive of information, history, gossip, and outright lies. Even simple searches for the names of relatives, however far-flung, who might be disabled or might have information about other disabled relatives can be a goldmine. Be careful to verify any information you find. While there are legitimate sources such as Archives.com, there are lots of scam artists out there.

• **Seek Out Public Records**
Public records are an amazing source for information that our families might not choose to share with us about our disabled relatives and ancestors. If you know of an institution, seek its records. If you know of a school that a disabled relative attended, seek out its faculty who might have known that person. Birth, death, and marriage records are easily accessible via the internet—for free!

• **Ask Nosy Questions, Politely**
Use neutral language to question family and extended kinship circles about relatives who might have had disabilities. Be polite—but a little nosy! Elders in particular might relish the chance to have an audience for their family stories.

- **Listen**

  This is perhaps the most important thing. Listen for where disability might be an important part of the story but not named as such. This is often true for mental disability, due to shame and stigma. People of different generations may use different, even ableist language to describe disabled family members; avoid correcting, and instead listen actively, asking questions to get a fuller picture and more precise information. Remember that you are constructing a narrative, remaking the family myth: by nature, different people will have different, sometimes conflicting, accounts of the same events. That's the nature of a family myth, after all.

- **Keep Going**

  Don't be stymied. Keep going with your search, even if you hit what seems like a dead end. If one family member is uncomfortable talking about Uncle Louie's deafness, ask another. It's a recursive search, not linear. New information might pop up long after you initially search it out. I view finding and building my family's disability lineage as a lifelong process.

- **Look for Absences**

  Who's missing? Who do you not recognize in a family photo? Ask questions about people who might be relatives who appear in family records, photos, and videos, and note any disappearances. With a little research, those absences, disappearances, and blots on the family record can turn out to be the most revealing.

- **Share**

  Talk to everyone and anyone you know about the disability lineages you have uncovered and how valuable they are to you. This may encourage others to speak up about other family members whom you didn't even know about and to help others in their quest to recover and value disability lineage.

- **Rethink What You Already Know**
  I always knew of Cousin XY, but I never thought of him as part of my disability lineage—or really part of my family story at all. I've always known Grandma Adina was deaf and that my mother was hard of hearing, but I didn't connect that to the larger disability narrative in my family. Finding our disability lineages is sometimes a matter of re-finding what we already know, valuing it anew.

- **Connect with Others**
  Families are more eager than ever to connect. Create a website about your family. Be open about your interest in disability, family, lineage, and ancestry. Use tools like Ancestry.com to build your lineage and to connect with others. Let your kinship network know about it; encourage them to contribute.

- **Extend Your Kinship System**
  Include nonbiological, extended, distant, and absent kin in your search. Expand your sense of family to include all the complex branches, far-flung limbs, and fallen leaves of your particular dysfunctional tree. This will help connect you to a larger sense of disability lineage.

- **Include Professional Care Workers**
  Care workers are not only part of your extended kin, but they will also have a different perspective on your disabled family members than your biological relatives will, as Kathy did of Rhona. Of course, they are not obligated to spend time or perform uncompensated labor on your project, but in my experience, they often will find it valuable to share their experiences. Demonstrate to them how valuable their work was and how much you appreciate them sharing their perspective. Compensate them if you are taking a significant amount of their time. Anything that takes more than fifteen minutes should be compensated fairly and fully.

- **Leave a Record**
Document your findings. Create a proud record of your family's disability experiences and identities. Use the photo album and photo stream as your runway! Let the living disabled people in your family determine where and how they wish to appear. Weave the fabric of your lineage together. Imagine your descendants as proud, vibrant disabled people. What do you want to say to them? Others in your kinship network may be interested in this information; there may be kin you don't even know about who would be interested as well. Therefore, make it as public as you can.

- **Keep Your Search Alive**
This work is never done. It's ongoing: a living legacy that morphs and changes as you and your family grow. Evolving and expansive, ever-changing rather than finite. An unfinished tapestry.

RECIPES FOR A REVOLUTION

REIMAGINING CARE AND COMMUNITY

Below I have listed some concrete suggestions for how to transform the culture of care. Note that I say *culture*: laws matter, but to truly change something as individual, familial, and embodied as care, we must change the culture in which it is produced. We are all potentially culture producers: the creators of a world in which all bodyminds matter, all deserve care. Informed by disability lineage, the familial as well as the communal, I hope these suggestions incite you to make your own lists.

- **Transform Parent Support Groups into Mutual Aid Groups**
  Parent networks already exist for parents of children with disabilities. REACH, Mommies of Miracles, The ARC, Easter Seals, and Variety Club all provide meaningful support to family members of disabled people. Yet they are often cut off from disability activism, and from the transformational work that disabled people are doing for themselves. Despite their group format, they often replicate the notion of disability as individual or familial, and construct the disability as a trauma—a problem to solve. They are focused on nondisabled parents, facilitated by nondisabled therapists, and centered on the experiences of everyone except those

with disabilities! You can work to transform such groups by valuing and unearthing disability lineage as part of successful disability parenting. Instead of focusing only on the individual, help the group connect to disability rights and justice organizations. Use the group to promote disability as identity. Create forums for materially supporting one another as well as fun cultural activities. Some can be online; others are in person. Even a monthly outing to a free and accessible park can build community.

- **Involve and Center Support Groups on Parents Who Themselves Identify as Disabled**

  Who are the parents in your community who share your child's disability? Who are other adults with your child's disability? Our family's relationship to our child's disability changed radically once we started connecting with nonspeaking autistic teens and adults. On the most basic level, it simply allowed us to see that there *were* adults and teens who were nonspeaking. Because of the legacies of institutionalization, de-lineation, and segregation, we'd had little direct, lived experience of this. More importantly, it demonstrated to my daughter that she could look forward to life as a nonspeaking adult fully integrated into her family and community. You can't be what you can't see. Placing your child in your family as part of a proud line of disabled people helps them—and you—find the adults and teens in your community.

- **Reject "Far-from-the-Treeism": Highlight Similarities and Honor Differences**

  Too often, disabled children feel isolated in their families. Their parents are their primary points of reference for what is "normal," acceptable, included. Parents should work actively to find and celebrate disabled ancestors, both close and far in time. And parents should connect their own disabilities and differences with their children's. Reject far-from-the-treeism! In the autism activist-parent community, a new aphorism has emerged: cats don't have dogs. Celebrate *both* differences and connections, and stop assuming that a disabled child is any more similar to or different from their parents than any other child.

- **Encourage Disability Identity**
  Often I hear how parents worry about their children being "defined" by their disability. They encourage their kids therefore only to assimilate, deny, and minimize their experiences. This presumes that disability identity is valueless. In my experience, it is key to finding community and feeling seen and celebrated. Encourage your child to form an identity as a disabled person and see how that connects them to others. Foster connections with others who share your child's particular disabilities. Give them both the space and the tools to forge their own identity as a disabled person. Finding and honoring your family's disability lineage can help normalize disability as part of the family identity.

- **Connect Your Child's Specific Disability to the Larger Activist and Disability Community**
  Both parents and children with a particular disability share specific experiences, can be rich sources of information about treatments, providers, and activities, and become an extended kinship network. Our world got so much richer and deeper once we created a local community of nonspeaking autistic kids and parents. Even if we are able to get together only once a month, we connect frequently via email and text. Our kids are closely bonded, seeing themselves reflected and honored in one another. It's been just as important to build a larger identity and community with parents and children with very different disabilities. Both finding your particular people and participating in a decentered coalition are crucial. Disability lineage allows us to find ourselves in a larger narrative of disability beyond our specific diagnosis.

- **Find Roles for the Nonjoiners**
  I am by nature not a joiner. Luckily, I'm married to someone who thrives in groups, is terrific at forming them, and is a natural and

generous leader. This is good not only for my daughter, as it helps her to accomplish the world-building approach to disability and identity I've outlined, but also for me. Why? I needed the community to better support and understand my daughter's disability and to provide context for our experience as a family with disabilities. Though I'll never be the group organizer and instigator that my spouse is, I am a good family historian. Finding my family's disability lineage helped me imagine and reach out to a larger community of disabled families, friends, adults, and caregivers. So if you're not a group person, perhaps you can find another role where you can take the lead, such as that of lineage finder. Neurodivergent people sometimes don't enjoy typical group activities; nonetheless, they may find sociality, community, and group identity helpful even if it doesn't involve conventional "groupy" activities. Center the group around the needs of its disabled members.

- **Expose the Systemic Racism and Sexism of Care**
  Let's talk about the unequal distribution of care. Let's work together to first surface and examine care inequities. Then, let's fix it. Where are the fathers in these "family" and "parent" groups? Why are care workers so underpaid and marginalized? What deprofessionalized care can be supplied to one another, by one another, in the disability community via mutual aid? What should and must be professionalized? What would fair compensation look like for such care? An honest conversation in every family and community must happen before any real, systemic, and sustainable reorganization of care occurs. Then, take concrete action, however small and local. Don't let your family be the site of the reproduction of patriarchal and racist care systems!

- **Normalize Diverse Developmental Narratives**
  In our everyday lives, we can normalize diverse models of family, kinship, and care, reminding our ableist friends and family that we all need care as infants and elders, and often along the way. But just as powerful is the story we tell ourselves about how a family

should form and function. Integrating care as a normal and permanent feature of life and rejecting the false developmental model of the fictional normate will lead to more just models of care. Normalize interdependence and diverse paths to adulthood.

- **Reimagine Cure, Charity, and Congregate Care**
  We often talk as though institutionalization—as well as its abuses—is a thing of the past. The case of the Judge Rotenberg Educational Center in Massachusetts, where until 2020, autistic adults were routinely tased as part of "treatment," demonstrates the persistence of institutional abuse.[1] The rhetoric of monstrosity and cure persists in many of the Race for the Cure events. Hospitals still literally wheel out disabled children in their advertisements to raise money. Engage, challenge, and transform these powerful institutions—and form alternatives. Be an advocate and activist, and encourage your disabled kin to become self-advocates in transforming these problematic institutions.

- **Center Disabled Kin—Including Kids—as Change Agents and Self-Advocates**
  Disabled children should be encouraged to advocate for themselves, make their own choices about treatment, and have both age-appropriate peers and adults who share their disability involved in their lives, communities, and choices. Some disabled children have difficulty articulating their needs and desires—which does not mean they don't have them! Presume competence. Parents must center disabled children as *subjects* in their own lives. Families must provide their disabled children with a disability lineage connecting them to a proud past: to disabled peers and community in the present, and to adults who share their disability, as well as the supports and tools to express their needs and desires.

ACKNOWLEDGMENTS

It took all my families to write *All Our Families*. My colleagues in the Program in Disability Studies at Georgetown University have provided incredible intellectual and moral support at various stages of this project. Julia Watts Belser provided invaluable feedback early on, and her scholarship was crucial to my rethinking of disability and the sacred. Lydia X. Z. Brown, Mimi Khúc, Quill Kukla, Toby Long, Sylvia Onder, Joel Michael Reynolds, and so many others have modeled what engaged disability scholarship, activism, and justice really mean. They have also created the most dynamic, inclusive, and supportive intellectual community I've ever encountered.

My deepest thanks go to Libbie Rifkin, founder of the Program in Disability Studies at Georgetown University and my colleague and co-conspirator for the better part of two decades. Libbie has modeled what being a true scholar, advocate, activist, and leader looks like. Her contributions to my chapters on care were invaluable. She continues to show me what care, inclusion, and disability lineage can and should be.

At Georgetown, Caetlin Benson-Allot, Marcia Chatelain, Pam Fox, Melyssa Haffaf, LaMonda Horton-Stallings, Robert Patterson, Amanda Phillips, Samantha Pinto, Nicole Rizzuto, and Michelle C. Wang have provided unwavering support. What does not kill us . . . makes us start the revolution! Ricardo Ortiz and Kathryn Temple provided leadership and support in the Department of English. My colleagues in Theater and Performance Studies gave me a warm second home.

Christopher Celenza was an incredibly supportive—and now much-missed—dean during the creation of this project. His encouragement and support were unparalleled. I thank Dean Soyica Colbert for continuing and expanding upon this legacy.

My talented agent, Amanda Annis, helped shape and advocate for this project; I am so grateful for her support for this and all my work. Joanna Green, my brilliant editor at Beacon Press, provided supportive yet rigorous feedback. I thank everyone at Beacon for their hard work and commitment to social justice. Jessica Flores's careful editorial eye helped save me from myself at the bloody end.

Heather Grey at Cosgrove Care was generous with her time and helped me track down Rhona and her story. Special thanks to Kathy, the care worker who clearly adored Rhona and gave me so much insight into her life and death, and to all the caring, committed members past and present of Cosgrove Care in Glasgow. Rhona's family members were open and generous in sharing Rhona's story.

Christine Evans provided laughs, dinners at Martin's, and her keen critical eye on early drafts. I am so grateful for her friendship and brilliance. D. Travers Scott and Corinne Manning were, as always, co-conspirators. I thank them for all the Zoom writing and complaining sessions! They got me through the pandemic, and so much more. Mattilda Bernstein Sycamore, sister in struggle-slash-writing, was always cheering me on and making me laugh, even in my darkest Potomac basement moments. John McGrath helped me navigate the Manchester chapter of this story, reliably made fun of my mispronunciation of Glasgow, and provided a sounding board for many of the key concepts in this book. For decades, he's demonstrated how care and conflict can—and must—coexist. Nina Miller, my dear inherited friend, illuminated my own ableism regarding my mother. Julie Laffin and her spectacular (in every sense!) work on the intersection of environmental degradation and disability continues to challenge and excite me. Our thirty-plus-year collaboration has been a joy. Émilie Claire and Eríc le Ménédu: *merci mille fois*, my Montreal *mishpacha* supreme. Genius Fred Moten has been an incredible mentor, friend, and fellow traveler, helping me hear the song in the noise.

My extended kinship-friendship network supported me through many bright and dark times. David Jackson Ambrose, Eleanor Bader, Rebecca Brown, Mary Caponegro, Kiera Coffee, Michael Cunningham, Stephanie Foster, Derek Goldman, Robin Cara Graff, Fanny Howe, Holly Hughes, Sikivu Hutchinson, Lisa Jarnot, Sonya Leathers, Melinda Lopez, Susan Lynskey, Eileen Myles, Carrie Nedrow, Aimee Parkison, Ralph Savarese, Frances Sorensen, Michelle Tea, Jeremy Tiang, Penelope Treat, and Lidia Yuknavitch: I thank you all.

I would like to thank the Lafferty Family Endowed Fund for English for their support for the research of this project during the summer of 2019. A fellowship and residency at Faber in Olot, Catalonia, that same summer was transformative; I thank the Faber and all the residents for their generous support of this work. Enormous gratitude to Emilia Ferrara and family for their continued support of me as well as the Program in Disability Studies.

Cara Abercrombie, David Freccia, Vikram Jaswal, Anshu and Kapil Kapoor, Tauna Szyminski, Audrey, Indie, Sophia, and all the rest of our DC letter-boarding crew: thank you for providing my family with such a rich community. Thanks also to Lesley Bumstead and all the poets, teachers, and therapists who have truly seen Nadia and helped her flourish. Special thanks to Rabbi Ariana Katz and all the Hineniks at Hinenu for including my family so joyfully in their incredibly inclusive Jewish community.

Thanks to all my students, past, present, and future, especially those I've had the honor of encountering in the Program in Disability Studies. You are my best teachers.

Those who've moved on to the ancestral plane: Robert Blanchon, Christina Crosby, Kevin Killian, José Esteban Muñoz, Nancy Ring, Lawrence Steger, Cousin Rhona, Adina and Hal Lewis, Rebecca and Benjamin Fink, Young Ho Sohn, *zichrnona livrachah*. I honor Stacey Milbern, who wrote with such imagination and elegance about crip ancestry. Stacey became my ancestor, even though I never met her in life.

Sarah Sohn has been a true partner: in parenting, in joy. Thank you for sharing this wild ride with me, and for your love. Nadia Sohn Fink, my daughter, is at the center of this project. She is why I wondered about disability lineage in the first place. Nadia is eager to tell her own story, on her own terms; I thank her for letting me tell it from my partial, parental viewpoint here. I thank all my families: Chaleffs, Feldmans, Felsteins, Finks, Margolins, Sohns, biological, chosen, ancestral, present, past. And future.

NOTES

INTRODUCTION

1. Eli Clare, *Brilliant Imperfection: Grappling with Cure* (Durham, NC: Duke University Press, 2017).

2. Allison C. Carey, Pamela Block, and Richard K. Scotch, *Allies and Obstacles: Disability Activism and Parents of Children with Disabilities* (Philadelphia: Temple University Press, 2020), 4.

3. Eva Feder Kittay, introduction and chapter 6, in *Learning from My Daughter: The Value and Care of Disabled Minds* (Oxford: Oxford University Press, 2019).

4. See Angel Miles, Akemi Nishida, and Anjali J. Forber Pratt, "An Open Letter to White Disability Studies and Ableist Institutions of Higher Education," *Disability Studies Quarterly* 37, no. 3 (2017).

5. I have changed the name of this person and other living members of Rhona's and Cousin XY's families to protect their identities. I am grateful that they were willing to share their experiences with me for the purposes of this book.

6. Alison Kafer, *Feminist Queer Crip* (Bloomington: Indiana University Press, 2013).

7. Talila "TL" Lewis, "January 2021 Working Definition of Ableism," *Talila Lewis Blog*, January 1, 2021, https://www.talilalewis.com/blog/january-2021-working -definition-of-ableism.

CHAPTER 1: DISABILITY AS TRAUMA, FAMILY LINEAGE AS REPAIR

1. Barbara Burstin, "Holocaust Survivors: Rescue and Resettlement in the United States," Jewish Women's Archive, https://jwa.org/encyclopedia/article/holocaust -survivors-rescue-and-resettlement-in-united-states, last updated June 23, 2021.

2. See "Why Accessibility?" on the Dreamscape Foundation website for these and other eye-opening statistics, https://dreamscapefoundation.org/why-accessibility.

3. Quora, Reddit, and many other such forums have threads such as "Is it wrong not to want to have a child with a disability?" often posed as a question, though the answer is always "no." Quotes accessed January 3, 2019, http://www.Quora.com (link defunct as of June 24, 2021).

4. Michael Oliver, *The Politics of Disablement* (London: Palgrave Macmillan, 1990). Oliver pioneered the social model of disability, which he explores at length in this and numerous other works.

5. This definition and example, which appear widely in discussions of trauma on the internet, originate from Oxford Lexico, https://www.lexico.com/definition /Trauma, accessed June 6, 2021.

6. Linda Garand et al., "Diagnostic Labels, Stigma, and Participation in Research Related to Dementia and Mild Cognitive Impairment," *Research in Gerontological Nursing* 2, no. 2 (2009): 112–21.

7. Dana S. Dunn and Shane Burcaw, "Thinking About Disability Identity," *Spotlight on Disability Newsletter*, American Psychological Association, November 2013, https://www.apa.org/pi/disability/resources/publications/newsletter/2013/11/disability -identity.

8. Andrew Solomon, *Far from the Tree: Parents, Children, and the Search for Identity* (New York: Scribner, 2012), 2.

9. Shirley Durell, "How the Social Model of Disability Evolved," *Nursing Times* 110, no. 50 (2014): 20–22.

10. Tom Shakespeare and Nick Watson, "Beyond Models: Understanding the Complexity of Disabled People's Lives," in *New Directions in the Sociology of Chronic and Disabling Conditions*, ed. Graham Scambler and Sasha Scambler (London: Palgrave Macmillan, 2010).

11. Daniel R. Morrison and Monica Caspar, "Intersections of Disability Studies and Critical Trauma Studies: A Provocation," *Disability Studies Quarterly* 32, no. 2 (2012), https://dsq-sds.org/article/view/3189/3073.

12. See Dunn and Burcaw, "Thinking About Disability Identity."

13. Lennard Davis, *Bending Over Backwards: Disability, Dismodernism, and Other Difficult Positions* (New York: New York University Press, 2002), 32, quoted in Tom Shakespeare, *Disability Rights and Wrongs Revisited* (London: Routledge, 2014), 52.

14. Rosemarie Garland-Thomson, *Extraordinary Bodies: Figuring Physical Disability in American Culture and Literature* (New York: Columbia University Press, 1997), 8.

15. Talila "TL" Lewis, "January 2021 Working Definition of Ableism," *Talila Lewis Blog*, January 1, 2021, https://www.talilalewis.com/blog/january-2021-working -definition-of-ableism, accessed August 20, 2021.

16. Alaina Leary, "Parents with Disabilities Are Often Overlooked in Society," *Good Housekeeping* (blog), April 16, 2021, https://www.goodhousekeeping.com/life /parenting/a36121631/exceptional-mom-and-dads-alaina-leary.

17. See Letty Cottin Pogrebin's chilling personal account of this sorting by hair color in the Holocaust in "Isaac/Near Enough to Reach," a monologue in the documentary theater piece by Anna Deavere Smith, *Fires in the Mirror* (New York: Anchor Books, 1993). See also "Is Beauty in the Eyes of the Colonizer?," https://www.npr.org /sections/codeswitch/2019/02/06/685506578/is-beauty-in-the-eyes-of-the-colonizer.

18. This definition is taken from TL Lewis's blog where TL (who does not use pronouns) posts a continually updated definition of *ableism*, keeping this concept fluid and in motion, https://www.talilalewis.com/blog, accessed January 12, 2021.

19. Liz Crow, "Including All of Our Lives: Renewing the Social Model of Disability," in *Encounters with Strangers: Feminism and Disability*, ed. Jenny Morris (London: Women's Press, 1996), 210.

20. Judith Butler, "Giving an Account of Oneself," *diacritics* 31, no. 4 (2001): 26. Cited in Libbie Rifkin, "'Say Your Favorite Poet in the World is Lying There': Eileen

Myles, James Schuyler, and the Queer Intimacies of Care," *Journal of Medical Humanities*, no. 38 (2017): 82.

21. Peter Wohlleben, *The Hidden Life of Trees* (Vancouver, BC: Greystone Books, 2016), 4.

22. See Sharon Marcus, "Queer Theory for Everyone: A Review Essay," for a survey of critiques of this construct in *Signs* 31, no. 1 (2005): 191–218, https://doi-org.proxy.library.georgetown.edu/10.1086/432743.

23. Pamela Bartram, "Melancholia, Mourning, Love: Transforming the Melancholic Response to Disability Through Psychotherapy," *British Journal of Psychotherapy* 29, no. 2 (May 2013), https://doi-org.proxy.library.georgetown.edu/10.1111/bjp.12002.

24. Emily Perl Kingsley, "Welcome to Holland," 1987, posted on Asperger/Autism Network (website), https://www.aane.org/welcome-to-holland.

25. Kingsley, "Welcome to Holland."

26. Cyrée Jarelle Johnson, "What Is Autism Neutrality?," TEDx talk, June 4, 2018, TED Video, https://www.youtube.com/watch?v=BNwhj3lhgDY.

27. For more on Emily Perl Kingsley's remarkable work, see "Emily Perl Kingsley: Global Advocate, Award Winning Author," Global Down Syndrome Foundation Board of Directors, https://www.globaldownsyndrome.org/our-story/leadership/adults-with-down-syndrome-task-force/emily-perl-kingsley.

28. Rather than give more airtime to this problematic genre, I recommend that readers instead seek out memoirs by disabled people themselves. Naoki Higashida's *The Reason I Jump: The Inner Voice of a Thirteen-Year-Old Boy with Autism* (New York: Random House, 2016) and Judith Heumann's *Being Heumann: An Unrepentant Memoir of a Disability Rights Activist* (Boston: Beacon Press, 2021) provide two very different accounts of how disabled people made sense of the family and social systems that excluded them and fought for the legal rights and cultural inclusion of all disabled people.

29. Anna Cvetkovich, *An Archive of Feelings: Trauma, Sexuality, and Lesbian Public Cultures* (Durham, NC: Duke University Press: 2003), 47.

30. Eve Kosofsky Sedgwick, *Touching Feeling: Affect, Pedagogy, Performativity* (Durham, NC: Duke University Press, 2003), 150.

CHAPTER 2: NAZIS, SORTING, AND SEGREGATION

1. See Carol Poore, *Disability in Twentieth-Century German Culture* (Ann Arbor: University of Michigan Press, 2007), 67.

2. John DiConsiglio, "The Holocaust Killing Centers: An Historical Nightmare for the Disabled," Columbian College of Arts & Sciences (blog), George Washington University, April 8, 2015. DiConsiglio provides a good popular account of Mitchell and Snyder's groundbreaking work on T4. Rather than merely publishing scholarly accounts of the T4 program, Mitchell and Snyder have created a pedagogy, a film made with their students and son, and other public, collective and accessible forms of engaging this important rethinking of disability in relation to the Holocaust. For more on this, see David Mitchell and Sharon Snyder, "Towards a Pedagogy of T4," Centre for Culture and Disability Studies, Liverpool Hope University, UK, available at https://www.youtube.com/watch?v=8p5s6GsYOkI.

3. Robert McGruer, "Compulsory Able-Bodiedness and Disabled Existence," in *The Disability Studies Reader*, 2nd ed., ed. Lennard Davis (New York: Routledge, 2006), 88–99.

4. For a discussion of the continued problem of sheltered workplaces for disabled people from a critical, disability rights perspective, see Roy Maurer, "Advocates Call for Integration of People with Disabilities," SHRM (Society for Human Resources) blog, September 9, 2011, https://www.shrm.org/resourcesandtools/hr-topics/behavioral -competencies/global-and-cultural-effectiveness/pages/integratedisabilities.aspx.

5. Edith Sheffer, *Asperger's Children: The Origins of Autism in Nazi Vienna* (New York: Norton, 2018). See especially chapters 4 and 6.

6. For a balanced discussion of the history of the two diagnoses, see "Asperger's Syndrome," Autism Society of America blog, https://www.autism-society.org/what-is /aspergers-syndrome.

7. Mitchell and Snyder, "Towards a Pedagogy of T4."

8. See James Q. Whitman, *Hitler's American Mode: The United States and the Making of Nazi Race Law* (Princeton, NJ: Princeton University Press, 2017).

9. Isabel Kres-Nash, "Racism and Ableism," AAPD (American Association for People with Disabilities) blog, November 16, 2016, https://www.aapd.com/racism-and -ableism.

10. Cyrée Jarelle Johnson, "A Paradoxical History of Black Disease," Disability Visibility Project (blog), May 14, 2020, https://disabilityvisibilityproject.com/2020 /05/14/a-paradoxical-history-of-black-disease.

11. Kim E. Nielsen, *A Disability History of the United States* (Boston: Beacon Press, 2012), 146–47.

12. Ruth O'Brien, chapter 2 in *Crippled Justice: The History of Modern Disability in the Workplace* (Chicago: University of Chicago Press), cited in Nielsen, *A Disability History of the United States*, 150.

13. Nielsen, *A Disability History of the United States*, 88.

14. Therí Alyce Pickens, *Black Madness: Mad Blackness* (Durham, NC: Duke University Press, 2019), 8.

15. Ivan Brown and John P. Radford, "The Growth and Decline of Institutions for People with Developmental Disabilities in Ontario: 1876–2009," *Journal on Developmental Disabilities* 21, no. 2 (2015), https://oadd.org/wp-content/uploads/2015/01 /41021_JoDD_21-2_v23f_7–27_Brown_and_Radford.pdf.

16. Nielsen, *A Disability History of the United States*, 95–98.

17. The first names have been changed. Out of respect for my family, I have changed the names of all my living family members whose lives I discuss in my study.

18. Christian Boltanski, *The Reserve of Dead Swiss*, 1990, Collection of the Tate Gallery, London, https://www.tate.org.uk/art/artworks/boltanski-the-reserve-of -dead-swiss-t06605.

19. See "Home, Not Institutions, for Children with Disabilities," Global Disability Rights Now!, April 9, 2018, https://www.globaldisabilityrightsnow.org/tools/homes -not-institutions-children-disabilities. The organization Global Disability Rights has analyzed the outcomes for children who grew up in institutional versus home settings around the globe.

20. "Spiritual abuse" is a term disability activists use to describe the forced conversion, religious and ritual practices, and erasure of disabled peoples' own spiritual and religious identities in violation of their basic human right to religious and spiritual self-determination. See Julia Watts Belser, "Judaism and Disability," in *Disability and*

World Religions: An Introduction, ed. Darla Schumm and Michael Stoltzfus (Houston: Baylor University Press, 2016).

21. See Brian Brock and John Swinton, *Disability in the Christian Tradition: A Reader* (Grand Rapids, MI: William B. Eerdmans, 2012).

22. Other regional resources for parents do exist that are secular, Jewish, and Catholic, such as Friendship Circle, Potomac Community Resources, but they do not provide overnight respite care.

23. Michael Bérubé, *Life as We Know It: A Father, a Family, and an Exceptional Child* (New York: Vintage, 1996), 28–30.

24. For more on this paradigm, see "Main Street: Redefining Inclusivity: A Rockville-Based Community in Rockville with National Aspirations," Main Street Blog, https://mainstreetconnect.org.

25. It's important to note that this deinstitutionalization is partial and uneven—people with disabilities and their advocates still struggle for the right of people with disabilities living in group homes to exercise self-determination. Like so many aspects of disability, institutionalization intersects with race, class, and gender. See *Barriers and Catalysts to Self-Directed Services and Supports for Adults with Disabilities: Results of the 2018 I/DD Provider Survey* (Spark Initiative, Optum, United Health Group, 2018), https://www.optum.com/content/dam/optum3/optum/en/resources/fact-sheets/spark-2018-provider-survey-report.pdf.

26. "The History of Emblems," International Committee of the Red Cross (ICRC) website, January 14, 2007, https://www.icrc.org/eng/resources/documents/misc/emblem-history.htm.

27. Switzerland's role in storing Nazi gold has recently been exposed, so its hands are not quite as clean as we previously thought. Nonetheless, the state was officially neutral, and its flag thus came to symbolize political neutrality in the bloody twentieth century. For more on Swiss banks' role in hiding Nazi gold, see "Swiss Banks and Nazi Gold," *Economist*, July 2, 1998, https://www.economist.com/europe/1998/07/02/swiss-banks-and-nazi-gold.

28. Note that the Muslim crescent and a neutral crystal shape have been added as emblems in order to separate the Red Cross from Christian symbolism, yet the name stands, and the red cross on a white background remains the most universally recognized symbol of the organization.

29. Benedict Anderson, introduction to *Imagined Communities: Reflections on the Origin and Spread of Nationalism*, rev. ed. (London: Verso, 2016).

30. Nicholas Watson and Tom Shakespeare, "The Social Model of Disability: An Outdated Ideology," *Research in Social Science and Disability* 2 (2002): 9–28.

31. Watson and Shakespeare, "The Social Model of Disability." Emphasis in the original.

32. For a summary of this argument, see Rosemarie Garland-Thomson, "Becoming Disabled," in *Beginning with Disability: A Primer*, ed. Robert McGruer (New York: Routledge, 2018), chapter 2.

33. Carrie Sandhal, "Queering the Crip or Cripping the Queer? Intersections of Queer and Crip Identities in Solo Autobiographical Performances," *GLQ: A Journal of Lesbian and Gay Studies* 9 (2003): 25–26.

34. Kafer, *Feminist Queer Crip*.

35. See Mia Mingus, "Changing the Framework: Disability Justice," *Leaving Evidence* (blog), February 12, 2011, https://leavingevidence.wordpress.com/2011/02/12/changing-the-framework-disability-justice.

36. Mingus, "Changing the Framework."

37. Sharon Barnartt, *Disability as a Fluid State*, vol. 5, ed. Sharon N. Barnartt and Barbara Altman (West Yorkshire, UK: Emerald, 2010), back cover text.

38. For a Tropicalia-inflected account of this period by one of its foremost figures, see Caetano Veloso's political and musical memoir, *Tropical Truth: A Story of Music and Revolution in Brazil* (Boston: Da Capo Press, 2003). My project owes a debt to Veloso that is tonal and aesthetic as well as political and intellectual.

39. See "How to Include People with Disabilities," Respectability (website), https://www.respectability.org/inclusive-philanthropy/how-to-include-people-with-disabilities, accessed January 12, 2021.

40. Eli Clare, *Brilliant Imperfection: Grappling with Cure* (Durham, NC: Duke University Press, 2017), 8.

41. Eli Clare, "Grappling with Cure," UC Berkeley School of Public Health Dean's Speaker Series, recorded March 2, 2017, available at https://www.youtube.com/watch?v=wO_Gr-n6aq8.

42. Clare, *Brilliant Imperfection*, 184.

43. Clare, *Brilliant Imperfection*, 184.

CHAPTER 3: GENES AND GENOCIDE

1. Pew Research Center Report, "Public Opinion on Abortion, Views on Abortion 1995–2019," Fact Sheet, August 29, 2019, https://www.pewforum.org/fact-sheet/public-opinion-on-abortion.

2. Harlan Lane, "Ethnicity, Ethics, and the Deaf-World," *Journal of Deaf Studies and Deaf Education* 10, no. 3 (2005).

3. I will not cite Newman's horrific text as I do not wish to give it any more attention. One of the best (of many) critiques, however, can be found here: Shannon Des Roches Rosa, "To Siri, with So Much Disappointment," *Squidalicious* (blog), March 1, 2018, http://www.squidalicious.com/2018/03/to-siri-with-so-much-disappointment.html.

4. Saidee Wynn, "Please Stop Spreading 'Inspiration Porn' About Disability," *The Mighty*, October 2, 2017, https://themighty.com/2017/10/please-stop-spreading-inspiration-porn-about-disability.

5. Michael Bérubé, *Life as Jamie Knows It: An Exceptional Child Grows Up* (Boston: Beacon Press, 2016), 18.

6. See Octave Mannoni, "Je sais bien, mais quand-meme . . . ," *Clefs Pour L'imaginaire ou L'autre Scene* (Paris: Editions du Seuil, 1969). Though rooted in Freudian thought, Mannoni provides this famous phrasing regarding the fetishist's thinking: "I know very well, but just the same."

7. Armand Marie Leroi, *Mutants: On Genetic Variety and the Human Body* (London: Penguin, 2005), 19. Cited in Tom Shakespeare, "Pass it On," *Farmer of Thoughts* blogpost, accessed August 20, 2021.

8. For an excellent, detailed layperson's description of CRISPR, see Aparna Vidyasagar, "What Is CRISPR?," *Live Science* (newsletter), April 21, 2018, https://www.livescience.com/58790-crispr-explained.html.

9. George Estreich, *Fables and Futures: Biotechnology, Disability, and the Stories We Tell Ourselves* (Cambridge, MA: MIT Press, 2019), xiv.

10. See the popular TED talk by Ellen Jorgensen, "What You Need to Know about CRISPR," TEDSummit, June 2016, with over two million views to date, https://www.ted.com/talks/ellen_jorgensen_what_you_need_to_know_about_crispr/transcript?language=en.

11. "Researchers Overcome Hurdle in CRISPR Gene Editing for Muscular Dystrophy," *Science Daily*, University of Missouri School of Medicine, January 8, 2019, https://www.medicine.missouri.edu/news/researchers-overcome-hurdle-crispr-gene-editing-muscular-dystrophy.

12. See Joel Hruska, "CRISPR Gene Editing May Have Unanticipated Side Effects," *Extreme Tech* (blog), July 24, 2018, https://www.extremetech.com/extreme/274110-study-suggests-crispr-gene-editing-could-have-unanticipated-side-effects.

13. My father, Gerald R. Fink of MIT, is one of the people at the forefront of this rethinking of the value of "junk" DNA. I thank him for assisting this layperson in her understanding of this complex field.

14. Sandy Sufian and Rosemarie Garland-Thomson, "The Dark Side of CRISPR," *Scientific American*, February 16, 2021, https://www.scientificamerican.com/article/the-dark-side-of-crispr.

15. See Jessica Wright, "Mutations Between Genes, Long Overlooked, May Be Key in Autism," *Spectrum*, May 27, 2019, https://www.spectrumnews.org/news/mutations-genes-long-overlooked-may-key-autism.

16. Steven Silberman, *Neurotribes: The Legacy of Autism and the Future of Neurodiversity* (New York: Penguin, 2015), 470.

17. See *About Us: Essays from the Disability Series*, ed. Peter Catapano and Rosemarie Garland-Thomson (New York: Liveright, 2019), for selections from the popular series.

18. See Eli Clare, "Defective, Deficient, and Burdensome: Thinking About Bad Bodies," personal website, http://eliclare.com/what-eli-offers/lectures/bad-bodies, accessed August 17, 2021.

19. Aaron Schaal, "Science Must Rise Up to Support People Like Me," *Nature*, April 18, 2018, https://www.nature.com/articles/d41586-018-04598-z.

20. Sarah Zielinski, "Science and Technology Could Do More to Help People with Disabilities, Experts Say," AAAS, February 11, 2014, https://www.aaas.org/news/science-and-technology-could-do-more-help-people-disabilities-experts-say.

21. Rosemarie Garland-Thomson, *Extraordinary Bodies* (New York: Columbia University Press, 1997), 8.

22. See "Overview and Landscape for Postsecondary Education," National Down Syndrome Society, for more statistics and analysis on the increasing presence of people with Down syndrome in postsecondary education, https://www.ndss.org/programs/ndss-legislative-agenda/education/postsecondary-education.

23. "Undergraduate Enrollment," US Department of Education Statistics, 2016, last updated May 2021, https://nces.ed.gov/programs/coe/indicator/cha.

24. Julian Quinones and Arijeta Lajka, "'What Kind of Society Do You Want to Live In?' Inside the Country Where Down Syndrome Is Disappearing," *CBS News*, August 14, 2017, https://www.cbsnews.com/news/down-syndrome-iceland.

25. "Acquired Disabilities," Respectability Employer Information (website), https://www.respectability.org/resources.

26. D. A. Caeton, "Choice of a Lifetime: Disability, Feminism, and Reproductive Rights," *Disability Studies Quarterly* 31, no. 1 (2011), http://www.dsq-sds.org/article /view/1369/1501.

27. Michelle Sie Whitten, "The Story of Two Syndromes," Global Down Syndrome Foundation, https://www.globaldownsyndrome.org/our-story/staff/michelle-sie -whitten. Whitten, the foundation's executive director, offers a commentary on this research, describing in detail how the outcomes of Down syndrome have so radically changed without any significant medication or medical breakthroughs in treatment.

28. Whitten, "The Story of Two Syndromes."

29. "The Rehabilitation Act of 1973, Sections 501 and 505," U.S. Equal Employment Commission, https://www.eeoc.gov/statutes/rehabilitation-act-1973.

30. US Department of Justice, *A Guide to Disability Rights Laws* (2013), https:// www.ada.gov/cguide.htm, and "The Equality Act of 2010 and the UN Convention," Gov.UK, 2019, https://www.gov.uk/rights-disabled-person/the-equality-act-2010-and -un-convention.

31. Sarah Zhang, "The Last Children of Down Syndrome," *Atlantic*, December 2020, https://www.theatlantic.com/magazine/archive/2020/12/the-last-children-of -down-syndrome/616928.

32. Dirksen Bauman and Joseph J. Murray, "An Introduction to Deaf Gain," *Psychology Today* (blog), November 13, 2014, https://www.psychologytoday.com/us/blog /deaf-gain/201411/introduction-deaf-gain.

33. See the Autism Self Advocacy Network website, https://autisticadvocacy.org, for resources on neurodiversity by people who themselves identify as autistic.

34. Thunberg has worked hard to displace the "deficit" narrative; one of many articles in which she makes this claim about how her autism shaped and helped her become a world-changing activist is Steve Silberman's "Greta Thunberg Became a Climate Activist Not in Spite of Her Autism, But Because of It," *Vox*, September 24, 2019, https:// www.vox.com/first-person/2019/5/6/18531551/greta-thunberg-autism-aspergers. See also Thunberg's book in which she describes her views of the role of her autism in her activism: *No One Is Too Small to Make a Difference* (New York: Penguin, 2019).

35. N. Barker, "'What Will You Gain When You Lose?' Disability Gain, Creativity, and Human Difference," *Serendipity Studio* (blog), November 28, 2014, https:// serendipstudio.org/oneworld/identity-matters-being-belonging-becoming/%E2%80 %9Cwhat-will-you-gain-when-you-lose%E2%80%9D-disability-gain.

36. Irene Lacher, "*Tribes'* Star Russell Harvard Talks Deaf Community Culture," *Los Angeles Times*, April 7, 2013, https://www.latimes.com/entertainment/arts/la-xpm -2013-apr-07-la-et-cm-tribes-russell-harvard-conversation-20130407-story.html.

37. "Russell Harvard Travels Between Tribes at the Taper," *This Stage LA* (blog), March 21, 2013, https://thisstage.la/2013/03/russell-harvard-travels-between-tribes -at-the-taper.

38. Author attended production. For details, see Monique Holt, "Russell Harvard on 'Lear,' Playing the Villain, and His Dream Roles," *American Theater: A Publication of the Theater Communications Group*, April 26, 2019, https://www.americantheatre .org/2019/04/26/russell-harvard-on-lear-playing-the-villain-and-his-dream-roles.

CHAPTER 4: DISAPPEARING IN PUBLIC

1. Melissa Blake, "Somebody Told Me I'd Never Model Because I'm Disabled," CNN.com, October 31, 2020, website comments deleted as of December 21, 2020.

2. Melissa Blake, "A Message to Parents Who Use My Face to Make Their Kids Cry," Refinery 29, August 26, 2020, https://refinery29.com/en-us/2020/08/9987054/new-teacher-challenge.

3. Blake, "A Message to Parents Who Use My Face to Make Their Kids Cry."

4. Itzia Crespo, "Accessibility Dissonance: The Disability Community's Overlooked Fight for Remote Learning," *State Press*, April 14, 2020, https://www.statepress.com/article/2020/04/spmagazine-accessibility-dissonance-the-disability-communitys-overlooked-fight-for-remote-learning.

5. Mia Mingus, "Access Intimacy, Interdependence, and Disability Justice," from the 2017 Paul K. Longmore Lecture on Disability Studies, San Francisco State University, April 11, 2017. Also posted on Mingus's blog, *Leaving Evidence*, April 12, 2017, https://leavingevidence.wordpress.com/2017/04/12/access-intimacy-interdependence-and-disability-justice.

6. See Ed Shanahan and Kimiko de Freytas-Tamura, "150-Foot Vessel Sculpture at Hudson Yards Closes After Third Suicide," *New York Times*, January 12, 2021, https://www.nytimes.com/2021/01/12/nyregion/hudson-yards-suicide-vessel.html, and Ashley Wong and Michael Gold, "Fourth Suicide at the Vessel Leads to Call for Higher Barriers," *New York Times,* July 29, 2021. https://www.nytimes.com/2021/07/29/nyregion/vessel-suicide-hudson-yards.html. For a more nuanced disability justice perspective, see Emily Sara, "Fighting the Art World's Ableism, Hyperallergic," August 2, 2019, https://hyperallergic.com/510439/fighting-the-art-worlds-ableism. The coda to this disturbing story is that *The Vessel*, as of this writing, has reopened—but now requires that people pay to visit, and do so only in groups! This would be the very opposite of access intimacy. See "The Vessel, a Tourist Draw, to Reopen with Changes After Several Deaths, *New York Times*, May 26, 2021, https://www.nytimes.com/2021/05/26/nyregion/hudson-yards-vessel-reopening.html.

7. Cameron Morgan, "The Unacknowledged Crisis of Violence Against Disabled People," Center for Disability Rights (blog), https://www.cdrnys.org/blog/advocacy/the-unacknowledged-crisis-of-violence-against-disabled-people.

8. See Susan Schweik's extensive discussion of Chicago's ugly laws and ordinances in chapter 8 of *The Ugly Laws: Disability in Public*, History of Disability Series (New York: New York University Press, 2009).

9. Schweik, *The Ugly Laws*, 65.

10. Rosemarie Garland-Thomson, "Staring at the Other," *Disability Studies Quarterly* 25, no. 4 (2005).

11. Petra Kuppers, *Studying Disability Arts and Culture: An Introduction* (London: Palgrave MacMillan, 2014), 96.

12. Garland-Thomson, "Staring at the Other."

13. Garland-Thomson, "Staring at the Other."

14. Riva Lehrer, "Circle Stories," Riva Lehrer art gallery website, https://www.rivalehrerart.com/circle-stories. See Riva Lehrer's website for visual examples: https://www.rivalehrerart.com/gallery.

15. For an excellent discussion of the pairing of the ugly laws with freakshows, see Kim E. Nielsen, *A Disability History of the United States* (Boston: Beacon Press, 2012).

16. "Our Mission," Sins Invalid, website https://www.sinsinvalid.org/mission, accessed August 18, 2021.

17. Schweik, *The Ugly Laws*, 102.

18. TL Lewis, "Sharing Disability," lecture, Georgetown University Disability Studies Series, November 9, 2020.

19. Abigail Abrams, "Black, Disabled and at Risk: The Overlooked Problem of Police Violence Against Americans with Disabilities," *Time*, June 25, 2020, https://time.com/5857438/police-violence-black-disabled.

20. *The Forty-Year-Old Version*, dir. Radha Blank (Los Gatos, CA: Netflix, 2020), film.

21. Kenneth Fries, ed., *Staring Back: The Disability Experience from the Inside Out* (New York: Plume, 1987), 1.

22. Peta Cox, "Passing as Sane, or How to Get People to Sit Next to You on the Bus," in *Disability and Passing: Blurring the Lines of Identity*, ed. Jeffrey A. Bruen and Daniel Wilson (Philadelphia: Temple University Press, 2013), 100.

23. See Kuppers, chapter 5, "Disability Culture," and chapter 7, "Freak Shows and the Theater," in *Studying Disability Arts and Culture*, for an excellent summary of the work of disability artists in this vein.

24. Michelle R. Mario-Redmond, Alexia M. Kemerling, and Arielle Silverman, "Hostile, Benevolent, and Ambivalent Ableism: Contemporary Manifestations," special issue, *Social Issues* 75, no. 3 (June 10, 2019), DOI: 10.1111/josi.12337.

25. Mia Mingus, "Moving Toward the Ugly: A Politic Beyond Desirability," keynote speech, Femmes of Color Symposium, Oakland, California, August 21, 2011, also published on *Leaving Evidence* (blog), https://leavingevidence.wordpress.com/2011/08/22/moving-toward-the-ugly-a-politic-beyond-desirability.

26. See, for example, Nina Golgowski, "Bones So Frail It Would Be Impossible to Walk and Room for Only Half a Liver: Shocking Research Reveals What Life Would Be Like If a REAL Woman Had Barbie's Body," *Daily Mail*, April 14, 2013. Interestingly, these "facts" about Barbie are often included in materials compiled by mental health professionals about eating disorders. See the "Get Real Barbie" Fact Sheet created by the South Shore Eating Disorders Collaborative for one intriguing example, https://www.chapman.edu/students/health-and-safety/psychological-counseling/_files/eating-disorder-files/13-barbie-facts.pdf.

27. For an excellent examination of this, see Nicholas Hudson, "From Nation to Race: The Origin of Racial Classification in Eighteenth-Century Thought," *Eighteenth-Century Studies* 29, no. 3 (1996): 247–64.

28. Nara Schoenberg, "At 39, DeKalb Activist Melissa Blake Is Modeling in Her First Runway Fashion Show—At New York Fashion Week," *Chicago Tribune*, August 16, 2020.

29. See Madeline Stuart's website for images and coverage. It appears that her mother is in charge of her image, career, and voice, http://www.madelinestuartmodel.com.

30. Schoenberg, "At 39, DeKalb Activist Melissa Blake Is Modeling in Her First Runway Fashion Show."

31. Blake, "Somebody Told Me I'd Never Model Because I'm Disabled."

32. Blake, "Somebody Told Me I'd Never Model Because I'm Disabled."

33. Melissa Blake's Twitter feed, https://twitter.com/melissablake?ref_src=twsrc%5Egoogle%7Ctwcamp%5Eserp%7Ctwgr%5Eauthor.

34. Mia Mingus, "Moving Toward the Ugly: A Politic Beyond Desirability," *Leaving Evidence* (blog), https://leavingevidence.wordpress.com/2011/08/22/moving-toward-the-ugly-a-politic-beyond-desirability, accessed August 17, 2021.

35. Nielsen, *A Disability History of the United States*, 153.

36. Scottish Equality and Human Rights Commission, *Disability Rights in Scotland: Supplementary Submission to Inform the CRPD List of Issues on the UK*, https://www.equalityhumanrights.com/sites/default/files/scotland_supplementary_submission_to_crpd_uk_loi_-_ehrc_shrc.pdf.

37. Anna Mollow, "Identity Politics and Disability Studies: A Critique of Recent Theory," *Michigan Quarterly Review* 43, no. 2 (2004), http://hdl.handle.net/2027/spo.act2080.0043.218.

CHAPTER 5: LINEAGES OF CARE

1. I am using "sex" to denote the biological and "gender" to denote the cultural sense of maleness and femaleness, though sex is not binary and gender identity is somewhat hard wired though socially constructed. For a nuanced, evidence-based analysis of the sex-gender binary and its failings, see Simon(e) D. Sun, "Stop Using Phony Science to Justify Transphobia," *Scientific American* blog, June 13, 2019, https://blogs.scientificamerican.com/voices/stop-using-phony-science-to-justify-transphobia.

2. "The Consequence of Son Preference and Sex-Selective Abortion in China and India," CMAJ 183, no. 12 (September 6, 2011): 1374–77. Offers an analysis of the persistence of this bias and its consequences.

3. Anna Mathur, "'I Don't Want a Boy'—The Secret Shame of Baby Gender Preference," *Medium* online, May 29, 2020 (link no longer available).

4. It's useful to consider the rise of the gender-reveal party as a performance of the anxieties that the medical and social understanding of sex as a spectrum expose. See Christen Perry, "How Gender Reveal Parties Reinforce a Harmful Binary," *Very Well Family* (blog), September 15, 2020, https://www.verywellfamily.com/how-gender-reveal-parties-reinforce-a-harmful-binary-5077547.

5. Sarah Sahagian, "Let's Stop Saying 'We Don't Care, as Long as Our Baby's Healthy,'" *Huffington Post*, December 17, 2014, https://www.huffingtonpost.ca/sarah-sahagian/baby-healthy_b_6336822.html.

6. Web MD, "Does Being Over 35 Put Your Pregnancy at Risk?," https://www.webmd.com/baby/over-35-pregnant#1, accessed August 17, 2021.

7. Ruth Hubbard, "Abortion and Disability: Who Should and Who Should Not Inhabit the World?," in *The Disability Studies Reader*, 2nd ed., ed. Lennard J. Davis (New York: Routledge, 2006), 93.

8. The role of gender norms versus biological, supposedly innate differences in both the diagnosis and the presentation of autism remains unclear. See Meng-Chuan Lai, Michael V. Lombardo, Bonnie Aeyeung, Bhismadev Chakravarti, and Simon Baron-Cohen, "Sex/Gender Differences and Autism: Setting the Scene for Future Research," *Journal of the American Academy of Child and Adolescent Psychiatry* 54, no. 1 (January 2015): 11–24.

9. Sahagian, "Let's Stop Saying 'We Don't Care, as Long as Our Baby's Healthy.'"

10. Articles such as "Long Slide Looms for World Population, with Sweeping Ramifications," by Damien Cave, Emma Bubola, and Chloe Sang-Hun, in the *New York Times*, May 22, 2021, and elsewhere blossomed like mushrooms after the rain following the pandemic, usually giving only lip service to care needs and fears as a primary source of this "crisis," despite numerous studies—cited in this very article, for example—of the profoundly gendered ways care fears impact women's choices regarding family formation and reproduction.

11. Nidha Sharma, Subho Chakrabarti, and Sandeep Grover, "Gender Difference in Caregiving Among Family—Caregivers of People with Mental Illnesses," *World Journal of Psychiatry* 6, no. 1 (March 22, 2016): 7–17, https://pubmed.ncbi.nlm.nih .gov/27014594.

12. David Brooks, "The Nuclear Family Was a Mistake," *Atlantic*, March 2020, https://www.theatlantic.com/magazine/archive/2020/03/the-nuclear-family-was-a -mistake/605536.

13. Brooks, "The Nuclear Family Was a Mistake."

14. TL Lewis website, blog post, 2021, https://www.talilalewis.com/blog, accessed August 27, 2021.

15. Feder Kittay, *Learning from My Daughter: The Value and Care of Disabled Minds* (New York: Oxford University Press, 2019), introduction and chap. 6.

16. See Kate Washington's recent study-cum-personal-account, *Already Toast: Caregiving and Burnout in America* (Boston: Beacon Press, 2021), 167.

17. April Verrett, "Home Care Workers Are Now Called Essential. But the History of the Profession Shows That the U.S. Has Never Treated Them as Such," *Time*, August 24, 2020, https://time.com/5882416/home-care-workers-racism.

18. Verrett, "Home Care Workers Are Now Called Essential."

19. Dominic Bradley and Sarah Katz, "Sandra Bland, Eric Garner, Freddie Gray: The Toll of Police Violence on Disabled Americans," *Guardian UK* online, June 9, 2020, https://www.theguardian.com/commentisfree/2020/jun/09/sandra-bland-eric -garner-freddie-gray-the-toll-of-police-violence-on-disabled-americans. It's beyond the scope of this project to consider the remedies at the structural level to this racist and ableist police violence. See legal scholar and activist TL Lewis for innovative, radical ways of addressing the intersections of ableism and racism in the criminal justice system, https://www.talilalewis.com.

20. Frank Edwards, Hedwig Lee, and Michael Esposito, "Risk of Being Killed by Police Use of Force in the United States by Age, Race-Ethnicity, and Sex," *Proceedings of the National Academy of Sciences* 116, no. 34 (August 20, 2019): 16793–798, https:// doi.org/10.1073/pnas.1821204116.

21. Kelly M. Hoffman, Sophie Trawalter, Jordan R. Axt, and M. Norman Oliver, "Racial Bias in Pain Assessment and Treatment Recommendations," *Proceedings of the National Academy of Sciences* 113, no. 16 (April 19, 2016): 301.

22. Allison Norlian, "For Mothers of Black Children with Disabilities, Living with Twice the Fear," *Forbes* online, June 9, 2020, https://www.forbes.com/sites /allisonnorlian/2020/06/09/for-mothers-of-black-children-with-disabilities-living -with-twice-the-fear.

23. See TL Lewis, "Why I Don't Use 'Anti-Black Ableism' (and Language Longings)", blog post, https://www.talilalewis.com/blog/archives/08-2020, retrieved August 17, 2021.

24. Grace Chang, *Disposable Domestics: Immigrant Women Workers in the Global Economy* (Chicago: Haymarket Books, 2016).

25. Evelyn Nakano Glenn, *Forced to Care: Coercion and Caregiving in America* (Cambridge, MA: Harvard University Press, 2012), 10.

26. Glenn, *Forced to Care*, 11.

27. For a summary of this study's findings, see "Disabled Children in Low Income Families: Private Costs and Public Consequences," Public Policy Institute of California, October 2000, https://www.ppic.org/content/pubs/rb/RB_1000MMRB.pdf.

28. "Caregiver Statistics: Demographics," Family Caregiver Alliance, https://www.caregiver.org/resource/caregiver-statistics-demographics.

29. Chang, *Disposable Domestics*, 12.

30. Washington, *Already Toast*, 167.

31. Nielsen, *A Disability History of the United States*, 64.

32. "Montgomery County Population," Montgomery County Demographics Summary, Maryland Demographics, https://www.maryland-demographics.com/montgomery-county-demographics#:~:text=Race%20%26%20Ethnicity,%25)%20and%20Black%20(17.9%25), accessed August 12, 2020.

33. "How a Post COVID-19 Workplace Can Embrace Accessibility—for Everyone," Guardian Insurance website, 2021, https://www.guardianlife.com/coronavirus/how-can-workplaces-support-people-with-disabilities.

34. "How a Post COVID-19 Workplace Can Embrace Accessibility—for Everyone."

35. Leah Lakshmi Piepzna-Samarasinha, *Care Work: Dreaming Disability Justice* (Vancouver, BC: Arsenal Pulp Press, 2018), 41.

36. Feder Kittay, *Learning from My Daughter*, 163.

37. Feder Kittay, *Learning from My Daughter*, 162.

38. See Colleen Flaherty, "Life as They Know It," *Inside Higher Education*, October 27, 2016, https://www.insidehighered.com/news/2016/10/27/michael-b%C3%A9rub%C3%A9-publishes-follow-his-1996-book-about-his-son-down-syndrome.

39. Ralph James Savarese, *Reasonable People: A Memoir of Autism and Adoption* (New York: Other Press, 2017).

40. Valerie Strauss, "Mom: People Don't Want to Hear the 'Ugly Details' of Our Struggle to Raise and Educate Our Son," *Washington Post*, March 12, 2019, https://www.washingtonpost.com/education/2019/03/12/mom-people-dont-want-hear-ugly-details-our-struggle-raise-educate-our-autistic-son-heres-truth-anyway.

41. See Marga Vicedo, *Intelligent Love: The Story of Clara Park, Her Autistic Daughter, and the Myth of the Refrigerator Mother* (Boston: Beacon Press, 2021).

42. Feder Kittay, *Learning from My Daughter*, 7.

43. Stacy Clifford Simplican, "Care, Disability, and Violence: Theorizing Complex Dependency in Eva Kittay and Judith Butler," *Hypatia* 30, no. 1 (Winter 2015). Thanks to Libbie Rifkin for suggesting this intervention into Kittay for the purposes of my project.

CHAPTER 6: REIMAGINING CARE

1. Dean Spade, *Mutual Aid: Building Solidarity During This Crisis (and the Next)* (London: Verso, 2020), 2.

2. Spade, *Mutual Aid*, 21.

3. Jia Tolentino, "What Mutual Aid Can Do During a Pandemic," *New Yorker*, May 11, 2020, https://www.newyorker.com/magazine/2020/05/18/what-mutual-aid-can-do-during-a-pandemic.

4. See John Ehrenberg, "What Can We Learn from Occupy's Failure?," *Nature*, July 4, 2017, https://www.nature.com/articles/palcomms201762.

5. Joanna Wuest, "Mutual Aid Can't Do It Alone," *The Nation*, December 16, 2020, https://www.thenation.com/article/society/mutual-aid-pandemic-covid.

6. Tolentino, "What Mutual Aid Can Do During a Pandemic."

7. Mia Mingus, "Access Intimacy, Interdependency, and Disability Justice," Paul K. Longmore Lecture on Disability Studies at San Francisco State University, April 11, 2017; posted on Mingus's blog, https://leavingevidence.wordpress.com/2017/04/12/access-intimacy-interdependence-and-disability-justice.

8. Mingus, "Access Intimacy, Interdependency, and Disability Justice."

9. Autistic Women and Nonbinary Network (website), January 2021, https://awnnetwork.org.

10. Critiquing "self-care" white consumer "feminist" culture is like shooting extremely well-moisturized fish in a barrel, and it has been done so scathingly and frequently that it has become a bit of a misogynistic trope in popular culture. For an examination of this, see André Spicer, "How a Radical Feminist Idea Was Stripped of Politics for the Mass Market," *Guardian*, August 21, 2019, https://www.theguardian.com/commentisfree/2019/aug/21/self-care-radical-feminist-idea-mass-market.

11. For an excellent critique of the ableist premises of the current wellness craze, see Carrie Griffin Basas, "What's Bad About Wellness? What the Disability Rights Perspective Offers About the Limitations of Wellness," *Journal of Health Politics, Policy, and Law* 38, no. 5 (2014).

12. Emily Paige Ballou, Sharon daVanport, and Morénike Giwa Onaiwu, eds., *Sincerely, Your Autistic Child: What People on the Autism Spectrum Wish Their Parents Knew About Growing Up, Acceptance, and Identity* (Boston: Beacon Press, 2021).

13. "Decolonizing Mad Pride, Reclaiming Healing Justice," Fireweed Justice Collective, Zoom presentation, Georgetown University, October 15, 2020.

14. "Our Framework," Fireweed Justice Collective website, https://fireweedcollective.org, accessed August 11, 2021.

15. Despite efforts by mainstream organizations like Autism Speaks to imitate disability justice approaches, they have for the most part simply adopted the lingo without changing their practices. See Sarah Luterman, "The Biggest Autism Advocacy Group Is Still Failing Too Many Autistic People," *Washington Post*, February 14, 2020, https://www.washingtonpost.com/outlook/2020/02/14/biggest-autism-advocacy-group-is-still-failing-too-many-autistic-people.

16. Alison Leigh Cowan, "Hospitals Send Bill If Mental Patients Win Suit," *New York Times*, December 25, 2010, https://www.nytimes.com/2010/12/25/nyregion/25damages.html.

17. See "Medicaid Program; Home and Community-Based Services (HCBS) Waivers; Center for Medicare and Medicaid Services. Advance Notice of Proposed Rulemaking," *Federal Register* 74 (June 22, 2009): 29453–456, cited in ASAN, *Keeping the Promise: Self Advocates Defining the Meaning of Community Living* (Washington, DC: Autistic Self Advocacy Network), https://autisticadvocacy.org/policy/briefs /keeping-the-promise-self-advocates-defining-the-meaning-of-community-living, accessed August 31, 2021.

18. Wuest, "Mutual Aid Can't Do It Alone."

19. Carol Stack, *All Our Kin* (New York: Basic Books, 1974), 124.

20. E. Patrick Johnson, "'Quare' Studies, or (Almost) Everything I Know About Queer Studies I Learned from My Grandmother," *Text and Performance Quarterly* 21, no. 1 (2001): 1–25, https://doi.org/10.1080/10462930128119.

21. "Transforming Family," in *Beyond Survival: Strategies and Stories from the Transformative Justice Movement*, ed. Ejeris Dixon and Leah Lakshmi Piepzna-Samarasinha (Chico, CA: AK Books, 2021), 82.

22. Maggie Nelson, *The Argonauts* (Minneapolis: Graywolf Press, 2015), 75.

23. Johnson, "'Quare' Studies, or (Almost) Everything I Know About Queer Studies I Learned from My Grandmother."

24. Faye Ginsberg and Rayna Rapp, "Family," in *Keywords for Disability Studies*, ed. Rachel Adamas, Benjamin Weiss, and David Serlin, Keywords Online Series (New York: New York University Press, 2015) (blogpost), https://keywords.nyupress.org /disability-studies/essay/family.

25. Mia Birdsong, *How We Show Up: Reclaiming Family, Friendship, and Community* (New York: Hachette, 2020), 8.

26. Birdsong, *How We Show Up*, 226. Emphasis in original.

27. Stacey Milbern, "On the Ancestral Plane: Crip Hand-Me-Downs and the Legacy of Our Movements," in *Disability Visibility: First-Person Stories from the Twenty-First Century*, ed. Alice Wong (New York: Vintage, 2020), 269.

28. Milbern, "On the Ancestral Plane," 269.

29. Leah Piepzna-Samarasinha, "Crip Lineages, Crip Futures: A Conversation with Stacey Milbern," in Piepzna-Samarasinha, *Care Work*, 242. This entire dialogue is visionary and stunning. It deserves to be read in its entirety.

30. Piepzna-Samarasinha, "Crip Lineages, Crip Futures," 244.

31. Trevor G. Gates, "Chosen Families," *The SAGE Encyclopedia of Marriage, Family, and Couples Counseling*, vol. 4, ed. Jon Carlson and Shannon B. Dermer (London: Sage, 2017), https://sk.sagepub.com/reference/the-sage-encyclopedia-of-marriage -family-couples-counseling/i2967.xml, accessed January 12, 2021.

32. Louis Althusser, "Ideology and Ideological State Apparatuses," in *Lenin and Philosophy and Other Essays*, trans. Ben Brewster (New York: Monthly Review Press, 1970), 121–76.

33. Feder Kittay, *Learning from My Daughter*.

34. Feder Kittay, *Learning from My Daughter*, 7.

35. Joshua Chambers-Letson, "The Queer of Color's Mother: Ryan Rivera, Audre Lorde, Martin Wong, Danh Võ," *TDR: The Drama Review* 62, no. 1 (2018): 46–59, muse.jhu.edu/article/686621.

36. Jessica Slice, "Imposter Syndrome and Parenting with a Disability," in Wong, *Disability Visibility*, 132.

37. For one of many commentaries on this phenomenon, see Bella DePaulo, "America Is No Longer a Nation of Nuclear Families," *Quartz*, June 30, 2015, https:// qz.com/440167/america-is-no-longer-a-nation-of-nuclear-families.

38. The term "high needs" is itself vexed. As many disability rights activists have pointed out, an individual's needs may be high at one moment and not in another, or in one context but not another. It also allows someone presumably without these particular needs to decide what constitutes a "high" need. However, I haven't found a better term to convey needs that must be met for an individual to have the fullest, most inclusive experience in a particular context.

39. Aimi Hamraie, *Building Access: Universal Design and the Politics of Disability* (Minneapolis: University of Minnesota Press, 2017), 6.

40. Hamraie, *Building Access*, xiv.

41. Birdsong, *How We Show Up*, 165.

CHAPTER 7: SEWING THE ANCESTRAL CLOTH

1. Jennifer Pastiloff, *On Being Human: A Memoir of Waking Up, Living Real, and Listening Hard* (New York: Penguin, 2019), loc. no. 287, Kindle ed.

2. Jennifer Pastiloff, "I'm Hearing Impaired and My Mask Taught Me to Ask for What I Need," *Forge* online, August 11, 2020, https://forge.medium.com/im-hearing -impaired-and-my-mask-taught-me-to-ask-for-what-i-need-d44f411a3a2d.

3. Elizabeth Wright, "Why Disabled People Don't Need to Overcome Their Disability," *Medium*, April 27, 2020, https://medium.com/age-of-awareness/why-disabled -people-dont-need-to-overcome-their-disability-ff4dfa6d791f.

4. Stacey Milbern, "On the Ancestral Plane: Crip Hand-Me-Downs and the Legacy of Our Movements," in *Disability Visibility: First-Person Stories from the Twenty-First Century*, ed. Alice Wong (New York: Vintage, 2020), 269.

5. José Esteban Muñoz, *Cruising Utopia: The Then and There of Queer Futurity*, 2nd ed. (Durham, NC: Duke University Press, 2019), 35.

6. Judith Halberstam, "Queer Temporality and Postmodern Geographies," *Caring Labor: An Archive*, July 30, 2010, https://caringlabor.wordpress.com/2010/07/30/judith -halberstam-queer-temporality-and-postmodern-geographies.

7. Alison Kafer, *Feminist Queer Crip* (Indianapolis: Indiana University Press, 2013), 27.

8. Kafer, *Feminist Queer Crip*, 20.

9. Milbern, "On the Ancestral Plane," 269.

10. See, for example, Dereckna Purnell, "Why Does Obama Scold Black Boys?," *New York Times*, February 23, 2019.

11. Carol Stack, *All Our Kin* (New York: Basic Books, 1974), 124.

12. It is far beyond the scope of this book to delineate the rich, complex, and multifaceted ways that Black and Indigenous North American communities have constructed lineage, family, disability, and time. Please see Kim E. Nielsen, *A Disability History of the United States* (Boston: Beacon Press, 2012); Roxanne Dunbar-Ortiz, *An Indigenous Peoples' History of the United States* (Boston: Beacon Press, 2015); and Carol

Stack, *All Our Kin* (New York: Basic Books, 1974), as starting places for a more thorough investigation of these crucial subjects.

13. Milbern, "On the Ancestral Plane," 268.

14. Milbern, "On the Ancestral Plane," 269.

15. Milbern, "On the Ancestral Plane," 269.

16. Milbern, "On the Ancestral Plane," 269.

17. Emily Burack, "Why Jews Say 'May Her Memory Be a Blessing' When Someone Has Died," *Hey Alma* (blog), November 21, 2020, https://www.heyalma.com/why-jews-say-may-her-memory-be-a-blessing-revolution-when-someone-has-died.

18. Burack, "Why Jews Say 'May Her Memory Be a Blessing' When Someone Has Died."

19. Mia Mingus, mission statement (homepage), *Leaving Evidence* (blog), https://leavingevidence.wordpress.com, accessed August 20, 2021.

20. Martin Luther King Jr., *Letter from Birmingham Jail* (London: Penguin UK Modern Paperback, 2018), 3.

21. Tom Shakespeare, "A Dead Man's Shoes," *Farmer of Thoughts* (blog), https://farmerofthoughts.co.uk/collected_pieces/a-dead-mans-shoes, accessed January 12, 2021.

22. Shakespeare, "A Dead Man's Shoes."

APPENDIX II: RECIPES FOR A REVOLUTION

1. A decade of work by disability activists led finally to ending the horrific practice of tasing at a residential school. For an account of this work, see Ed Pikington, "It's Torture: Critics Step Up Bid to Stop US School Using Electric Shocks on Children," *Guardian* online, November 16, 2018, https://www.theguardian.com/us-news/2018/nov/16/judge-rotenberg-center-massachusetts-electric-shocks.

INDEX